Land Ownership and Taxation in American Agriculture

Land Ownership and Taxation in American Agriculture

EDITED BY

Gene Wunderlich

Westview Press

BOULDER • SAN FRANCISCO • OXFORD

This Westview softcover edition is printed on acid-free paper and bound in library-quality, coated covers that carry the highest rating of the National Association of State Textbook Administrators, in consultation with the Association of American Publishers and the Book Manufacturers' Institute.

Copyright © 1993 by Westview Press, Inc., except for chapters 1, 2, 3, 4, 7, 9, 17, 18, and 20, which are works of the U.S. government

Published in 1993 in the United States of America by Westview Press, Inc., 5500 Central Avenue, Boulder, Colorado 80301-2877, and in the United Kingdom by Westview Press, 36 Lonsdale Road, Summertown, Oxford OX2 7EW

A CIP catalog record for this book is available from the Library of Congress.
ISBN 0-8133-8646-2

Printed and bound in the United States of America

The paper used in this publication meets the requirements
of the American National Standard for Permanence of Paper
for Printed Library Materials Z39.48-1984.

10   9   8   7   6   5   4   3   2   1

Contents

PART THREE
Options

PART FOUR
Land Information

Foreword

Land economics is one of the most venerable subjects within economics. The classical scholars—Smith, Ricardo, Malthus, Mill, and others—all had a great deal to say about land. They were interested in its contribution to production, in the way it is held, and how its natural attributes affect its social use. The early neoclassical economists, especially Marshall, also had a deep appreciation for the economic and social problems associated with the way land is held and used.

Agricultural economists have also accorded importance to land, and for several decades they have nurtured a subfield of study called land economics. More recently, this specialization has been largely replaced by resource economics. Even though the labels have changed, the basic policy problems associated with land remain.

It is to the credit of Gene Wunderlich and his colleagues in the Economic Research Service that they have recognized the continuing importance of these problems and have done something about it. This 20-chapter anthology is indeed a comprehensive treatment of agricultural land. It is clear that a diligent search was made for the talent necessary to discuss the many dimensions of the social control of land. These dimensions include economics, politics, philosophy, geography, and the law.

Clearly, the subject is a timely one. Because we are a mobile people and live in a changing society, agricultural land use is an important part of the rural landscape. The way that space is used is also of interest to the larger society. The larger society can be expected to reflect its interest through a range of public policies, including but not necessarily limited to, land-use control, taxation, and environmental regulation. This can be expected to heighten interest in those institutions (governing rules, formal and informal) that affect agricultural land. And, of course, the agricultural land area is not fixed over time. It can be expected to change in response to new technology, settlement patterns, and numerous other influences.

Personally, I am pleased that land economics continues to receive attention. Recent work in neoclassical economics has emphasized short-run problems and equilibrium conditions. There has been serious discussion in this context as to whether land economics can be justified as a subject for special study. This argument holds that all factors of production can be reduced to labor and capital and that land should be considered as capital. Such a point of view may be tenable for certain problems, but full acceptance of it would mean that economists would be mute on many of the problems of our time. Land-use controls of various kinds may be crude instruments for the accomplishment of some social objectives, but they may be the only means available to those who wish to influence the use of rural space. It is to the credit of those who decided to produce this volume that they chose not to be mute and influenced and encouraged others accordingly.

Emery N. Castle
Oregon State University

Preface

The origins of this volume trace to a 1990 conference on the social collection of rent in the then Soviet Union, sponsored by the Robert Schalkenbach Foundation. In the course of discussions about what converting from a planned to a market economy entails, several of us became aware of real property institutions often taken for granted in the United States. These are the institutions that guide the marketing and allocation of land as an asset, factor of production, and consumption good. We thought a revisit of the American land ownership,* tenure, and taxation system would be helpful not only for those seeking a transition from a planned to a market economy but also for those hoping to improve the performance of the American version of a market economy. This volume examines the foundations of the system for owning and taxing agricultural land in the United States.

The U.S. property system of landownership includes hundreds of interests that are created, enforced, adjudicated, and transferred. The economy requires that these interests be easily and efficiently accessed. Specialists in brokerage, appraisal, leasing, regulation, recordation, management, and finance aid in the transfers. Some of the services are separately priced, and the cost of others is imbedded in the price of land. In either case, a property system that assembles, stores, and moves information requires resources. Brokerage fees, insurance premiums, closing expenses, and recording charges give real meaning to the abstraction *transaction costs.* The property system is not free.

Nor does *market price* adequately represent all the values implied by our property system. In this volume, we consider the conditions of land policy at several levels of government and question some of the historical views of progress. We examine fundamental features of ownership interests and the nature of valuing and pricing land. We analyze the contracts between those who hold land and those who use it. We even

---

*The term *landownership* refers to the state or condition of being a landowner. *Land ownership* refers to the relationship among persons toward a specific object, land, hence, the ownership and taxation of land, or land ownership and land taxation.

compare the U.S. system to that of Britain, source of many of our institutional roots.

In 1990, the Bureau of the Census had just published the results of a special survey of agricultural landownership, the Agricultural Economics and Land Ownership Survey. That survey produced some unprecedented information on the structure of agricultural landownership and information on trends toward concentrated, nonoperator ownership of farmland. Data from the survey appear in several chapters of this volume. The role of land information at all levels, from aggregative national and state statistics to data on individual parcels, is present throughout this volume. Indeed, we premise a better property system on better information.

Gene Wunderlich
Washington, D.C.

Acknowledgments

The Robert Schalkenbach Foundation initiated, encouraged, and substantially supported the creation of this volume. The Farm Foundation, Economic Research Service, and Institute for Land Information also provided valuable assistance for the volume's publication. Mason Gaffney and Lowell Harriss were particularly helpful in the early planning phases of the enterprise. James Hildreth, John Miranowski, Lowell Harriss, and Fred Harrison sharpened the focus of each of the four parts of the volume. John Lee, administrator of the Economic Research Service, challenged and encouraged the contributors and the editor. Melody Mathis-Pace assisted in many aspects of assembling the manuscript. Denise Rogers assisted the editor throughout the preparation of the volume. Jean Shirhall exercised outstanding editorial skills and transformed what might have been an arduous task into a pleasure. For the many minds and hands that put it all together, I am grateful.

G. W.

PART ONE

Description

The land is the source or matter from whence all wealth is produced. The labor of man is the form which produces it: and wealth in itself is nothing but the maintenance, conveniences, and superfluities of life.

—R. Cantillon, *Essai*, 1755

1

Agricultural Landownership and the Real Property Tax

Gene Wunderlich

Agriculture occupies nearly two-thirds of the private land in the United States, 878 million acres. Ownership of agricultural land is unevenly distributed among 3 million owners, who exercise their separate judgments about who will use the land and how and when it will be used. The pattern of landownership determines who will gain and who will lose from private and public decisions about what happens on the land.

Three dimensions of real property—ownership, tenure, and taxation—are examined in this volume to help readers gain a better understanding of, and stimulate discussion about, how land is used, valued, transferred, and held in agriculture and the rural economy. Two conclusions flow from the papers in this volume. First, simplistic notions of private property are a disservice to those seeking to understand the basic issues of valuation, control, and use of land. Rather, public and private interests should be examined as supporting dimensions of an integrated property system. Second, an effective, just, and efficient property system requires better, and possibly more accessible, land information.

Ownership, Values, and Taxes

Land information, and the knowledge it supports, nourishes millions of public and private decisions about the use of and investment in land. Private decisions about land use are made within a wide variety of tenure arrangements, the scope and variety of which enable farmers and landowners to gain access to land they need and to proffer land they do not need. This volume includes two chapters on leasing as a means for bridging between the ownership and the use of land. Leasing arrangements, which account for 45 percent of the farmland operated in the United States, provide for flexibility in the size and composition of farms and help distribute the risks of production and marketing.

To provide comparable insight into the public dimension of the private property system in agriculture, several papers in this volume address the nature of the real property tax in the United States. Approximately one-fifth of the return to farmland in the United States is paid as real property taxes to local governments. The real property tax thus represents a substantial public interest in agricultural land. Administered under the laws of 50 states and thousands of local governments, the real property tax assumes a wide variety of forms and levels.

 Underlying tenure arrangements and taxation—private or public decisions—is value. For land, value means rent. Rent provides the backdrop for all discussions of ownership, transfers of rights and obligations, the terms of tenure, and the levy of taxes. The land value thread runs through the entire fabric of this volume.

In this introductory chapter, I present a few facts about ownership, largely to provide an overview of trends in the structure of landownership. I argue that the mixed private/public property system of the United States is derived from social contract, rather than a natural right. Also, I hold that property rights are based on a pluralistic ethic, only one element of which is efficiency. I caution about premises. Mostly, I expose uncertainties and plead for knowledge, and thence data and information, about ownership, values, and taxes.

Who Owns What?

Who are the landowners? How did they become landowners? How is landownership distributed? The more profound answers to these questions that follow in subsequent chapters will be abetted with a few facts about landowners and the extent of their holdings. From there, one can better understand what landownership does for owners and for those who are not owners.

The principal landowner in the United States, in terms of area, is the U.S. government. Of the 2.3 billion acres in the United States, 690 million acres (nearly 30 percent) are owned by the federal government. About 144 million acres of federal land are in agriculture. State and local governments and Indian reservations hold 165 million acres, less than half of which are in agriculture. Virtually all government-held agricultural land is suitable only for grazing.[1] About 55 percent of the private land in agriculture is cropland and the remainder is grassland and pasture.

Private landowners are individual persons, combinations of persons, or legal entities. According to the Agricultural Economics and Land Ownership Survey (AELOS; see Chapter 4), 86 percent of private landowners are individuals or families and they own 69 percent of the privately held agricultural land. Another 11 percent of private owners, holding 24 percent of the agricultural land, are partnerships or family corporations. One percent of owners, with 4 percent of the agricultural land, are nonfamily corporations. A miscellany of estates, trusts, and other legal entities, another 2 percent of private owners, hold 3 percent of the agricultural land. Thus, most decisions about agricultural land are made by people directly, that is, without a complex organizational hierarchy. From this directness, and the large absolute number of landowners, one could conclude that decision making about agricultural land is widely dispersed.

Landownership, however, is by no means evenly distributed. The 4 percent of private owners with the largest holdings own 47 percent of the agricultural land, which represents 25 percent of the value of land and buildings. The 30 percent with the least land hold only 2 percent of the agricultural land, which is worth 11 percent of the value of land and buildings. In addition, the number of landowners relative to the population as a whole is small. Available evidence indicates that the proportions of land held among private landowners in 1988 were about the same as midcentury, but the total number of landowners shrank from 5 to 3 million.

How active are private landowners in agricultural decision making? First, 56 percent of the landowners are farm or ranch operators and, presumably, are immersed in farming decisions. That means that 44 percent of the owners of farmland are not operating farms and may be only passively involved in decisions pertaining to farming. About half of all farm landlords do not live on their own or any other farm. Most farm landlords have no farming experience—62 percent are neither farming nor retired from farming.

The available facts point to fewer agricultural landowners in the future and to those landowners having less experience and involvement in agricultural operations. The number of farmers, especially full time, will decline in number and in proportion to owners of farmland, potentially leaving renters in a stronger position than landlords.

The Idea of Landownership

The idea of property is rather like an iceberg. It is more complicated than it looks, and much of its significance is submerged.

—Kenneth Minogue[2]

A few characteristics of nominal landowners and the distribution of their holdings barely begin to describe landownership. Landownership represents the unique system of interests and claims emerging from a community's property institutions and land qualities. Later chapters will describe the institutions of real property, the valuation of interests in land, and the mechanisms society uses to influence either the interests in land or the value of those interests. Here, I hope only to underscore the social foundation of private property, particularly as it pertains to agricultural land.

Property interests are often described through the analogy of sticks in a bundle of rights.[3] A more apt analogy might be the ingredients of a recipe. A property "recipe" accommodates the idea of blending, merging, and modifying interests. The use of an easement for ingress/egress, for example, may be conditioned on when, by whom, and for what purpose and may be periodically renegotiated. A leasing contract is a special recipe for behavior, a blend of local conventions and individual innovations created by landlord and tenant.

Under the umbrella of landownership may be significant classes of interests, that is, rights, duties, liabilities, and privileges. Common classes of interests include easements, leaseholds, mineral rights, security/collateral, water rights, air rights, development rights, and eminent domain. At any one time, any or all of such interests could be in negotiation, contest, or transfer. Each class of interests will be expressed within socially sanctioned laws and related rules. Specific interests will be identified, negotiated, and agreed by interested parties, but within a social system.

The creation, articulation, and enforcement of the rights and obligations in a property system or in an individual contract incur costs. Locating a parcel, negotiating a lease, transferring a deed, releasing a lien, or appraising a property—all require information and effort, known as *transaction costs*. Because land has no cost of production, the economic success of a landownership system can be reduced, more or less, to gains from shifts from one land use to another minus the transaction costs.

Kenneth Minogue said, "The problem of property ... is a problem of justification."[4] If the transfer of land was only a matter of placing the use decision in the hands of the most efficient decision maker, the problem of justification would be simple. But the issue of who ought to own the land is not that simple. Justice says that efficiency is but one of many bases for ownership.[5] Further, there are as many efficient solutions as there are distributions, so the problem begins with distribution. Presumably, public policy will reflect value judgments about the means by which land can be acquired, held, and transferred.

The Land Question

Whose land is it? Whose land should it be? The question of landownership takes two forms, one expository, the other ethical. Both are essential to understanding land issues and forming land policies. Neither provides a complete answer to the land question, however. The papers in this volume contain descriptions, analyses, and prescriptions pertaining mainly to agricultural land, but they do not lose sight of ownership and control in the larger context of the property system. Perhaps a few words of background will set the stage for the papers and aid in relating them to that larger context of property.

The shape of landownership in America was cut in 1787 by the Northwest Ordinance,[6] in the 1830s and 1841 by the Preemption Acts, in 1862 by the Homestead Act,[7] and in the 1900s by a series of conservation measures.[8] The style of landownership was set in the summer of 1787 by Manasseh Cutler, who upstaged the formation of the U.S. Constitution with a real estate deal in which he acquired 1.5 million acres for the Ohio Company and another 3.5 million acres for private speculation.[9] From such public policies and private enterprise perspectives has emerged the mixed-ownership, market-driven, landownership system of the United States.

Within wide limits, parties are unrestricted in the transfer of private land. Patterns of landownership are the product of market forces and individual decisions. Ownership of agricultural land, as noted, is divided among a declining but still large number of owners. A public interest in the conservation of agricultural land arrived with the dust bowl drought of the 1930s. Today, that public interest takes the form of such measures as the Conservation Reserve Program, Nature Conservancy, and the preferential taxation of agricultural land. Land policies, historically and currently, are influenced by a number of underlying issues, which may surface in forums as diverse as federal legislation and private transactions. These issues include absenteeism, equality of holdings and opportunities to acquire land, entitlements and moral authority, valuing and pricing, and the obligations of ownership.

Absenteeism

The negative connotation of *absentee* reflects a community's apparent antipathy to the immigrant, stranger, or outsider. One problem with the notion of absenteeism is definitional. At what point does a pioneer become a resident? What is an absentee owner of farmland? A resident of a parcel abutting land rented to another farmer? A farmland owner living in a nearby town in the same county? Same state? Same nation? Another connotation of absenteeism is *detachment*, or *insularity*. Distance can be physical, economic, social, or psychological. In the administration of commodity support programs by the Agricultural Stabilization and Conservation Service, for example, landlords with share leases, which involve the sharing of farm management, share in program benefits, whereas landlords with cash leases, who tend to be passive to farm decisions, do not receive program benefits. The issues surrounding absentee landlords also go beyond production and marketing decisions to control of wealth, flows of income into and out of communities, conservation, long-term capital investment, and the draw on, and payment for, public services.

Equity

The question, Who should own the land? goes to the question of how much. How far from equality of holdings is too much inequality? Or is the distribution of wealth the necessary result of a freely working economy? Is the ownership of farmland by 3 million owners too concentrated in a population of 250 million? In a population of 30 million or 3 million? Is inequality inequitable? Inequality of wealth holding, including landownership, is of concern for reasons of justice and fairness and for reasons of efficiency and monopolistic behavior. Except perhaps in some individual communities or situations, the concentration of holdings of agricultural land is probably less significant for matters of monopoly or efficiency than it is for matters of justice or fairness. The issue may be related also to the absentee issue: large-scale ownership by a landowner-farm operator is more easily countenanced than large-scale ownership by a distant (impersonal, corporate) owner.

Desert

The question of who deserves to own agricultural land is present in many policies. Affording an access preference to owners of land adjacent to public land suggests the special worthiness of locals. Policies to encourage "keeping farmland in the family" suggest that lineal descendants of farmers deserve to own land more than new or nonfamily farmers. Restrictions on corporate owners suggest that one form of organization is more deserving of the opportunity to own land than another. The same argument holds for foreign as opposed to domestic owners. In addition to purely economic criteria of efficiency, there are notions of worthiness based on ethnicity, ancestry, social or political standing, occupation, and reward. Veterans of military service, for example, have been given grants for land and preferences in financing. Tenants under the Farm Security Administration were able to purchase the land they farmed on favorable terms. Contrariwise, ethnicity resulted in the loss of the North American continent by native Americans to European settlers, and farmland owned by Japanese-Americans was expropriated by the government during World War II.

Authority

Land-use decisions are made in some cases by the exercise of special authority. Local governments may influence land use by virtue of their duty to protect community health, safety, and morals. Planners may create community designs that, through public regulation, effectively limit the options of nominal owners. Public utilities may exercise eminent domain authority for easements. Strong activist groups may pressure owners through moral suasion. Churches have acquired land on authorities presumably beyond the usual governmental or market forces. Although authority in public policy is commonly thought of in terms of government, authority can come from other sources, including public opinion.

Valuing, Pricing

Perhaps the primal issue pertaining to landownership is *who benefits.* Stated as a utilitarian or economic precept, land is an instrument for enhancing utility or satisfaction. When alternatives exist, utilities are relative and prices guide traders of resources and goods, such as land. Land is priced as a factor of production or as a final good. Agricultural land is typically conceived as an input to producing food and fiber stock. For some owners, farmland may be a final good and its ownership in farming retained long after its price in an alternative use has exceeded its price for farming. Farmland may be retained in farming even when it has been priced out of farming because there is no more profitable way of holding for asset appreciation. At issue is who should capture the appreciation in price due to the working of market forces if no additional effort or investment is made by the owner. Within the utilitarian or conventional economic framework, some payment is needed for owners to manage the use of land. Payments guide changes in the use of land. Broadly speaking, such payments are the costs of the property system; they are information and command costs, required under private, public, or mixed ownership. But what of the surplus above information and command costs? Does a society want to pay owners for their information and command services or for their luck or manipulative abilities? Should owners be paid for their work or for their "rent-enhancing" capacity?

Responsibility

The arguments of the papers in this volume rest primarily on utilitarian premises and concepts. Other philosophic bases for examining the ethics (perhaps even the economics) of landownership must be acknowledged, however. Reasoning about the use, control, pricing, and taxation of land might proceed from, say, a neo-Kantian basis. Arguments might center on the responsibility of landownership rather than the rights of landownership. Policy might regard landowners as custodians rather than masters of territory.

Premises, Premises

Each of the logical/rhetorical arguments presented in the papers of this volume originates from assumptions or premises, which often are unstated.[10] The authors of these arguments were selected in part for their diversity, not likemindedness. Thus, the careful reader will search out the authors' premises, critically noting the implicit.

In the spirit of an open covenant with the reader, I present some premises that I believe are widely, if not universally, accepted. First, the ownership interests in land—private, public, or quasi-private—are socially created institutions. Private property arises and continues because an organized society with a monopoly of power, usually government, perceives economic benefits of dispersed decision making, risk sharing, and accountability; political benefits of stability and dispersed power holding; and social benefits of justice and equity.

Second, taxation, as in the real property tax, represents a claim or interest of the public in the object taxed. Like *freehold, leasehold,* or *easement,* a *"taxhold"* is a set of rules by which the state exercises an interest in land, particularly a claim on the value—rent in the case of land.

Third, the value of land is socially created. The additions to value due to individual effort are, by and large, capital. Real estate consists of combinations of land and capital, in varying proportions.

Fourth, all interests created or sustained by society can be modified or withdrawn by society, and all values created by society can be claimed by society. I call this the Frank Knight premise because of his statement that "property is a social institution; society has the unquestionable right to change or abolish it at will, and will maintain the institution only so long as property-owners serve the social interest."[11]

These premises are suitable for an assessment of the land ownership, tenure, and taxation system of the United States. Alternative premises are also possible. The premises are not primitives. They can be restated as issues; they do not yield tautologies. The general conclusion that follows from the premises is that, subject to the rules it imposes on itself, society can attach what it creates, either the property rights or the value of the rights.

From Facts and Information, Knowledge

Knowledge about the character and workings of the private property system is essential to its survival and improvement. Unfortunately, Arthur Young's homily, "property turns sand into gold," suggests to some the simplistic view that unattended private property will itself ensure efficiency, equity, happiness, and the family farm. But as Henry George remarked,

> It is not the magic of property, as Arthur Young said, that has turned the Flemish sands into fruitful fields. It is the magic of security of labor. This can be secured in other ways than making land private property, just as the heat necessary to roast a pig can be secured in other ways than by burning down houses.[12]

The system of private property in land in American agriculture includes a variety of owners and possessors. Over every plot of ground hover claimants whose invisible hands vie for the control and fruits of the land. Knowledge of claimants and the rules that control them is an important ingredient of the property system. Property *is* information. A warranty deed is not a deed (action), it is a document, a datum.

Knowledge about landownership includes the condition or status of landholdings and the transfers, changes, or modifications of interests in land. This volume contains knowledge of both types, but attention seems naturally to turn to the elements of change, the action at the margin. Transfers of ownership involve sales and inheritances, to be sure. But transfers also encompass changing land-use regulations, creating leases or easements, selling mineral rights, reassessing, and restricting the drainage of wetlands. Transfers imply a specification of interests and a shift in control or decision options.

Knowledge for making the system work, as the papers in this volume testify, comes in many forms and at many levels. National surveys, state investigations, and local recording, surveying and assessing are a few of the varied sources of facts and information. Land information plus experience and analysis become knowledge for brokers, assessors, planners, analysts, and others who serve and support the property system.

Part One of this volume describes the status, or condition, of landownership in American agriculture. Chapter 2 emphasizes leasing as a feature of the private sector's tenure mechanism for assigning land-use control. Chapter 3 emphasizes the real property tax as a feature of the public's interest in farmland. Chapter 4 describes the Census Bureau's AELOS program, a large-scale data source that provides an overview of national and state landownership patterns.

Part Two offers knowledge about landownership by interpretation or analysis. Property in land is meticulously dissected and interests in land are related to choices and values (Chapters 5 and 6). Special attention is devoted to easements and interests in unique property. The relation of tenure to the environment is captured in Chapter 7, which shows that, under some conditions, share leasing reduces negative externalities. Chapters 8 and 9, on valuing and pricing land (among other things), contribute substantially to knowledge about the separation of land and capital in agricultural real estate. Because real estate is such an important factor in the agricultural industry—70 percent of farm assets—its taxation is likewise important. Thus, Chapters 10 and 11, on the land wealth of agriculture and the real property tax, examine the pivotal economic relationship of taxation to ownership.

Part Three presents views and prescriptions on the settlement and use of land and insights about the proper role of government (Chapters 12-15). The subject of Part Three could be called "policy." The chapters on the United Kingdom (14 and 15) provide a contrast to the open, easy U.S. land system.

Part Four returns full circle to data and information and closes on the knowledge issue. The chapters (16-20) focus largely on the sources, limitations, and potential for collecting, assembling, and dispensing facts. Land facts are the raw material of the land information and knowledge needed for successful operation and development of the real property system.

Where Now?

The boundaries among and between private and public interests have been defined and redefined throughout the history of the nation. Each era submits its concerns to the forums of public opinion, legislatures, and the courts. The place of property was contended by the drafters of the Declaration of Independence.[13] As the nation achieved independence, expansion, development, ascendancy, and maturity, it called for different roles for property. The contemporaries of Lewis and Clark attached a different meaning to landownership than do the contemporaries of Armstrong, Aldrin, and Collins. Planetary awareness grew out of space exploration in the 1960s, and the nation gained a better grasp of global interdependence and ecological destruction. The unrestricted rights of owners to use land as they chose was challenged in the name of public interest. "Externalities" visited on one's downstream, downwind, and immediate neighbors became bases for litigation and legislation. Economists, philosophers, and politicians sought knowledge of how best to represent the interests of those who own land and those who do not.[14]

Early in 1992, three cases involving landownership were brought before the U.S. Supreme Court.[15] None pertained to agricultural land, but all had a bearing on the limits of private property in relation to the public. The cases represent yet another swing in the public-private pendulum of rights of landownership. The court cases, a number of property rights bills,[16] and the entreaties of developer and property rights lobbies are a more visible dimension of a larger movement of landholders chafing at regulation, a movement similar to, and possibly including a portion of, taxpayers in "revolt." In response to the property rights movement, environmentalists and public interest groups have been working to counter the perceived threat of unrestrained use of property to earth and atmosphere. Just how far the pendulum will swing is uncertain. This volume is intended to suggest to the reader the possibilities for, and potentials of, alternatives in land policy.

Notes

Gene Wunderlich is a senior economist, Economic Research Service, U.S. Department of Agriculture. The views expressed are the author's and do not necessarily represent policies or views of the U.S. Department of Agriculture.

1. From A. Daugherty, *Major Land Uses of Land in the United States: 1987*, AER-643 (Washington, D.C.: U.S. Department of Agriculture, 1991):14. The 2.3 billion acres include Alaska, which has little agricultural land. All other figures exclude Alaska. Daugherty shows 830 million acres of cropland, grassland, pasture, and range in private ownership. The 1987 Census of Agriculture shows 964 million acres of "land in farms." The AELOS survey, based on the 1987 Census of Agriculture, excludes some railroad land as being public and did not include institutional owners or horticultural operations; hence, the "nonpublic" lands reported for operating and nonoperating owners is 833 million acres. The AELOS survey is described by Blackledge in Chapter 4 of this volume, and a comparison of acreages, by definitions, is contained in G. Wunderlich, *Owning Farmland in the United States*, AIB-637 (Washington, D.C.: U.S. Department of Agriculture, 1991):11.

2. K. Minogue, "The Concept of Property and Its Contemporary Significance," in J. Pennock and J. Chapman, *Nomos XXII: Property* (New York: New York University Press, 1980):10. One can hardly overstate the importance and diversity of the ideas of property in history or contemporary economy and society. At the risk of serious omissions, the following references are provided: B. Ackerman, ed., *Economic Foundations of Property Law* (Boston: Little, Brown, 1975); R. Schlatter, *Private Property: The History of an Idea* (New York: Russell and Russell, 1973); D.R. Denman, *Origins of Ownership* (London: George Allen and Unwin, 1958); M. Harris, *Origin of the Land Tenure System in the United States* (Ames: Iowa State College Press, 1953). For readers seeking data-rich historical perspectives on agricultural land ownership and tenure in the United States, see L.C. Gray, C. Stewart, H. Turner, J. Sanders, and W. Spillman, "Farm Ownership and Tenancy," in U.S. Department of Agriculture, *The Yearbook of Agriculture* (Washington, D.C., 1923):507-600; and E.A. Goldenweiser and L. Truesdell, *Farm Tenancy in the United States*, Census Monograph IV (Washington, D.C.: U.S. Department of Commerce, 1924).

3. Discrete rights or classes of rights have been used to describe property. Noyes, for example, has an extended discussion of the bundle of rights. See particularly, C. Noyes, *The Institution of Property* (New York: Longmans, Green 1936):306-311. Textbooks following in the bundle-of-rights tradition: R. Ely, *Land Economics* (Madison: University of Wisconsin Press, 1964):76-77; F. Dovring, *Land Economics* (Boston: Breton, 1987):332-333. Hohfeld developed a system of rights, duties, privileges, immunities, etc., which was adopted by the American Law Institute and has become a standard for thinking about property. W. Hohfeld, *Fundamental Legal Conceptions*, ed. W.W. Cook (New Haven: Yale University Press, 1923). Bromley, more recently, rests his entitlements terminology on Hohfeldian symmetry: D. Bromley, *Economic Interests and Institutions* (Oxford: Basil Blackwell, 1989):44-46. See also Youngman (Chapter 5) and Schmid (Chapter 6) in this volume.

4. Minogue, "The Concept of Property and Its Contemporary Significance," 3.

5. Efficiency is among the nine canons of justice in N. Rescher, *Distributive Justice* (Washington, D.C.: University Press of America, 1965). Over two decades after J. Rawls' *Theory of Justice* (Cambridge, Mass.: Harvard University Press, 1971), interest in the issue of distribution continues to grow.

6. Description and text of the Northwest Ordinance can be found in R. Perry and J. Cooper, *Sources of Our Liberties* (Chicago: American Bar Association, 1978):387-398; and *The Annals of America*, Vol. 3 (Chicago: Encyclopedia Britannica, 1968):191-196.

7. P. Gates, *History of the Public Land Law Development* (Washington, D.C.: Public Land Law Review Commission, 1968):219-247.

8. F. Steiner, *Soil Conservation in the United States* (Baltimore: Johns Hopkins Press, 1990):xii-xvii.

9. C.D. Bowen, *Miracle at Philadelphia* (New York: Little, Brown, 1966):172-174.

10. Formally, enthymemes, or enthymematic arguments, may be valid even if all premises are not explicit. However, in the logic of everyday conversation on controversial issues, suppressed premises can lead to misunderstanding and pointless dispute.

11. F. Knight, *Risk, Uncertainty, and Profit* (1921) (New York: Augustus Kelley, 1964):360.

12. H. George, *Progress and Poverty* (1879) (New York: Robert Schalkenbach Foundation, 1984):399.

13. Despite his feelings for the political importance of property, Jefferson chose not to use the language of the Continental Congress's Declaration of Resolves ("life, liberty, and property") for the Declaration of Independence ("life, liberty and the pursuit of happiness"). D. Malone, *Jefferson and His Time*, Vol. One, *Jefferson the Virginian* (Boston: Little, Brown, 1948):226-228; Bowen, *Miracle at Philadelphia*, 71.

Private property rights advocates may connect John Locke with a libertarian perspective of property. This simplistic, and incorrect, perception of Locke's position on property is thoroughly analyzed by Tully: "According to Locke's argument, if men agreed to private property in land it would be purely conventional and it would be justified only if it were a prudential means of bringing about a just distribution of property in accordance with the natural right to the product of one's labour and the three claim rights." J. Tully, *A Discourse on Property: John Locke and His Adversaries* (New York: Cambridge University Press, 1980):168.

14. Probably every major economist, philosopher, and politician has had something to say about property, and many about landownership. An early 1960s view is the now classic article by H. Demsetz, "Toward a Theory of Property Rights," *American Economic Review* 57, May (1967):347-359. Demsetz, Cheung, and others have been extended with Barzel's emphasis on transaction costs in Y. Barzel, *Economic Analysis of Property Rights* (New York: Cambridge University Press, 1989). The principal issue in property, in my opinion, is that of justice, for which a body of literature begins with Rawls, *A Theory of Justice*. The issues of efficiency and equity are brought together thoughtfully by A. Buchanan, *Ethics, Efficiency, and the Market* (Totowa, N.J.: Rowman and Allanheld, 1985). See also Bromley, *Economic Interests and Institutions* and Youngman (Chapter 5) and Schmid (Chapter 6) in this volume.

15. *Lucas v. South Carolina Coastal Council; Yee v. City of Escondido, California;* and *PFZ Properties v. Rodriguez.* The Lucas case arose from the exercise of building restrictions in South Carolina's Beachfront Management Act. Lucas alleged that he was entitled to compensation because the act prevented him from building on a lot that he had specifically purchased for the purpose of building a beachfront home. The trial court agreed, but the state supreme court overturned the trial court's decision. The Supreme Court reviewed the case and then remanded it to the state court for further review. The Court's decision does not appear to represent a radical change in property rights law, but it may restrain state regulation of land use. The PFZ case, which arose over a conflict between development and protection of a mangrove forest in Puerto Rico, was dismissed by the Supreme Court without explanation on the basis of a procedural error in filing the case. In the Yee case, the owner of a trailer park alleged that a rent control ordinance lowered the sale value of the property and thus took property without compensation. The Supreme Court, in an opinion delivered by Justice O'Connor with all justices either joining or concurring, held that a rent control

that merely has the effect of transferring wealth from owners to the mobile home tenants does not constitute a taking of property. All of these cases, regardless of the court's holding, go to the issues of public and private interests in, and values of, property.

16. In 1991, a spate of bills, e.g., HR 905 and S 50, were introduced in the U.S. House and Senate, respectively, under the title of Private Property Rights Act. The essence of these bills, many of which were incorporated into the language of other bills, is that no regulation can become effective until the Attorney General assesses its potential for the taking of private property. Similar bills, e.g., Virginia's HB 1029 and SB 514, are being submitted in state legislatures.

2

Leasing Farmland

Denise M. Rogers

Land leasing plays a vital role in U.S. agriculture. It allows landlords to receive monetary returns from land they do not wish to operate, and it allows tenants to acquire use rights to land. Since 1900 the proportion of agricultural land that is leased has consistently exceeded 30 percent (Figure 2.1). In 1988, 45 percent of agricultural land was leased and 41 percent of all farmers operated at least some leased land.[1]

Although leasing has always been an important part of U.S. agriculture, attitudes toward leasing have changed over time. Early on, tenants and landowners viewed leasing as just a means of entering agriculture, a step on the agricultural ladder toward full ownership. Leasing was also associated with full tenants, those operators who lease all the land they operate. In 1940, tenant operators made up 39 percent of all farm operators. By 1988, however, tenants constituted only 12 percent of all operators, and they operated 15 percent of the land in farms. Part owners, farmers who own part and rent part of the land they operate, have taken the place of full tenants. In 1988, part owners operated 67 percent of rented agricultural land in the United States.

Tenants and landowners no longer see leasing only as a step toward full ownership. They now perceive it as an effective way to gain control of land resources. Leasing can be used to expand or contract the farm operation, conserve limited capital for financing farm operations, enhance management flexibility, and reduce risk. Leasing also permits farmers to phase out their involvement in farming.

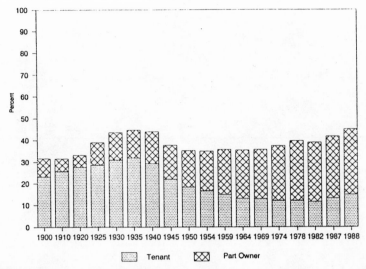

FIGURE 2.1 Percentage of total farmland leased, by tenure of operator (selected years). *Source:* O. Kula and D.M. Rogers, *Farmland Ownership and Renting in the United States 1987*, AGES-9130 (Washington, D.C.: U.S. Department of Agriculture, 1991); and Bureau of the Census, *1987 Census of Agriculture*, Vol. 3, *Related Surveys*, Pt. 2, *Agricultural Economics and Land Ownership Survey*, AC87-RS-2(Washington, D.C., 1990).

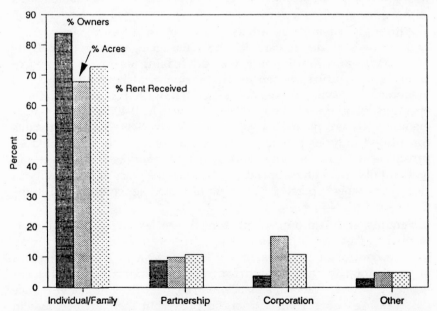

FIGURE 2.2 Type of farm organization: percentage of owners, acres, and rent received. *Source:* Bureau of the Census, *1987 Census of Agriculture*, Vol. 3, Pt. 2.

Agricultural Landlords

According to the 1988 Agricultural Economics and Land Ownership Survey (AELOS), a follow-on survey to the 1987 Census of Agriculture, excluding public owners (federal and state governments, Indian reservations, railroads and institutions), there are 2.95 million owners of agricultural land in the United States. One and one-half million of these agricultural landowners lease 332 million acres of farmland to others under 1.9 million leases. Over 90 percent of this land is leased out by nonoperating owners.

Nonoperator-owners do not operate any of the land they own; they lease out all or part of their land. Nonoperator-owners own 338 million acres, of which they lease 299 million acres under 1.7 million leases to others.[2] Owner-operators, who own all the land they operate, own 495 million acres of land. They operate 93 percent of those acres and lease the remainder—33 million acres—to others.

The AELOS program classifies landowners into individual/family, partnership, corporate, and other owners. Most of the farmland owners (84 percent) who lease land to others are individuals or families. These landowners lease out 68 percent of all leased acres and earn 73 percent of the total value of farmland rent received (Figure 2.2). Nine percent of all landlords are partnerships. Corporations, both family and nonfamily held, make up 4 percent of all owners who lease land to others. These corporations, however, lease out 17 percent of all acres leased to others and they earn 11 percent of the total value of rent received. The "other" landlord type consists primarily of trust or estate forms of ownership. It also includes lawsuit judgments and foreclosures. This category constitutes about 3 percent of all owners and 5 percent of the acres leased to others.

Although agricultural leasing is an important phenomenon nationally, it varies significantly by region. Over 40 percent of agricultural land is leased in the traditional farming areas of the Midwest and the Plains. The East North Central (45 percent), West North Central (43 percent), and West South Central (48 percent) regions all have high levels of leasing. Leasing is also common in the Pacific region (45 percent). In other areas, especially those along the eastern seaboard, agricultural leasing is much less common.

Individual/Family and Partnership Landlords

The AELOS program also provides data on the personal characteristics of individual/family and partnership owners, who constitute 93 percent of all farmland owners who lease land to others.

Agricultural landowners who lease land to others are older than the all-owner average: Sixty-five percent are aged 60 or older and 39 percent are aged 70 or older. Agricultural landlords who are aged 60 or older account for a disproportionately higher percentage of acres leased, value of land and buildings, and rent received. The percentages decline for landlords who are aged 70 or older, which may be attributable to an increased rate of disposal of land, through sales or transfer to other family members, by older individuals.

Most agricultural landlords are not actively engaged in farming—only 8 percent list their primary occupation as operating a ranch or farm. As noted, approximately 90 percent of farm landlords are non-operating owners. Over 50 percent of farm landlords are retired, either from farming or nonfarm-related business.

Most individual/family and partnership landlords live near the farmland they rent to others. Thirty-seven percent live on the land they rent. Of those landlords who do not live on the rented farm, over 56 percent live within 25 miles of the rented land, and 25 percent live over 150 miles from the land they rent to others.

White landowners make up 98 percent of all owners who lease land to others, and they rent out 99 percent of all the land leased by individual/family and partnership owners. Black ownership of farmland has declined precipitously since the late 1970s. In 1978, black landowners owned 6.3 million acres of farmland. By 1988, they owned slightly under 2 million acres. Despite this decline, black landowners still constitute the largest percentage (71 percent) of minority landowners who lease land to others.

Women are an important force in the farmland leasing market. Forty percent of individual/family or partnership landlords are women, 31 percent are men, and 29 percent are joint (male and female) landlords. Women control a large part of the land in the rental market—40 percent of the land rented to others by individual/family and partnership landlords. These numbers are expected to increase as the farm population continues to age.

Landlords' Relationship to Farming

Until the late 1960s, most agricultural landlords were closely associated with farming. Even nonoperator-landlords were usually retired farmers, members of farm families, or long-time residents of farming communities. They often participated closely in the planning and implementation of operations on the land they rented to others.[3] Now, however, 62 percent of landlords are neither engaged in nor retired from any agriculturally related activity.

The disengagement of landlords from farming has a number of important implications. Studies suggest that the contributions landlords make to the management of the land they rent to others has declined in recent years.[4] This trend may be related to the fact that now almost 90 percent of all landlords do not operate farms. Nonoperator-landlords are likely to lack the experience and the interest in farming necessary for active managerial participation. They are also more likely to leave management decisions to their tenants. This trend may also reflect the desire for independent decision making on the part of tenants, many of whom rent parcels of land from several landlords.

The AELOS questionnaire asked landlords to indicate whether the following five management decisions were made by the landlord, the tenant, or jointly: selection of fertilizer and chemicals, cultivation practices, selection of crop variety or livestock breed, harvesting decisions, and marketing of agricultural products. There is little variation in the division of decision-making responsibility for the first four management decisions. Those decisions are made in 7-8 percent of leasing arrangements by the landlord alone, in 77-82 percent by the tenant alone, and in 11-15 percent jointly by landlord and tenant. The division of decision-making responsibility for the marketing of agricultural products does differ, however. Landlords participate more in marketing decisions, and tenants assume less sole decision-making responsibility.

Landlord disengagement from farming may also have long-term implications for the productivity of land. Renters may be less willing than owners to invest in long-term land improvement or soil conservation, especially if their future tenure is uncertain or they are not compensated in some way for the value of the improvements at the termination of the lease. If renters have less incentive to invest in land and are not required by landlords to make such investments, and if landlords are not active in the management of the farm operation, the long-run productive capacity of agricultural land may be reduced.

Another aspect of landlord disengagement from farming is an increased use of cash leases. Share leases generally involve more negotiation, owner supervision, and coordination than cash leases. The higher level of landlord participation is a disadvantage for landlords who do not want to be actively involved in management decisions. Over the past 20 years, the percentage of farmland rented under cash versus share leases has steadily increased. The only exception was a slight shift toward more share leases during the economic upheavals and uncertainty in the agricultural sector during the mid-1980s.[5]

Lease Type

Various arrangements are used for leasing agricultural land. Cash leases are the most common lease type: They constitute 64 percent of all leases. Sixty-seven percent of all owners use cash leases, and 65 percent of all leased acres are leased for cash rentals.

Under a cash lease, the tenant makes a fixed cash payment per acre and assumes all the risks associated with fluctuations in the level of output and market prices. The landlord still must assume the risk of nonpayment of rent by the tenant and the risk that the tenant will abuse the land.

Some cash leases provide for adjustments in rent payment for unusual circumstances, including drought, hail, other adverse weather conditions, and above-normal yields due to exceptional growing conditions. This lease type combines the risk-sharing advantages of share leases with the management flexibility of cash leases. About 6 percent of the cash leases are adjustable, but 12 percent of acres rented for cash are under adjustable leases.

Share leases account for 30 percent of all leases and all acres leased. Under a share lease, the tenant pays the landlord a specified share of the crop. The landlord shares the risk because the rent paid varies directly with the level of output and the market price. Share leases, as noted, typically allow for greater participation by the landlord in the management of the farm operation and the sharing of expenses between landlord and tenant.

Cash/share leases involve some combination of cash and share leases. The AELOS program defines a category of "other" leases, which may include tenants who use the land rent free or in return for a fixed quantity of product, payment of taxes, or maintenance of buildings.

Rents under share leases would be expected to be higher than under cash leases due to the sharing of expenses between landlord and tenant, the participation of the landlord in farm management, and the additional risk to the landlord. The average gross rent for share leases is $46.44 per acre, compared with $27.30 per acre for cash leases. These gross rents, however, do not account for the operating expenses paid by owners, the largest of which are real estate taxes. Real estate taxes constitute 42 percent of all operating expenses paid by landlords. Under cash leases, owners generally pay only for real estate taxes. Under share leases, landowners typically pay a share of the operating expenses in proportion to the share of the crop they receive, in addition to real estate taxes.

A part of the difference between rents under cash leases and share leases is a return to the managerial input of the landowner under a share lease. It is likely, however, that any remaining differential between cash rents and share rents represents a risk premium paid to the land-owner for assuming a part of the risk of share leasing.

Although most leases are for cash in all nine geographic areas of the United States, the proportions of cash and share leases vary widely by region (Figure 2.3). Cash leases are most predominant in the eastern portion of the country. In the New England, Middle Atlantic, and South Atlantic regions, from 82 to 85 percent of all leases are cash leases. In these areas, 78 to 94 percent of gross rentals are earned from cash leases. The lowest incidence of cash leases is in the East North Central and West North Central regions—with 57 and 54 percent cash leases, respectively.

Share leases are more common in regions with a higher percentage of leased land. These are the major farming regions of the Midwest and the Plains, specifically the East North Central (39 percent share leases) and West North Central (40 percent) regions. Share leases are least common in the New England (5 percent), Middle Atlantic (2 percent), and South Atlantic (10 percent) regions.

Conclusion

Land leasing has always been an important part of U.S. agriculture, but it has become increasingly important over the past 25 years. It is now widely perceived to be an effective way to gain control of land resources. Over time, the character of leasing has changed: Today, the largest group of renters are part owners, not tenants, as was the case in the early 1900s. These part owners may lease land from several landlords.

With the increase in the number of nonoperator-landlords, many of whom may have little knowledge of agriculture, and with the increased use of cash leases, many landlords are leaving farm management deci-sions to their tenants. Will an increasing number of absentee landlords mean reduced investment in the land? Will tenants be willing to make investments in the long-run productivity of the land? Can leases be structured so that the productivity of the land is protected? These kinds of questions are being raised with increasing urgency as more and more agricultural landlords disengage from farming.

Notes

Denise M. Rogers is an agricultural economist, Economic Research Service, U.S. Department of Agriculture. The views expressed are the author's and do not necessarily represent policies or views of the U.S. Department of Agriculture.

24

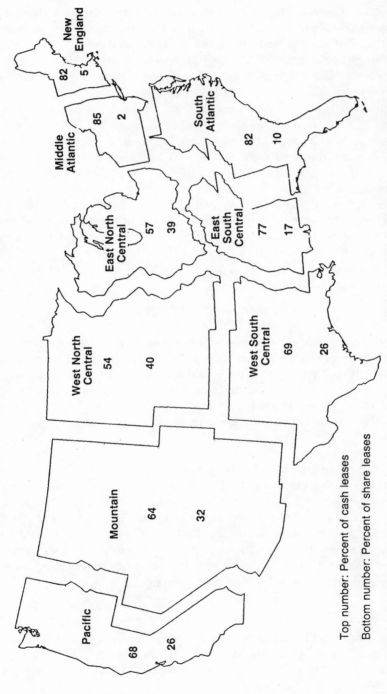

Top number: Percent of cash leases

Bottom number: Percent of share leases

FIGURE 2.3 Lease type, by region. *Source:* Adapted from D.M. Rogers, *Leasing Farmland in the United States,* AGES-9159 (Washington, D.C.: U.S. Department of Agriculture, 1991):9.

1. Unless otherwise noted, the data presented in this paper are from the 1988 Agricultural Economics and Land Ownership Survey (AELOS). See Bureau of the Census, *1987 Census of Agriculture,* Vol. 3, *Related Surveys,* Pt. 2, *Agricultural Economics and Land Ownership Survey,* AC87-RS-2 (Washington, D.C., 1990). Blackledge (in this volume) describes how the AELOS program was established, the survey methodology used, and how the results should be interpreted.

2. The 39 million acre (11 percent) difference between what is owned and what is rented out is agricultural land or land associated with former farm units. The land includes idle pasture and cropland as well as 1.5 million acres set aside in conservation reserve programs. The land in homestead units for the nearly 600,000 owners who live on farms rented to others is also included.

3. D. Baron, "The Status of Farmland Leasing in the United States," in J.P. DeBraal and G. Wunderlich, eds., *Rents and Rental Practices in United States Agriculture* (Oak Brook, Ill.: Farm Foundation, 1983).

4. D. Baron, "The Effects of Tenancy and Risk on Cropping Patterns: A Mathematical Programming Analysis," *Journal of Agricultural Economics Research* 34, no.4(1982); R. Reinsel and B. Johnson, *Farm Tenure and Cash Rents in the United States,* AER-190 (Washington, D.C.: U.S. Department of Agriculture, 1970).

5. B. Johnson, L. Janssen, M. Lundeen, and J.D. Aiken, "Agricultural Land Leasing and Rental Market Characteristics: A Case Study of South Dakota and Nebraska," University of Nebraska, Lincoln, 1987.

3

Taxing Farmland

J. Peter DeBraal

Real estate taxes—taxes that affect real estate values, income, and communities—are an important source of income to local governments for financing schools, police and fire protection, parks, and many social programs. But, according to the Federation of Tax Administrators, although property taxes (real and personal) may be rising as a percentage contribution to combined state and local revenues, they have been declining at the national level, from approximately 46 percent in 1960 to 30 percent in 1988.[1] Meanwhile, the share of state and local income taxes rose from about 10 to 26 percent of revenues between 1960 and 1988. Sales taxes provided from 32 to 36 percent of the revenues and miscellaneous taxes about 10 percent. In 1988, sales taxes represented the largest source of state and local revenues in 31 states, and the property tax was the principal source in 13 states. State and local income taxes were the largest source of revenue in 5 states.

The Farm Real Estate Taxes (FRET) Data Series

The U.S. Department of Agriculture (USDA) maintains a data series on farm real estate taxes (FRET), by state and nationally, that dates from 1890/1909—1890 for taxes per acre and 1909 for total taxes and taxes per $100 of full market value. The Bureau of Economic Analysis, predecessor to the Economic Research Service (ERS), made initial estimates in 1922, and further estimates during 1934-1936 made it possible to extend the series back to 1890/1909. Since the mid-1930s, adjustments have been made in the methods used in computing these taxes but the procedures remain generally the same. (Figure 3.1 shows the trend in farm real estate taxes per acre and per $100 of full market value from 1909 to 1990.)

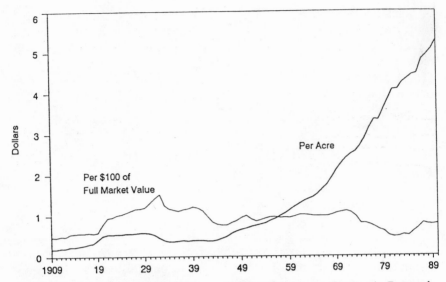

FIGURE 3.1 U.S. farm real estate taxes, 1909-1990. *Source:* Economic Research Service, U.S. Department of Agriculture, 1992.

Because of the social and economic impact of real estate taxation, public policy in agricultural affairs is directly affected. Congress, under the Agricultural Adjustment Act of 1938, specifically directed USDA to collect FRET data, which are then used as a component in USDA's prices-paid index for commodities and services, interest, taxes, and farm wages. The data are also used, for example, to assess farm expenditures.

The FRET data are estimates of real property taxes levied on farm and ranch land and buildings by state and local governments. Special assessments for improvements, such as drainage and irrigation (presumably based on benefits received rather than value itself), are excluded. The data are obtained from a nationwide survey of approximately 4,200 taxing jurisdictions that provide tax and acreage information on 10 farm or ranch parcels in their jurisdiction for the current and preceding years. Respondents in jurisdictions with fewer than 10 parcels are requested to provide information on all parcels in the jurisdiction. For 1990, the response rate from the 4,200 jurisdictions was about 66 percent. To expand the survey data to state- and national-level estimates, ERS uses Census of Agriculture data on acres of land in farms and farmland values. For noncensus years, the data are adjusted based on the percentage change in land in farms reported by the National Agricultural Statistics Service and ERS's annual estimates of farm real estate values. ERS uses taxes levied (the tax bill) rather than taxes paid because of taxpayer challenges or delinquencies, both of which may take several years to resolve. In the long run, ERS assumes, taxes levied and those paid are about equal.

Taxes levied on farm real estate (land and buildings) by state and local governments totaled $4.6 billion in 1990, up 3.5 percent from 1989. (These data do not include Alaska because of difficulties in determining the amount of privately owned taxable farmland in the state.) The U.S. average tax per acre was $5.27, up from $5.06 in 1989. The increase in taxes per acre was slightly greater than the increase in farmland values so that the average tax per $100 of full market value on U.S. farm real estate rose slightly, from $0.76 in 1989 to $0.78 in 1990. (See Figures 3.2 and 3.3, which display the divergence among states of taxes per acre and taxes per $100 of full market value, respectively.)

Compared with 1989, average taxes per acre in 1990 were higher in 39 states and lower in 10. Taxes per $100 of full market value were higher in 34 states, lower in 13, and unchanged in 2. Taxes varied widely among the states. For example, 1990 average taxes per acre ranged from $0.40 in New Mexico to $48.22 in Rhode Island (Figure 3.2). State taxes also varied within regions. In the Corn Belt, for example, taxes per acre ranged from $2.51 in Missouri to $15.24 in Illinois. Similarly, taxes per acre in the Southeast ranged from $1.32 in Alabama to $11.97 in Florida. Taxes per $100 of full market value ranged from $0.08 in Delaware to $3.30 in Michigan (Figure 3.3). Within the Mountain region, they ranged from $0.21 in New Mexico to $2.10 in Arizona.

Variations in farm real estate taxes among states are partly due to (1) the degree that states rely on real estate taxes as a source of local revenue, rather than income or sales taxes, and (2) the extent that states provide tax relief, such as preferential land-use assessment, homestead and old age exemptions, veteran's preferences, and so forth.

As of December 31, 1988, all 50 states had laws on preferential (or deferred) land-use assessment of farmland.[2] These laws provide that farmland devoted to a qualifying use be assessed on the basis of its use as farmland and not on its market value. Not unexpectedly, these laws vary from state to state. Some states have a minimum acreage requirement or require that the land be in its qualifying use for a number of years, or both. Other states require that the landowner receive a certain percentage of his or her yearly gross income from the land. Nineteen states have laws providing for preferential assessment with no penalty if there is a conversion to a nonqualifying use. Twenty-seven states have programs with a deferred (or rollback) tax—a penalty that is applied when the land is converted to a nonqualifying use. The tax is equal to the amount of taxes that would have been paid for a specified number of years had there been no preferential assessment. Six states, in addition to having preferential assessment laws, have laws providing for

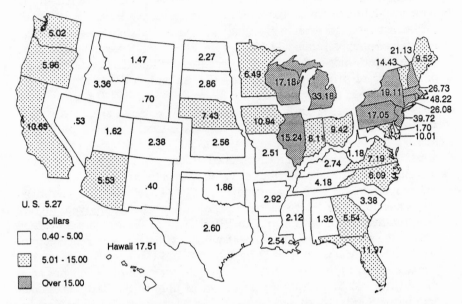

FIGURE 3.2 Farm real estate taxes, average per acre, 1990. *Source:* Economic Research Service, U.S. Department of Agriculture, 1992.

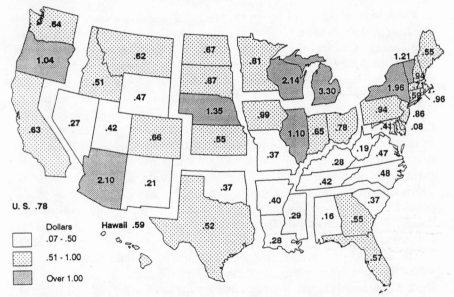

FIGURE 3.3 Farm real estate taxes per $100 of full market value, 1990. *Source:* Economic Research Service, U.S. Department of Agriculture, 1992.

restrictive agreements—an agreement that the landowner enters into with the state or local government restricting the land use in exchange for tax concessions. The penalty for breaking an agreement is essentially a deferred tax. Two states, New Hampshire and Pennsylvania, each have two programs, one based on preferential assessment and the other on restrictive agreements.

The FRET data are published in a variety of forms—this volume, for instance; a summary in USDA's *Agricultural Situation and Outlook* report on farmland values; and a USDA statistical bulletin covering the entire series from 1890 to date and providing a more elaborate discussion of how the data are gathered and analyzed. ERS uses the data to analyze the impacts of preferential assessment laws on tax returns, in particular, differences before the laws were enacted by the states and in years following enactments, and to examine tax differences between land with buildings and land without buildings.

Other Sources of Farm Real Estate Tax Data

There are other sources of farm real estate tax data. The Census Bureau's Agricultural Economics and Land Ownership Survey (AELOS) provides extensive data on farm real estate taxes. The bureau's Census of Governments is a potential source of such data. ERS's Farm Costs and Returns Survey provides farm real estate tax data for farm operators.

The AELOS data are comprehensive, but noticeably divergent from FRET data. For 1988, AELOS reported total taxes of $4.8 billion, taxes per acre of $6.08, and taxes per $100 of market value of $0.85. This compares with FRET total taxes of $4.3 billion, taxes per acre of $4.92, and taxes per $100 of market value of $0.77. These differences may be ascribed to the sources of information and the method of sampling. The AELOS data are from a one-time sample of farm real estate taxes *paid* by landowners, whereas the FRET data are from an annual survey of all taxing jurisdictions in which the local taxing authority provides the taxes *levied* for a sample of parcels. Nevertheless, the two surveys are complementary. The FRET series provides trend data, whereas AELOS provides data for cross-sectional analysis for the year of the survey for such items as financing, type of owner, method of acquisition, size of holdings, and so forth.

The two other sources of data on farm real estate taxes have serious limitations. The Census of Governments is heavily urban oriented. The Farm Cost and Returns Survey covers farm operators, who cannot be expected to have reliable real estate tax information on land they do not own.

Notes

J. Peter DeBraal is an attorney, Economic Research Service, U.S. Department of Agriculture. The views expressed are the author's and do not necessarily represent policies or views of the U.S. Department of Agriculture.

1. Federation of Tax Administrators, *Tax Administrators News* 54, no. 3(1990):34-35.

2. J.D. Aiken, *State Farmland Preferential Assessment Statutes*, RB 315 (Lincoln: University of Nebraska, 1989).

4

Collecting and Interpreting Farmland Data: The AELOS Program

John Blackledge

The 1988 Agricultural Economics and Land Ownership Survey (AELOS) was the most comprehensive survey of ownership of agricultural land ever undertaken in the United States. The results provide a broad range of information about the 3 million owners of agricultural land—who they are, how they acquired their land, what they do with it, and the extent to which they participate in management decisions on the land they rent to farm operators. As an integrated survey covering economic relationships and landownership, AELOS provides information at the state and regional level.

The AELOS was part of the 1987 Census of Agriculture program.[1] The Census of Agriculture is a quinquennial program that collects detailed information on the number of farms, land in farms, production of crops and livestock on farms, use of agricultural inputs, and characteristics of farms and farm operators for every county and state in the United States. The 1987 census provided the sampling frame for selecting the original mail file for AELOS.

Background

Researchers and policymakers have had few tools with which to study ownership of agricultural land. The only previous nationwide surveys of the number of agricultural landholders were associated with the 1900 and 1945 censuses of agriculture.

In the 1900 census, enumerators collected the name and address of the owners of all "rented farms," that is, farms operated on a tenant basis by individuals who did not own any of the land in the farm unit.

This excluded the landlord or owner involved in part-owner operations, which was the case for about 450,000 (8 percent) of the farms in 1900. The published results included the number of owners, acres owned, and number of tenants for tenant farms in 1900. The 1.9 million tenant farms were owned by 1.3 million owners.[2]

As part of the 1945 Census of Agriculture, enumerators collected the names and addresses of a sample of landowners while enumerating farms. Survey forms were mailed to the 130,000 landowners identified in the census processing. The U.S. Department of Agriculture (USDA) issued a report based on 38,000 responses to the survey. The report included information on how land was acquired, how the owner expected to transfer the land to children or relatives, owner's age and occupational characteristics, and whether land was rented out on a cash or share basis.[3]

The farm finance surveys associated with the 1959, 1964, 1969, and 1978 censuses of agriculture measured the farm-related capital investment, debt, and cash operating expenses provided by operators and their associated landlords for the farm unit. The surveys also detailed the characteristics of farm operators and landlords. However, the "landlords" represented the number of leases or rental arrangements associated with farm operations, not the actual number of landowners.

During the planning phase of the 1987 Census of Agriculture, the Bureau of the Census received numerous requests to satisfy the long-standing need for current information on landownership and to continue providing baseline financial data from the farm finance surveys. The Census Advisory Committee on Agriculture Statistics, agribusiness representatives, policymakers, academicians, and economic analysts were among those making such requests. Finally, in 1987 the Census Bureau, with financial assistance from USDA, established a single data collection program for the agricultural sector—AELOS. This program restored the financial series that had been discontinued in 1979 and placed equal emphasis on collecting landownership data.

Planning

Once the financial commitment had been made for AELOS, planning was quickly begun. A number of steps had to be taken if the report forms were to be mailed out on schedule in January 1989, only 14 months away. In particular, the survey designers had to get as much input from potential data users as possible on content issues.

After several months of meetings with representatives of various agricultural organizations and state and federal agencies, the survey designers resolved the final data content issues. There was neither sufficient money nor time to carry out a full-scale pretest. As an alternative, staff in the Census Bureau's Agriculture Division held approximately 20 meetings with farm operators in five states. At the meetings, participants completed either a landlord or operator report form and provided written and oral evaluations of the various questions asked on the forms. The meetings resulted in rewording and other modifications to the report forms and their instructions.

Identifying Landowners

Under ideal survey conditions, a sample of agricultural landowners would be selected from an inventory of all agricultural landowners. Because such an inventory was not available, the AELOS program had to use a different method to select its list of agricultural landowners. All agricultural landowners can be distinguished as either owner-operators or nonoperator-owners based on whether they operate a farm at a given point in time. Lists of owner-operators and nonoperator-owners were made by collecting landownership data from a sample of all farm operators and their associated landlords enumerated by the 1987 Census of Agriculture.[4]

The collection of data on farm operators and landlords was conducted in two stages. In stage 1, the report forms were mailed to the stratified sample of all farm operators from the 1987 Census of Agriculture. From those returns, a mailing list of landlords associated with farm rental land was developed. In stage 2, report forms were mailed to the landlords identified by farm operators in stage 1.

Additional steps were necessary to identify landowners. Owner-operators were readily identified from the operator reports, but additional processing was necessary to identify nonoperator-owners among the landlords. This was done to exclude public landlords, identify landlords who did not operate farms, and ensure that any landlord renting land to more than one tenant was included only once as a nonoperator-owner.

Public landlords include federal and state agencies, railroad companies, and Indian reservations. They were identified while the landlord mailing list was being processed and excluded from the ownership data.

The identification of landlords not operating farms was exhaustive. The landlord report form included the question, "Did you operate a farm or ranch in 1988?" Landlords who responded yes were compared with the 1987 census mail file. They were reclassified as not operating a farm if they were not located or located as a "nonfarm" in the 1987 census file. This was necessary because landlords are assumed to have a bias to respond as "farming" and to conform to the census definition of a farm. The landlords who did not respond to the question about operating a farm or ranch in 1988 were also matched to the 1987 census file and classified as a farm operator if identified in that file as a "farm."

To ensure that a nonoperator-owner was not duplicated, computer programs identified probable matches based on name and zip code. The probable matches were then manually reviewed to locate all landlords reported by two or more tenants. Such multiple landlords were coded to ensure that their acreage and personal characteristics were included only once in the landownership data if they qualified as a nonoperator-owner.

Use of the census as a sampling frame for follow-on surveys such as AELOS is economically efficient. The census provides a valid universe for sampling. Much of the information already collected in the 1987 Census of Agriculture was also used directly in the AELOS program to enhance the content without making report forms too long. For example, 1987 census data on the characteristics of the farm operators and the classifications of farms were used in the AELOS program.

Mailout and Response

Report forms were mailed to 44,000 farm operators. After four follow-up mailings, the final response rate was 82 percent. Of the 47,000 landlord names collected from operator reports (stage 1), report forms were mailed to 44,000 (stage 2). The remaining 3,000 were public landlords and those for whom there was an insufficient address for mailing. The response rate for the landlord survey was 78 percent.

Obtaining the names and addresses of landlords for stage 2 was one of the more difficult and time-consuming processing steps. A large number of the names and addresses were illegible or missing, and farm operators had to be recontacted to obtain adequate names and addresses. Even after careful review of the names and addresses reported by farm operators, a major effort was required to remail successfully a large number of originally undeliverable report forms to landlords throughout the country.

Editing the Data

Nonresponse and Missing/Inconsistent Data

The response to both mailings was substantial considering the complex nature of the report forms. Nonresponse to the operator report form was accounted for by reweighting the sample of farm operators. Missing data for nonrespondent landlords and landlords who returned reports without providing basic information on acres owned and the like were accounted for by an imputation process. This was necessary for two reasons, sample expansion and farm unit data. Expanding the sample to represent the universe of landlords was controlled by the farm operator file used in the stage 1 mailing. Each landlord had the same final expansion weight as the associated farm operator. If a nonrespondent landlord for an operator had not been included in the final file, the expansion of landlord data would have been short of the true estimate. It was also necessary to account for each landlord associated with a farm operator in order to estimate accurately the financial and physical contributions of the landlord(s) to an associated farm unit.

Imputation of data for nonrespondent landlords was accomplished by a combination of clerical and computerized editing. The basic data—acres of land rented to the operator and type of ownership—were obtained by using the landlord name and acres leased as reported by the farm operator. Such items as value of land and buildings, landowner-ship characteristics, taxes, and landlord characteristics and occupation were imputed by computerized editing programs. The imputation was based on the characteristics of landlords with similar acreage in the same geographic area. Responses to questions about participation in management decisions, net cash income, and characteristics of corporate landlords (sections 5, 8, and 10B of the landlord's report form) were not imputed on the grounds that those items were not necessarily related to acres rented out or owned. Approximately 590,000 (33 percent) of the 1.8 million landlords were accounted for by imputation.

The most serious response problems were with the landlord report form. Although the landlord response rate of 78 percent was only 4 percentage points short of the response rate for operators, the quality of the reports returned by landlords was not as good. (The 78 percent response rate includes landlord reports returned blank or incomplete and accounted for in the imputation process.) A few examples of problems with the landlord reports follow:

- Some landlords were obviously confused about what they were to report as expenditures. In response to questions about expenditures, a comment such as "ask the operator" was their only reply. This indicates that they did not understand they were to report expenditures they made as a landlord on the land rented to a specific farm operator. When this occurred, the landlord may not have included expenses associated with the land leased to the tenant.
- Some farm operators leasing the land completed the landlord report forms. Such instances were identified by comparing the

name of the person completing the landlord report with the name of the farm operator. Apparently some landlords chose to put the response burden on the tenant. This may have resulted in accurate estimates of expenditures the landlord made for the farm unit but less accurate detail on landownership data and landlord characteristics.

- Some landlords skipped the questions relating to the number of leases and value of rent received in error. Landlords who had not purchased land in 1988 were instructed to skip to the next item, item 7. However, it became obvious that some did not see item 7 and skipped directly to *section* 7, which immediately followed item 7. The operator report form had the same wording but it did not create a problem. because the sequence of questions was different.

- About 10 percent of all landlords are also farm operators. A few landlords who operate farms were obviously confused by the landlord report form. Some farm operators who rented land to others included financial data for their own agricultural activities in addition to their contribution to the tenant(s) for whom they were to respond. This had no impact on the landownership data because those landlords, by definition, were owner-operators and excluded from the ownership data.

Steps were taken during the data processing to minimize the impact of nonresponses to items or sections of the report forms and to salvage as much information from remarks or attached notes as possible. All report forms were manually screened prior to data keying. Respondents answering no to debt or operating expenses were identified and coded during this review. Difficult problems and all preidentified large-scale operations were also referred to an analyst for review prior to data keying.

After the data were keyed, computerized editing programs were used to make comprehensive checks for consistency among related data items and to check individual entries. The editing programs corrected erroneous or inconsistent data and supplied missing data based on similar reports within the same geographic area. Large changes and predetermined data relationships were identified in the editing and flagged for manual review and correction.

Because "no debt" for landlords and operators and "no expenses" for landlords were manually precoded, the editing program was able to recognize nonresponses to the expenses and/or debt questions. For nonresponses the program would determine if expenses or debt should be added to the report and the dollar amount to be imputed. The decision to impute and the dollar amount were based on indicators held in the editing process from similar reports. Key items for the farm operator reports were also compared with 1987 census data and major inconsistencies were flagged for manual review.

Reconciling Operator and Landlord Reports

The initial reviews of the landlord and operator reports were conducted independently to save time. It would have delayed processing to hold the farm operator reports until the associated landlord reports were returned and available for review in conjunction with the operator reports. As processing progressed, however, a review (or reconciliation) of the major comparable data items in the two reports was completed.

Four categories of data were matched during the reconciliation process. The number of acres and the value of land and buildings the farm operator reported for rented land were compared with equivalent values reported by the landlord(s). The levels of expenditures and assets provided by the landlords were compared with the scale or overall size of the farm unit.

The reconciliation phase identified some of the reporting problems described earlier, such as landlords including gross expenditures instead of expenses associated with the acres leased to the specified farm operator. The reconciliation also identified reporting or imputation errors for land values, expenditures, and other data items.

Large or Unusual Landownership Reports

At the onset of the data collection, AELOS staff were concerned about what type of ownership structure existed for landlords and how it might affect data collection. Would a number of farm operators report holding companies or bank trusts as landholders? How many landlords used agents to handle the leasing of their property? If a significant number of landlords or acres were involved in holding companies, would the quality of data on the characteristics of landlords/nonoperator-owners be compromised?

Although these questions cannot be answered definitively, there were relatively few instances of landholding companies being involved. There were instances in which companies held significant tracts of nonagricultural land, such as land for mineral or timber resources, but data on nonagricultural lands were deleted during processing.

Real Estate Tax Data

Real estate tax data published in the AELOS report relate farm operator characteristics to tax rates. Data of this nature are unique and are not available from USDA's annual series on real estate taxes. For example, in 1988 the real estate tax paid by landlords on farms with losses was $4.13 per acre compared with $6.61 per acre for farms with gains.

The real estate taxes paid and the tax rate per acre were estimated from responses to questions about acreage and real estate taxes. Operators and landlords were instructed to include the information on acres taxed and real estate taxes paid from all tax bills in 1988 for the farm and ranch land, buildings, and other improvements.

The next step was to establish the real estate taxes paid for each farm unit. This was necessary because the real estate tax is an important component of the operating expenses paid by the operator as well as the landlord for the farm unit. Real estate taxes for the farm unit exclude the taxes paid on land the operator rents to others and include only the taxes paid by the landlord on the acres leased to the farm unit.

To arrive at the estimated real estate taxes for the farm unit, the report for taxes paid and acres taxed for all land owned was used to establish a "tax rate per acre" for each operator and landlord. The tax rate per acre multiplied by the acres owned and included in the farm unit for each landlord and operator was summed to arrive at the estimated real estate tax for the farm unit. The method implies that the acres in the farm unit are taxed at the same rate as any acres not in the farm unit.

The question arises as to whether taxes on residential property have an effect on the farm data. This may be more prevalent for landlords than operators. As an example, if a landlord has a contiguous parcel of land that includes his or her residence and rents all but the residence to a farm operator, would the data from the tax bill include the residence? If the answer is yes, and assuming the tax rate per acre is higher for the residence and its associated lot than for the farm, the estimated tax on the property rented to the farm operator will be overstated.

Limitations of AELOS Data

The survey sample was designed to provide estimates with an average error of 15 percent or less for state estimates. The results included both sampling and nonsampling error. At all points, care was taken to identify and correct respondent errors and to avoid introducing processing error. Some nonsampling-type errors related to the design of the report forms were described above. In addition, the methods used to account for nonresponses contributed to both sampling and nonsampling errors.

Some data limitations derive from the method used to arrive at estimates for owners of agricultural land. The AELOS estimates are not an absolute total for 1988. The sample selected excluded "abnormal" farms and horticultural specialty farms, or nearly 37,000 farms and 58.7 million acres included in the 1987 Census of Agriculture. This was consistent with procedures used in prior farm finance surveys.

Abnormal farms (55 million acres or nearly 6 percent of all land in farms) were excluded because of their unusual ownership and resulting financial characteristics. Abnormal farms are primarily institutional farms, research and experimental farms, and farms on Indian reservations.

Including the 35,000 horticultural specialty farms in 1988 would have added 2 percent to the number of owner-operators if all operators were indeed owners. All horticultural farms were included in the 1988 Census of Horticultural Specialties and therefore excluded from AELOS to reduce the burden on respondents.[5]

The number of owners also does not include all the individuals who share interest in agricultural land. By census definition, there is only one operator per farm unit. The same principle was applied to landownership. This method does not measure the number of family members, partners, or stockholders who have interest in landownership.

Changes in the status of the farm operation from 1987 to 1988 are also not reflected in the AELOS data. There were 3,148 operators from the 1987 census who returned AELOS report forms but were no longer farming in 1988. When expanded, those observations represented 232,000 farms with 68.1 million acres and $7.5 million in sales, based on acres and sales in the 1987 Census of Agriculture. No attempt was made to include new farm operations (or "births") started in 1988 in the survey.[6]

Current Use and Future Prospects for AELOS

In addition to the wealth of AELOS information already available in printed form, special tabulations can be constructed from the microdata files used to compile the AELOS report. Some of the data presented in various chapters of this volume include the results of special tabulations using the AELOS microdata files. The Census Bureau, however, does not release any reports or tabulations that might reveal individual responses. The microdata files can be accessed only by Census Bureau staff and sworn agents acting on behalf of the bureau. As with any information collected by the Census Bureau, safeguarding the confidentiality of individual reports is a primary concern and responsibility.

The Census Bureau has no plans for including an AELOS program in the 1992 Census of Agriculture program. Requests for the Commerce Department to continue the AELOS program in the future have been circulated. The scope, content, and likelihood of AELOS-type surveys in the future, however, will depend in part on the influence of the users.

Notes

John Blackledge is a statistician, Census of Agriculture, Bureau of the Census. The views expressed are the author's and do not necessarily represent policies or views of the U.S. Department of Commerce.

1. Bureau of the Census, *1987 Census of Agriculture,* Vol. 3, *Related Surveys,* Pt. 2, *Agricultural Economics and Land Ownership Survey,* AC87-RS-2 (Washington, D.C., 1990).

2. See Bureau of the Census, *Twelfth Census of the United States,* Vol. 5, *Agriculture,* Pt. 1, *Farms, Livestock and Animal Products* (Washington, D.C., 1902):Tables 21-25.

3. For further details, see B.T. Inman and W.H. Fippin, *Farm Land Ownership in the United States,* Misc. Pub. No. 699, Bureau of Agricultural Economics (Washington, D.C.: U.S. Department of Agriculture, 1949).

4. The enumeration of a sample of operators and their landlords served multiple purposes in the integrated AELOS program. The sample of farm operators and associated landlords was used to tabulate financial data for farm units, Tables 1-65 of the AELOS report (see note 1). The information for owner-operators and nonoperator-owners was combined to describe "owned land in farms," Tables 66-113 of the AELOS report.

5. Bureau of the Census, *1987 Census of Agriculture,* Vol. 4, *Census of Horticultural Specialties,* AC87-HOR-1 (Washington, D.C., 1991).

6. The appendixes to the AELOS report provide a complete list of definitions used in the survey, descriptions of the data collection procedures and statistical methodology, and copies of the report forms and information sheets mailed to the respondents. Further information about the survey can be obtained from the AELOS report (see note 1).

PART TWO

Explanation

The accumulation ... of property ... and its security to individuals in every society must be an effect of the protection afforded to it by the joint strength of the society in the execution of its laws. Private property therefore is a creature of society, and is subject to the calls of that society.

—B. Franklin, *Writings*, 1789

5

Concepts of Property and Taxation

Joan M. Youngman

The most common method of examining the interaction of concepts of property, taxation, and land policy considers specific connections among these separate areas. For example, preferential methods of taxing agricultural land clearly use the tax as an instrument of land policy.[1] However, these areas are also united by their relationship to a larger system of rights governed by legal concepts of property. Concepts of property and of taxation, in turn, touch upon basic political and social issues concerning the delineation of rights among individuals and between individuals and the state.[2]

Concepts of Property in the Treatment of Partial Interests: The Case of Easements

The legal concept of property does not denote the tangible or intangible objects that are termed property in common speech. Rather, *property* as a legal concept refers to rights and interests in such objects.[3] Nonetheless, references to the objects of those rights as property persist in legislative and judicial statements dealing with the taxation of land and buildings. As James Bonbright observed,

> Because the law of early capitalism concerned itself so largely with rights of full, undivided ownership, and because these rights attached mainly to specific, tangible objects, like land or chattels, the property rights in these objects were closely identified with the objects themselves.... A court, no less than a layman, will sometimes refer to a tract of land or a shipment of wheat as property, and will sometimes refer to the interests of people in this land or this shipment as property.[4]

This distinction was central to the concept of legal relations developed by the legal philosopher Wesley Hohfeld. He wrote,

> Sometimes [*property*] is employed to indicate the physical object to which various legal rights, privileges, etc. relate; then again—with far greater discrimination and accuracy—the word is used to denote the legal interest (or aggregate of legal relations) appertaining to such physical object.[5]

Property rights and interests may take a number of forms. They may consist of the permanent rights associated with full ownership, limited only by superior claims of the sovereign or the governing body, or they may constitute rights of temporary use or possession, such as a leasehold. They may also include rights to restrict the use to which land or buildings are put by other parties, rights to share in the proceeds of productive use or transfer, and rights to direct future use or ownership to other parties. In each case, a preexisting legal structure provides the setting within which private parties arrange their economic affairs.

The *easement* is a property right that illustrates many of the difficulties and potential benefits of such divided legal claims. An easement is an interest, either positive or negative, in land in the possession of another.[6] A positive easement allows its holder to make some specified use of the property. An easement of way, for example, prevents the holder's entry on the property from constituting trespass. A negative easement prevents the owner or possessor of the affected property from taking some otherwise permissible action with regard to it. In this manner, an easement of air and light prevents the owner of an adjacent lot from erecting structures on a given location or above a given height. In Hohfeldian terms, grantors of easements of way relinquish their right to keep the grantees from their property and have instead a position of "no-right" to protest such intrusion. Correspondingly, the grantees exchange their duty to refrain from trespass for a privilege of entry.[7]

These examples illustrate a special characteristic of many easements. Unlike a mortgage, life interest, or lease, an easement in specific property was traditionally held by the owner of a neighboring estate. Such an *appurtenant* easement could follow the ownership of the benefited, or dominant, estate, and the obligations of the easement could correspondingly run to future owners of the burdened, or servient, estate.[8] This situation further complicated the concepts of property rights and ownership, for the easement came to be considered as belonging to the dominant estate. As explained in *American Law of Property*,

The relation between a dominant tenement and an easement appurtenant to it is often described as though the easement belonged in some way to the tenement. Since an easement is an aggregate of legal relations and since such relations exist only between legal persons, to describe an easement as belonging to anyone other than a legal person is to use figurative language.[9]

In *The Common Law,* Oliver Wendell Holmes ascribed this confusion to the survival in legal language of terms proper to a concept of property as itself a legal person, "where an axe was made the object of criminal process":[10]

As easements were said to belong to the dominant estate, it followed that whoever possessed the land had a right of the same degree over what was incidental to it. If the true meaning had been that a way or other easement admits of possession, and is taken possession of with the land to which it runs, and that its enjoyment is protected on the same grounds as possession in other cases, the thought could have been understood. But that was not the meaning of the Roman law, and, as has been shown, it is not the doctrine of ours. We must take it that easements have become an incident of land by an unconscious and unreasoned assumption that a piece of land can have rights. It need not be said that this is absurd, although the rules of law which are based upon it are not so.[11]

Most commentators have accepted the traditional classification of an easement as an *incorporeal hereditament.*[12] A hereditament, says Blackstone, "is by much the largest and most comprehensive expression: for it includes not only lands and tenements, but whatsoever may be *inherited,* be it corporeal or incorporeal, real, personal, or mixed."[13] Hohfeld commented,

It is clear that only legal interests as such can be inherited; yet in the foregoing quotation there is inextricable confusion between the physical or "corporeal" objects and the corresponding legal interests, all of which latter must necessarily be "incorporeal" ... The legal interest of the fee simple owner of land and the comparatively limited interest of the owner of a "right of way" over such land are alike so far as "incorporeality" is concerned; the true contrast consists, of course, primarily in the fact that the fee simple owner's aggregate of legal relations is far more extensive than the aggregate of the easement owner.[14]

Hohfeld considered easements, like other partial interests in property, to be aggregates of rights (or claims), privileges, powers and immunities vested in the "owner" of the interest.... For this reason it is a serious obstacle to close analysis and clear thinking that courts and writers habitually deal with the easement (as they do with all other legal interests) as if it were a simple unity to be described adequately by a few loose and ambiguous terms such as "property," "title," "ownership," "*right* of ownership," "right," "privilege," "incorporeal (!) right," etc.—terms utterly insufficient to indicate the precise elements involved.[15]

Attachment of the benefit of an appurtenant easement to a specified parcel of land led in turn to the common practice of assessing that benefit as part of the taxable value of the dominant estate. The character of the property tax as a tax *in rem*, one against the land and not against the owner personally, encouraged the fallacy of imputing the characteristics of a legal person to real property. Hohfeld quoted with admiration from Holmes's opinion in *Tyler v. Court of Registration:* "All proceedings, like all rights, are really against persons. Whether they are proceedings or rights in rem depends upon the number of persons affected."[16] Hohfeld then expanded and elaborated upon the approach of this opinion to draw a distinction between rights *in rem* and those *in personam:*

A paucital right, or claim (right *in personam*) is either a unique right residing in a person (or group of persons) and availing against a single person (or single group of persons); or else it is one of a *few* fundamentally similar, yet separate, rights availing respectively against a few definite persons. A multital right, or claim (right *in rem*) is always *one* of a large *class* of *fundamentally similar* yet separate rights, actual or potential, residing in a single person (or single group of persons) but availing *respectively* against persons constituting a very large and indefinite class of people.[17]

By drawing a distinction on the basis of the number of persons affected and the existence of similar rights of the same class, Hohfeld once again attacked any reliance upon a concept of property as the physical object itself. An action *in rem* existed within the same universe of rights, interests, privileges, and duties held by human beings as did the concept of property itself.

Use of Easements for Agricultural Preservation

The seemingly esoteric issues of jurisprudence and legal theory discussed above have important practical consequences for ordering economic affairs that concern real property. They play a central role in current efforts in the United States to use easements to conserve agricultural land.

An agricultural preservation easement, like a historical preservation easement or an open-space easement, restricts the affected land to certain uses—in this case, to specified agricultural uses.[18] This is accomplished not through a personal contractual agreement with the owner, but through a conveyance of specific elements of the owner's rights, such as the right to undertake commercial development. In effect, the grant of a negative easement in the land itself has taken the place of an individual agreement with the present owner.

Current preservation efforts that make use of easements include the 1990 Farms for the Future Act,[19] which authorizes government purchase of scenic easements and building rights in agricultural areas threatened by development, and a program of the Farmers Home Administration that forgives debt on environmentally sensitive lands in exchange for conservation easements on that property.[20] Similar programs for agricultural preservation have been undertaken by state and local governments[21] and private conservation organizations.[22] Conveyance of a property right through the creation of an easement can offer greater permanence than individual and time-limited contractual agreements for land preservation.

In the area of contractual agreements, the Conservation Reserve Program (CRP) administered by the U.S. Department of Agriculture constitutes the major program for preservation of agricultural land in the United States.[23] It offers farmers cash payments for agreeing to retire specified land from crop production for a 10-year period. Thus far, it has enrolled over 35 million acres of land, an area equivalent to the state of Illinois.[24] Future decisions on the effect of changes in ownership on such contractual agreements will provide important guidance on their potential to serve as alternatives to easement programs.[25]

The success of a conservation or preservation easement program depends largely on the status of an easement under property law and its effect on assessments for property tax purposes. If such easements are not accorded the permanence and transferability traditionally granted appurtenant easements, their existence will be threatened by any change in ownership. Similarly, if the effect of an easement on value is not recognized in the property tax assessment process, owners will be reluctant to agree to such restrictions unless the payment to them compensates for this tax burden.[26]

The correct procedure for taxing land subject to an easement has raised legal, administrative, and legislative controversy.[27] If the transfer of rights pursuant to the grant of an easement is equivalent to a transfer of property, the easement should result in a reduction in the property tax assessment of the underlying land. However, an assessor may be unwilling to reduce the local property tax base by reason of a preservation policy set by a different level of government, particularly if that policy has already resulted in a significant transfer payment to the owner now seeking a tax reduction.[28]

These disputes give evidence of unresolved questions about the nature of property rights and ownership. For example, an owner may argue that payment received for an easement provides no grounds for refusing to lower the valuation of the remaining property from its unencumbered level. From the owner's point of view, the easement constitutes the sale of a portion of his or her interest in the property, and the payment confirms that the assessment should now be upon a lesser set of rights. Yet to the extent the easement is operationally similar to the Conservation Reserve Program and similar contractual agreements, this argument is undercut. Under these programs, the payments received by the owner reflect the value of the land subject to tax. The Conservation Reserve Program may in turn be compared with payment in kind for not raising particular crops.[29] Both are payments for a particular use of the land, and both provide a basis for imputing rental income—and therefore a higher assessed value—to the owner.[30] This illustrates the ambiguities in the distinction between property transfers and contractual agreements that must be clarified before their effects on property taxation can be determined.

Legal Concepts of Taxation

The legal concept of *taxation* is equally affected by recognition of property as a set of legal rights in a given object. Because those rights may be divided among multiple parties, including the sovereign or the state, a property tax may be considered the payment made to the holder of one set of those rights by the holder of another set for the privilege of their continued use and enjoyment. In effect, the property tax has taken on many characteristics of a rental payment under a lease.[31]

Another uncertain boundary to the concept of a *tax* concerns the distinction between a tax and a user charge. This distinction has grown in importance as governments at all levels attempt to respond to taxpayer discontent by increasing their reliance on charges for revenue. It poses a legal issue insofar as restrictions on either taxes or charges must be interpreted for application to a particular levy.[32] It is also an economic issue; the analysis of a tax as a fee for government services is most plausible for local government taxes on property within its jurisdiction.

The choice between a fee and a charge has obvious implications for redistribution of the tax burden among classes of taxpayers. The political turmoil engendered by the "community charge" in the United Kingdom was only the most recent and dramatic demonstration of this phenomenon.[33] In a more subtle fashion, the contrast between the systems of payment for higher education in the United States and in the social democracies of Western Europe illustrates the same point. Taxpayer levies that fund European universities constitute a "tax" insofar as they satisfy the criterion of a compulsory charge unrelated to the use of specific services. When compared with tuition payments in the United States, however, they demonstrate how such a tax can, as a social and economic fact, take on many of the attributes of a fee for private consumption.[34]

Property Taxes and Property Rights

The legal view of property as a set of rights in and to a specific object permits a deeper understanding of the distinctions among systems of property ownership. A simple dichotomy between private ownership and state ownership overlooks both their common features and alternatives that incorporate elements of each.[35]

The universal existence of some form of public restriction on an owner's use of private property shows that a nominal owner or titleholder in fact never possesses the entire set of rights that together make up the property as a whole. An owner who holds property subject to zoning restrictions, building and use restrictions, environmental restrictions, and historic preservation restrictions, among others, by no means possesses all rights in it. Strictly speaking, the titleholder does not own the entire property. Conversely, a system of state ownership of property that grants tenure rights to businesses and residents at subsidized or controlled rents has in fact transferred important property rights to those tenants.[36] Legally enforceable property rights of these kinds do not require the existence of a formally sanctioned market; even if such rights cannot be openly bought and sold, the owner's ability to protect his or her rights in land or buildings raises those rights to the level of a property interest.

The fact that the titleholder or other specified party is designated as the taxpayer under property tax statutes does not negate this division of "ownership" among multiple parties. The taxing jurisdiction may, for administrative convenience, value the parcel as a single unit and send one notification of the assessment and one tax bill. This does not affect the division of total value among all parties with an interest in the property—or all "owners."

A division of property interests between a landlord and tenant, or between co-owners, or between a life tenant and the holder of a

remainder interest clearly does not require a taxing jurisdiction to ap-
portion an assessment among each of the parties according to the value
of their interests. In order to accomplish such an apportionment, the
assessor would have to evaluate the terms of each lease, deed, or trust
agreement creating the division of interests and make an annual adjustment to the relative shares of the parties as the lease term or life interest
expired.[37] The designation of a specific party as the taxpayer for administrative purposes has no bearing on the status of the holders of other
interests as a matter of property law. Nor does it affect their actual responsibility for payment of the tax according to the terms of the lease or
other agreement among themselves.

A tax on land and buildings can thus be considered one form of a
state or public interest in property. Just as a tenant must pay rent to
continue occupancy of leased premises, so must the landlord or other
titleholder arrange for the payment of property taxes to ensure his or
her continued possession of this property. No analysis of the distribution of property rights in a given economic or political system can be
complete without an understanding of the component of taxation.

A striking example concerns the California tax-limitation measure
popularly known as Proposition 13. Adopted by citizen initiative in
1978, this amendment to the state constitution restricted the valuation of
property for tax purposes to its 1975-1976 market value, or its acquisition price if purchased later, and imposed a 2 percent ceiling on annual
inflation adjustments in the absence of a sale.[38] Given the enormous rise
in California housing prices over the past 15 years, this provision has
amounted to a massive redistribution of the tax burden among owners
of otherwise equivalent property, depending on the time of acquisition.[39] It is clear that owners in California do not in fact hold equivalent
property rights once the government's claim to a specified tax payment
is taken into account, just as tenants of physically identical buildings do
not hold the same property interests if their leases call for radically different rental payments.

The parallel between the tax provisions of Proposition 13 and explicit
tenure rights has grown even more pronounced in California since the
measure's initial passage. The statutory definition of a change in ownership requiring a new assessment at market value provides an example
of what is, in form, a technical implementation measure but, in fact, a
determination of substantive property rights. Both the legislature and
the voters readily excluded from this category any transfer between
spouses, to the survivor on the death of a spouse, and between former
spouses as part of a divorce settlement.[40] An exception for a transfer to
the owner's children poses far more difficult issues of horizontal equity
and the intergenerational shelter of accumulated wealth. Experience

throughout the world has shown that revaluation becomes more disruptive and politically unacceptable the longer the period between revaluations—and therefore the greater the changes in assessed valuations.[41] The California legislature was thus understandably reluctant to expand this particular exception to the definition of a change in ownership and limited it to disabled children and minor children. This approach was completely reversed by referendum in 1986. By popular vote, California revised the definition of a change in ownership to exclude all transfers of a primary residence between parents and children and all transfers of additional property of up to $1 million in value.[42]

Several aspects of this legislation are of interest with regard to the interaction of concepts of property, taxation, and land policy. A definitional adjustment to a technical valuation provision has substantially expanded the property rights held by a very specific and not readily identifiable class: members of a family unit in which property held by the parents is suitable for use, as a residence, as income-producing property, or for some other purpose, by their surviving children. Just as the right of tenants to occupy specific premises in systems of nominal state ownership constitutes property, rights to preferential tax treatment are no less a form of property for their convoluted and arbitrary nature. In fact, as in the case of tenure rights, their disguised nature permits them to escape political scrutiny even as it magnifies their distortion of the economic process. Surely a lively debate would have followed the introduction of an explicit spending measure designed to benefit only persons enjoying intergenerational multimillion-dollar wealth. Surely even more questions would have been raised had this subsidy been conditioned upon the economically inefficient requirement that the younger generation occupy the same physical quarters as their parents, with no option of putting that property on the market and buying another home.

Henry George, Property Rights, and Taxation

The link between taxation provisions and tenure rights brings the consideration of contemporary problems full circle to the social and political issues identified by Henry George more than a century ago.[43] George argued that the value of land that preexists any building or other improvement should accrue to society rather than to the owner holding title. That value, due to location and natural resources rather than to any human effort, he saw as rightfully claimed by the community rather than by the individual holding legal title to it. Thus, the distinction between the ownership of property as a unitary entity and possession of some subset of all rights in specified land and buildings is central to George's work. Ownership can be identified with the right to productive use of the land, rather than any right to withhold the land from production in hope of speculative gains.   Significantly, George's proposal for reclaiming this land value for the community did not involve a transfer of legal title. Instead, he called for a tax on the rental value of the land, economically equivalent to an expropriation of some or all of that value—and therefore of some or all of that property— depending on the level at which the tax was set. In this way, a system of private ownership could coexist with a socialization of rental value.[44]

Far from diminishing in importance with the passage of time, George's ideas are as timely for consideration as current debates, heard from Vermont to Tokyo,[45] concerning the appropriate method of taxing speculative land gains. Yet his ideas yield no simple nor universal prescription for resolution of this issue. The same factors that draw these property tax questions from the domain of finance and administration into the realm of political, economic, and social organization require that suggestions for their solution be informed by an equally wide range of disciplines and perspectives.

No economy today exists in a state of nature; it would be difficult indeed to convince an owner who had just purchased a plot of land with the accumulated savings of a lifetime of productive effort that the value of that bare land represented a social asset appropriate for a confiscatory tax. It would be no less difficult to persuade an impoverished peasant in an economy with the extreme stratification of wealth typical of many developing nations that land similar to that he farms should bear no higher tax by reason of the lavish hotel or office building constructed on it. Around the world, governments facing revenue shortfalls will find it difficult to reduce or eliminate any portion of a long-standing tax, particularly in an era when the general trend, led by income tax reform, is toward a broadening of the tax base and a corresponding reduction in tax rates. Practical assistance in addressing these issues requires that a theoretical understanding of the interaction of property rights, land policy, and taxation be combined with an equal appreciation of the specific political, social, and cultural settings in which these issues arise. This is a challenging task, and one that cannot be attempted within the confines of any single discipline.

Conclusion

A consideration of the legal structure of property law and of tax policy quickly raises fundamental issues of social organization because both fields involve decisions as to the distribution of rights: rights of ownership, rights of occupancy, rights of society and of the state. Such choices are an expression of underlying social values. "Property is not thought to be a right because it is an enforceable claim: it is an enforceable claim only because and in so far as the prevailing ethical theory holds that it is a necessary human right."[46] A recognition of these connections will enrich studies of land policy and taxation by permitting comparative reference between the two fields. Such a recognition will also help place studies in both areas within the context of the basic social and political structures within which they operate.

Notes

Joan M. Youngman is senior fellow, Lincoln Institute of Land Policy.

1. See generally, S. Redfield, *Vanishing Farmland: A Legal Solution for the States* (Lexington, Mass.: Lexington Books, 1984):95-130. For an argument that "the local real property tax system is the most important of the land use control systems," see N. Williams, "The Three Systems of Land Use Control," *Rutgers Law Review* 25 (1970):80, discussed in D. Myers, "The Legal Aspects of Agricultural Districting," *The Agricultural Law Journal*, 1980-1981 Annual:627, 631.

2. "No one will doubt that the institution and the concept of property are central to the current debates about capitalism, socialism, and such problems of 'post-industrial' society as the rights of the individual, the corporation, and the state." C. Macpherson, ed., *Property: Mainstream and Critical Positions* (Toronto: University of Toronto Press, 1978):i.

3. See, e.g., American Law Institute, *Restatement of the Law of Property* (St. Paul, Minn.: American Law Institute Publishers, 1944):Sec. 5 ("The word 'interest' is used in this Restatement both generically to include varying aggregates of rights, privileges, powers and immunities and distributively to mean any one of them"); Sec. 8 ("The term 'real property,' as it is used in this Restatement, means those interests in land described herein in sections 14-18 inclusive"); Sec. 9 ("The word 'estate,' as it is used in this Restatement, means an interest in land which (a) is or may become possessory; and (b) is ownership measured in terms of duration.").

4. J. Bonbright, *The Valuation of Property* (New York: McGraw-Hill, 1937), Vol. 1:100, 101.

5. W. Hohfeld, "Some Fundamental Legal Conceptions as Applied in Judicial Reasoning," *Yale Law Journal* 23(1913):16, 21.

6. A.J. Casner, ed., *American Law of Property* (Boston: Little, Brown, 1952), Vol. 2:Sec. 8.5.

7. See Hohfeld, "Some Fundamental Legal Conceptions as Applied in Judicial Reasoning," 16.

8. Casner, *American Law of Property*, Vol. 2:Secs. 8.71, 8.75.

9. *Ibid.*, Sec. 8.13.

10. O.W. Holmes, *The Common Law*, ed. M. Howe (London: Macmillan, 1968):297.

11. *Ibid.*, 299.

12. E.g., Comment, "Taxation of Easements in Airspace," *Maryland Law Review* 33(1973):159; C. Sweet, "The True Nature of an Easement," *Law Quarterly Review* 24(1908):259.

13. W. Blackstone, *Commentaries,* Vol. 2:*17. The definition of hereditament is taken from Sir Edward Coke, *Institutes,* Vol. 1:*6.

14. Hohfeld, "Some Fundamental Legal Conceptions as Applied in Judicial Reasoning," 16.

15. W. Hohfeld, "Faulty Analysis in Easement and License Cases," in W. Hohfeld, *Fundamental Legal Conceptions* (New Haven, Conn.: Yale University Press, 1923):162 (emphasis in original).

16. 175 Mass. 71, at 76, 55 N.E. 812, at 814 (1900), cited by Hohfeld in *Fundamental Legal Conceptions,* 75.

17. Hohfeld, "Some Fundamental Legal Conceptions as Applied in Judicial Reasoning."

18. See, e.g., "Comment, Forever a Farm: The Agricultural Conservation Easement in Pennsylvania," *Dickinson Law Review* 24(1990):527.

19. P.L. 101-624, Secs. 1465-1470, 104 Stat. 3359, 3616-19 (1990).

20. This is the Section 118 Farm Debt Restructuring and Conservation Set-Aside Program, described in A. Miller and J. Wright, "Report of the Subcommittee on Innovative Growth Management Measures: Preservation of Agricultural Land and Open Space," *The Urban Lawyer* 23(1991):821, 830.

21. See, e.g., "Comment, Forever a Farm."

22. Although exact estimates differ, the American Farmland Trust is reported to have assisted in the protection of 38,833 acres of farmland in 18 states through the use of conservation easements. Founded in 1980, it has 20,000 members and donors, including conservationists, farmers, and business owners, and an annual budget of $3 million. C. Shetterly, *States News Service,* March 8, 1991; "Leaders in the Field," *Los Angeles Times,* November 29, 1990:10.

23. This provides payments to farmers who agree to remove environmentally sensitive land, such as property in danger of erosion, former wetlands, or lands posing a potential threat to sources of drinking water, from production for 10-year periods. It was first instituted by the 1985 Food Security Act, 16 U.S.C. Sec. 3831. Similar programs have been undertaken in other countries, particularly those in the European Community. The Netherlands, for example, has retired 100,000 hectares from production in order to reduce nitrate contamination in its aquifers. A. Manale, "European Community Program to Control Nitrate Emissions from Agriculture," Bureau of National Affairs, *BNA International Environment Daily,* July 3, 1991.

24. S. Hodge, "Pork Chop: Budget Questions for Your Congressman," *The Heritage Foundation Policy Review* Fall(1991):58. As the title indicates, this article is extremely critical of the Conservation Reserve Program. It charges that "most of this land was highly marginal cropland to begin with and probably would not have been in production had it not been for the myriad of other crop subsidy programs. This program should be cancelled and the other subsidy programs should be reviewed for their effect on encouraging wasteful farming practices." For other critical journalistic commentary on the CRP, see, e.g., C. Trueheart, "P.J. O'Rourke, Down on Farms," *Washington Post,* July 17, 1990:B7, and

C. Wholforth, "Anchorage Postcard," *New Republic*, November 12, 1990:10. For an extremely thoughtful and scholarly review of agricultural preservation programs in general, see W. Church, "Farmland Conservation: The View from 1986," *University of Illinois Law Review* (1986):521. Professor Church is generally supportive of the CRP but he argues that short-term, time-limited programs are a misguided response to the threat of a farmland shortage that is unlikely to occur until well within the next century.

25. A few disputes of this type have arisen already. *Weimerskirch v. Leander*, 52 Wash. App. 807, 764 P.2d 663 (1988), affirmed a judgment that conservation reserve contracts could not be terminated by the lessor of the property without the consent of the lessee who had also been a party to the contract. However, this result depended on a finding that the lessor and lessee had not reached a contrary agreement under the terms of their lease.

26. "Although it was recommended at the enactment of this program [The Wisconsin Scenic and Conservation Easement Program] that property assessment be limited to fee value minus easement rights sold, this has frequently not been the case.... Landowners have been unwilling to participate in the program because in many instances local assessors have simply increased the assessment of the remaining property rights after sale of an easement to the pre-existing full fee value." T. Heller, "Property Taxation and Land Use Restrictions," *Wisconsin Law Review* (1974):751, 785(n. 77).

27. See, e.g., D. Massey and M. Silver, "Property Tax Incentives for Implementing Soil Conservation Programs Under Constitutional Taxing Limitations," *Denver Law Journal* 59(1982):485.

28. E.g., *Village of Ridgewood v. The Bolger Foundation*, 104 N.J. 337, 517 A.2d 135 (1986).

29. In *Federal Deposit Insurance Corporation v. Hartwig*, 463 N.W.2d 2 (Iowa 1990), the court found that CRP payments constituted "rents and profits" inuring to the benefit of the receiver following foreclosure. The court recognized that a difference of opinion existed among tribunals considering this question. *Matter of Butz*, 86 Bankr. 595, 598 (S.D. Iowa 1988), found CRP payments, like the earlier payment in kind (PIK) contracts, so "attenuated" from the land as not to constitute "rents and profits." On the other hand, *In re Waters*, 90 Bankr. 946, 979 (N.D. Iowa 1988), reached the opposite conclusion, citing the long-term nature of the contract, its conditions requiring specific conservation practices, and the use of the term "rent" in the CRP agreement. The *Hartwig* court agreed: "On balance, we find the reasoning of *Waters* more persuasive. Unlike the one-year contracts for "PIK bushels earned," see *Liebe*, 41 Bankr. at 970, the CRP contracts obligate the program participants (as well as their successors and assigns) to engage in specified planting and soil conservation practices for ten years. Given this fact, we think the CRP contracts "run with the land," rather than exist independent from it."

30. One case has arisen in which a taxpayer sought a reduction in the property tax valuation of his land by reason of a CRP agreement. In *Watley v. Board of Equalization of Holt County*, 236 Neb. 549, 462 N.W.2d 426 (1990), the court rejected "the assertion of appellants [i.e., taxpayers] that the voluntary decision to retire irrigated land to a reserve program converts it into a lesser classification of

farmland at the option of the owner." The court upheld the position of the Department of Revenue that "classification at the time of enrollment should be used in valuing land voluntarily placed in the reserve program."

31. See "Land Tax as Rent," pp. 17-18 of F. Dovring, "Concepts of Land, Value and Wealth," in G. Wunderlich, ed., *Land—Something of Value* (Cambridge, Mass.: Lincoln Institute of Land Policy, 1982).

32. *Emerson College v. City of Boston*, 391 Mass. 415, 425, 462 N.E.2d 1098 (1984) (relationship to cost of providing services insufficient in itself to classify an exaction as a fee rather than a tax: "Fees are legitimate to the extent that the services for which they are imposed are sufficiently particularized as to justify distribution of the costs among a limited group (the 'users,' or beneficiaries of the services), rather than the general public."); L. Zielke, "User Fees in Lieu of Taxes: Avoiding Constitutional Limitations," *Urban Lawyer* 23(1991):439.

33. The original rationale for replacement of residential rates (property taxes) with a "community charge" was presented in a 1986 Parliamentary Green Paper, *Paying for Local Government*, Cmnd. No. 9714 (London: Her Majesty's Stationery Office). See generally, S. Bailey and R. Paddison, eds., *The Reform of Local Government Finance in Britain* (London: Routledge, 1988). Commenting on the unpopularity of this plan, *The Economist* argued that "the government needs to come up with a scheme that is simple (so that its essence can be explained in one sentence) and seen to be fair (the duke pays more than the dustman)." "Farewell, Poll Tax," *The Economist*, February 23, 1991:17.

34. Professor J. Langbein points out that the 1987 tuition, room, and board payments at Johns Hopkins University, a representative private institution, totaled 31 percent of a family income of $50,000. In 1960 the same charges at Johns Hopkins represented 15 percent of an equivalent inflation-adjusted family income. J. Langbein, "The Twentieth-Century Revolution in Family Wealth Transmission," *Michigan Law Review* 86(1988):722, 734.

35. There is great variety among what are commonly thought of as market economies with regard to the treatment of rights to minerals or other natural resources found on land not in the public domain. G. Delaume, in "Economic Development and Sovereign Immunity," *American Journal of International Law* 79(1985):319, 324(n. 27), cites a number of resolutions of the United Nations General Assembly recognizing the sovereign power of a state to control the ownership of its natural resources.

36. See T. Chen, "Emerging Real Estate Markets in Urban China," *International Tax and Business Lawyer* 8(1990):78.

37. "Titles to real estate are frequently very complicated. There may be life estates absolute or defeasible, vested or contingent, leasehold interests, mortgages or lienors of various kinds.... And it is to be remembered that in many cases the collector is not learned in the law...." *Worcester v. Boston*, 179 Mass. 41, 60 N.E. 410, at 411 (1901). "It is practically impossible for a county assessor to know all easements, building restrictions and the like which exist in his county. Indeed, in this very case the assessor testified that he acted in ignorance of the building restriction here involved. Landowners themselves are ofttimes, as in this case, so confused as to the existence of such interests in land that they have to go to the courts to get them settled." *Hayes v. Gibbs*, 110 Utah 54, 169 P.2d 781, 789 (1946) (concurring opinion).

38. California Constitution, Article XIIIA ("Proposition 13").

39. The *New York Times* reported 20-fold disparities in California tax assessments among neighbors who purchased their properties at different times. L. Fisher, "Justices to Decide Macy Suit on Proposition 13 Realty Tax," *New York Times*, June 4, 1991:D1. That news report dealt with a decision by the U.S. Supreme Court to hear a constitutional challenge to Proposition 13 brought by the retail chain R. H. Macy & Company to protest the disparity between its assessment and those of similar department stores. Because a leveraged buy-out of its stock was deemed a "change in ownership," the Macy's store in question was reassessed at an amount 2.5 times that paid by its competitors in the same shopping center. Before the reassessment, the rates paid per square foot of retail space had been approximately equal. After the Supreme Court agreed to hear the case, fear of consumer retaliation against it for threatening Proposition 13 led Macy's to drop the action altogether. L. Fisher, "Macy's Ends Tax Challenge in California," *New York Times*, June 8, 1991:35.

40. See K. Ehrman and S. Flavin, *Taxing California Property*, 3d ed. (Deerfield, Ill.: Callaghan & Co., 1989), Vol. 1: Sec. 2:22.

41. Failure to maintain assessment rolls at anything approaching current value contributed to the demise of traditional residential rates in the United Kingdom. Although the law required revaluation every five years, this goal was rarely met. The only revaluations in England and Wales after World War II were in 1956, 1963, and 1973. Predictably, infrequent and therefore drastic changes in assessed valuation provoked political opposition. Protests against the 1985 revaluation in Scotland led to plans for the eventual elimination of the tax altogether. See P. Richards, "The Recent History of Local Fiscal Reform," in Bailey and Paddison, eds., *The Reform of Local Government Finance in Britain*.

42. California Constitution, Article XIIIA, Sec. 2(h).

43. Henry George (1839-1897) was the author of *Progress and Poverty* (1879), which proposed a confiscatory tax on the full value of all economic land rent. See generally, C. Lowell Harriss, "Lessons of Enduring Value: Henry George a Century Later," *American Journal of Economics and Sociology* 44(1985):479.

44. "What I like best about Henry George is the way he combines radical egalitarianism with an equally radical belief in free market capitalism." M. Kinsley, "George on My Mind," *New Republic,* November 6, 1989:8; "George's blend of radicalism and conservatism can puzzle one until it is seen as a reconciliation of the two. The system is internally consistent but defies conventional stereotypes." M. Gaffney, "Henry George," in J. Eatwell, M. Milgate, and P. Newman, eds., *The New Palgrave: A Dictionary of Economics*, Vol. 3 (New York: Stockton Press, 1987).

45. For an analysis of the Tokyo land market, which incorporates many elements of Henry George's work, see S. Tsuru, "The Political Economy of Urban Land: The Right of Property and the 'Price Revolution,'" in S. Bowles, R. Edwards, and W. Shepherd, eds., *Unconventional Wisdom: Essays on Economics in Honor of John Kenneth Galbraith* (Boston: Houghton-Mifflin, 1989):205-228.

46. Macpherson, *Property: Mainstream and Critical Positions*, 3.

6

Economic Interpretation of Property in Land

A. Allan Schmid

Many of us are fascinated by the drama of events in Eastern Europe. Questions of land tenure are on the agenda in a dramatic way. For some, the policy issues seem quite settled. The market and private property are in; central ownership and direction are out. Just pass a law saying that private property is allowed and disband the government-owned firms and sell them or give them away as fast as possible. Throw out the old bureaucratic rule books and just trust to people's greed to create the best of all possible worlds. The most efficient arrangements will be worked out among exchanging, maximizing parties. This is an illusion.

The illusion cannot be maintained after reading Joan Youngman's 1983 paper, although that was not its main purpose.[1] The paper is an inventory of how people have created a variety of different interests in real property and how those arrangements affect the observable market value. She asks just what exactly constitutes the property to be valued. If the property subject to tax is obvious as to definition, then a simple law declaring private property would suffice. If it is not obvious, as Youngman argues, then the former Socialist countries have a lot of decisions to make, which will keep the former public employees busy as lawyers and judges.

Youngman takes off from and is driven to answer the pessimism of J. Bonbright in his 1937 treatise, *The Valuation of Property*. Bonbright found that different courts ruled in a contrary manner, and he questioned the ability of appraisers and value theorists to settle the questions. He believed that, "The trouble lies far too deep to be cured by either of these economic skin specialists. It lies in the absence of any valid philosophy

for the general property tax or for the general real-estate tax."[2] Youngman would like to find a role for technical legal analysts that would give
them something to say without the necessity of any moral judgment.
She suggests analysts proceed inductively from specific disputes to general conclusions. A major ingredient of this reasoning would be the
search for a rule that can be used in a variety of different but related
cases. On this basis, a definition of property that can be used in cases
involving leases, specialty property, and easements is superior to a definition that covers only one of them. Consistency with other valued elements, such as administrative feasibility, horizontal equity, and
assessment at highest and best use, further increases a principle's attrac-
tiveness. This is so even if some of the other elements conflict and the
justification for the rates of trade-off among them is not obvious.

Several major questions are on the agenda of this volume. Can analysts find a principle of taxation that is independent of a moral judgment
about income distribution? (Is this what Bonbright meant by a "philosophy"?) More broadly, can analysts find a principle of property in general without a judgment about income distribution? Is the taxation
example a good vehicle for discovering implications for the broader
question? I think it is. Taxation reflects an interest. In an exchange economy the tax base is tantamount to an ownership interest. A tax and a
rental fee or a stock dividend have some similarities. With complete
state ownership, there is no need for taxes to support government. The
state is the residual claimant. There is a rule for what constitutes wages
rather than a rule for what constitutes taxable value. In a private economy an untaxed asset is one in which the public has no interest. Taxes
on private land are instrumentally equivalent to rental fees on publicly
owned land, and both are sources of government revenue. Just as a tax
represents a public interest in private land, preferential access to public
land represents a private interest in public land. Administrative rules
determine just who in the public has use of public land. People do not
know what they own unless they know the prices they face, including
tax prices. The U.S. ownership and interest system is in fact quasi-
private, or is it quasi-public?

I do not know what to expect of newly democratic legislatures in
Eastern Europe, but the old champions of private property are wonderfully vague in their definition of the basis for taxation. In the United
States, statutes speak of "fair market value," "actual cash value," "full
and fair cash value," "just value," or "true and fair value." These are
practically worthless principles. Youngman's candidate for a technical
principle is the concept of valuation based on fair market rent of the
total undivided property regardless of its actual division among parties.
This is termed the *summation of interests approach.*

Valuation of Property Subject to a Long-Term Lease

Suppose a property is subject to a long-term lease with many years to go; the lease was written many years ago and is unfavorable to the lessor. Should the tax assessment be based on the actual sale price of the owner's interest or on the sale price that would be offered if no lease existed? The majority of courts and Youngman prefer assessment based on the value of the entire property rather than the sale value of the owner's remaining interest. The courts speak of the "whole land," but it is a particular person that pays the tax. For administrative reasons, sending separate tax bills to a host of parties is undesirable.

Suppose also that at the time of the original contract both parties regarded the terms as fair. Now, however, the value has changed and the lessee has realized a particularly good deal. The tax assessor sees the current value, which the parties could not see with certainty, and wants to tax it. The owner claims that paying the tax on the new value was not anticipated when the deal was struck. The value may be there, but it is not available to the lessor. Youngman speaks of appropriate taxation as if the assets were part of an integrated firm. But, if the owner and lessee were a single firm, the unexpected gain would be shared according to their stock ownership. Is there a basis for taxation that can avoid the question of how to divide the unexpected increase in total value?

In her 1983 paper, Youngman argues that, "A landlord's interest in property burdened by an unfavorable lease is diminished by reason of the encumbrance by exactly the amount of the 'bonus value' enjoyed by the tenant—the present value of the difference between contract and market rent" (p. 726). This suggests that there is some value that is invariant with the choice of business organization. If that were true, institutions would not matter. But why do parties choose to be related by contract rather than the hierarchy of the integrated firm? Oliver Williamson would argue that whatever form exists is the most efficient.[3] This suggests that total value is higher with the market division of interests than with an undivided single firm. But this efficiency is a matter of expectations and not necessarily what actually happens.

For now, the only point I want to make with this conceptualization is that society is not indifferent as to the form of business organization. If the choice of a lease exposes the lessor to unpredictable tax obligations, a lease would be chosen for reasons other than the expected realization of total output. The integrated firm approach may be chosen to prevent what is equivalent to an opportunistic behavior by the lessee/tenant leaving the owner with the tax obligation from increased value.

Several courts have ruled that the state of the owner's title should not affect the assessed value. Youngman approves of this summation of interests approach. But again, it is the nominal owner that pays the tax, and not the other putative or eventual owners. The value depends on the investments made by the owner, but can the owner proceed with risky investments if other owners might come forward and claim part of the income? Is not there an unexamined relationship here between distribution and the realization of product?

Valuation of Property Subject to Easements

The landmark case regarding easements involved a golf course that was built as part of a housing development and that enhanced the value of the residential lots.[4] The developer retained ownership of the course after subjecting it to an easement ensuring its use for golf. Later, the course owner in fact was losing money on the course and asked the court for a zero tax assessment based on capitalized income. A Washington court agreed. Youngman does not, arguing that the summation of interests be the standard and that the owner has received compensation in the form of profits from the development, out of which the tax can be paid. She assumes that the integrated interests have the greatest value. Is it possible that the divided interests are worth more? The developer had the option of keeping the integrated golf course and houses and leasing both, in which case the capitalized contract rent would be the total return to the integrated firm. Apparently, the expected value of the integrated interest was less than that from dividing the property. Another option consistent with summation is for the home buyers to buy the course. But if they are not skilled in management, the productivity will be less although summed as an integrated firm. The summation approach need not produce the same total value in each case.

The sale price of the encumbered golf course is obviously irrelevant. But what is the relevance of the fact that homeowners without open space might pay a considerable sum for the land? This price is not invariant to history. The buying price of the land if not already owned is different today (after the subdivision is a success) than it would have been if, at the time of development, would-be home buyers had formed a group to bid for it (ignoring transaction costs in doing so). And the house owners are not mobile with respect to combining house site and golf course, so not all potential sites are competitors after the project that were before the project—the proximate land available for golf is now in a monopoly position.

Is the value that golf adds to nearby residences additive and accounted for in residential assessments? Youngman objects to the additive concept arguing that the reduction in value of the servient land is not exactly offset by the increased value of the dominant land. This is a good point, for gains can be expected from trade. So what is the remaining value in the servient estate?

But what if there is no value left, as in the case of the profitless golf course? Youngman advocates the imputation of payment (p. 798). The owner of the servient estate presumably received a payment for it. While there is no continuing flow of income from the encumbered land, which has zero sales price, there is a capital equivalent from the lump-sum purchase price.

If a farm owner farms the land, he or she would pay a property tax and an income tax. If the owner leases the land, the owner still pays a property tax and an income tax on the annual rental income (and the lessee would also pay an income tax). If the land is leased for a lump sum, should the owner escape the property tax? Often the courts say no (with Youngman's approval). But in the Twin Lakes golf case, the Washington court said yes, as noted above. Youngman (and I) argue that there is little instrumental difference between a long-term lease and an easement—both allow another party to have an interest. Why should the asset disappear for property tax purposes just because there is an easement rather than a lump-sum lease? The local assessor sees the land and cannot believe it has no value even if encumbered.

There are two problems here. One is inherent in markets and the second is an artifact of institutional choice. The imputation theory rests on the concept of perfect markets, which convert flows to equivalent stocks without any cost. This is unreal. If the process was perfect, people would not care about what form their assets were in. There is a reason why landowners convert land to a financial asset. They do not want to look backward at stock considerations but rather forward, where only success is taxed as income. As noted above, there is a problem in anticipating the stock tax when you have cut yourself off from receiving any flow income from any higher stock value.

The second problem is institutional. Local governments are now largely dependent on property taxes, and thus they care whether something is taxed as property or income, even if the totals are the same. There is now no institutional equivalent of the government as an integrated firm that would be indifferent to the form of wealth. In this setting, there are distributive issues among taxpayers of different kinds and taxpayers in different taxing jurisdictions.

Valuation of Specialty Property

Specialty property refers to an improvement uniquely suited to its current owner. It does not present a problem of divided interests, as in the above case of leases and easements, but it is included here and by Youngman because it raises the same question about the usefulness of observable sales data as the basis for taxation. The landmark case in this instance involved the New York Stock Exchange building.[5] The building is uniquely suited to only one user and no one else would want it, except as cleared land. In some cases there might be negative salvage value. Yet the assessor cannot believe the tax value is zero. The court ruled that the depreciated reproduction cost was the value. This is relevant only if the owner would rebuild if the building was lost. But, the owner's intention is partly a subjective matter.

The problem also arises with buildings of unusual architectural merit, which are often built as a symbol for a company and useful to it to create goodwill, which translates into profits. But that same value is not available to another buyer. Is the sale price to be the basis for taxation? In a case involving Seagram and Sons, the court ruled that the depreciated reproduction cost was relevant because the owner must have thought the cost was worthwhile.[6] Youngman objects, however, and says that, "Substitution of value to the owner for sale price risks taxation of prestige, sentiment, or business values rather than real estate values alone" (p. 768). She deplores the lack of objective criteria and says, "The judge's sense of fairness, and little else, determined the amount of the tax" (p. 763). There is that feared philosophical word *fairness* again.

Youngman, however, concludes that the problem of specialty valuation does not permit of single and general solution and that strict adherence to sales values would be unacceptable (a bit of philosophy is allowed). She urges that specialty application be kept as narrow as possible to contain the need-for-philosophy disease. She is aware of the potential because numerous types of property may be of greater value to their owners than to the market (i.e., others). Part of Youngman's objection would be overcome if legislation had defined a public purpose served by encouraging architecture whose extra cost is free of tax, such as is sometimes done for other public amenity features or as is done for use-value taxation of agricultural land.

In this paper I can only discuss a few of the choices that must be made about what interests are subject to tax. Youngman advocates the summation of interests approach in preference to the additive approach. I do not wish to defend the latter. I only want to say that implementation of the former is not free of moral judgment.

The broader issue is not just what interests to tax, but what interests are to be given rights and, thus, opportunities. The case most relevant to the issue in Youngman's 1983 article is one involving whether a tax sale can extinguish the interests of the beneficiaries of an easement. The courts are clear that payment of taxes in the past on the value of one's property emanating from a property interest does not guarantee the continuance of that right (although popular opinion would probably support such a contention). Legislation often prescribes that a tax-sale title be free and clear of all encumbrances, but the courts leave restrictive covenants in place. Youngman objects and argues that the beneficiaries have the option of collective action to pay the taxes themselves and thus avoid the tax sale (p. 787). This assumes that a right is only as good as one's ability to protect it. If transaction costs get in the way, that is too bad. This surely requires a distributive judgment. Certain legal and economics scholars, such as Cooter and Ulen,[7] advocate that the law give the right to the person who would purchase it if the transaction costs were zero. This is also value presumptive because transaction costs are often the instrument of certain groups' interests and what one can afford to pay is a function of prior public choices of income distribution.

Taxation as a Behavioral Incentive

The previous discussion was about the basis for the property tax used to pay for the general functions of government. The focus here is on taxation intended to alter people's behavior, such as the practice of farmland conservation and pollution control. A tax on a farmer's activity says the farmer does not own any or all of the resource in question, but he or she can buy any quantity at will at a given price. The implicit owner, for the moment, cannot refuse to sell. The only difference between a tax on an activity and ordinary asking prices for goods offered for sale is that a tax can be collected by an agent for the owners and tied to the use of a product other than the one actually used and owned by others. For example, if underground water or downstream watercourses are owned by nonfarmers, a tax can be imposed on the use of fertilizers or pesticides or as some function of the number of animals fed. The groundwater owner does not have the expense of collecting the selling price or actually proving that the farmer used the owner's resource.

In other words, a tax is like a surrogate lease price charged by the owner of the resource and collected by an agent, who is perhaps also part owner. To make it symmetrical to private property, perhaps the nonfarm beneficiary should pay a property tax on that interest. In any case, Youngman's theme that leases and easements are instrumentally similar can be expanded to taxes themselves, which are the instrument for a property interest and may be considered as substitutes and complements with direct redistribution of rights, cost sharing, prohibition, and liability to achieve a certain economic performance, including the distribution of income and opportunities.[8]

Conclusion

In closing, I would like to emphasize several concepts useful in thinking about property interests:

- Institutions matter. The performance (value) of different kinds of transactions may not be the same.
- Distribution cannot be separated from allocation. The distribution of taxes and other rights affects performance. There is no technical basis for choice of rights in law or welfare economics that escapes the need for moral judgment on distribution.
- Uncertainty matters, and rights relative to opportunistic behavior matter.
- Land is not an ordinary commodity.

Notes

A. Allan Schmid is professor, Department of Agricultural Economics, Michigan State University.

1. Joan M. Youngman, "Defining and Valuing the Base of the Property Tax," *Washington Law Review* 88(1983):713-812.

2. J. Bonbright, *The Valuation of Property* (New York: McGraw-Hill, 1937):508.

3. O. Williamson, *The Economic Institutions of Capitalism* (New York: Free Press, 1985).

4. *Twin Lakes Golf and Country Club v. King County*, 87 Wn. 2d 1, 548 P.2d 538 (1976).

5. *People ex rel. N.Y. Stock Exch. Bldg. Co. v. Cantor*, 221 A.D.193, 223 N.Y.S. 64 (1927).

6. *Joseph E. Seagram & Sons, Inc. v. Tax Comm'n*, 18 A.D.2d 109, 238 N.Y.S.2d 228 (1963).

7. R. Cooter and T. Ulen, *Law and Economics* (Glenview, Ill.: Scott, Foresman, 1988).

8. A. Schmid, *The Idea of Property: A Way to Think About Soil and Water Issues.* Department of Agricultural Economics Staff Paper No. 88-100 (East Lansing: Michigan State University, 1988).

7

Share Leasing and Externalities

Robert G. Chambers, Hyunok Lee, and John Quiggin

Much attention has been given to explaining contractual relations between landlords and share tenants in developing economies.[1] Relatively little attention has been given, however, to U.S. share-leasing practices.[2] This lack of attention is striking because a large amount of land is operated under some type of share arrangement in the United States. For example, over one-third of Corn Belt farmland is operated under share arrangements.[3]

The empirical literature on share leasing is largely devoted to examining whether share leases are Marshallian "efficient." This literature (e.g., Heady[4]) starts from the simple observation that share contracts, by allowing the tenant only a portion of the marginal returns from his or her efforts, blunt incentives. The result is the apparent underutilization of productive resources. The literature on whether this actually occurs is mixed. Some studies find strong support but others do not.

From our perspective, such studies seem little more than an exercise in what Coase calls "blackboard economics."[5] The fact that share leasing is so persistent and pervasive suggests that it plays a key economic role, one that will not disappear no matter how inefficient professional economists judge it to be. Most of the recent theoretical literature (beginning with Johnson[6]) on share leasing in developing economies does, in fact, take this same view.

This paper is a preliminary attempt to unravel some of the economic mysteries enshrouding current U.S. share-leasing practices. A logical way to start is to note that U.S. agricultural production practices depart widely from the stylized models used in the share-leasing literature developed in the context of developing countries. Unlike the situation in developing countries, U.S. agriculture has well-developed capital and, thus, land markets. In particular, U.S. farms are among the most capital- and chemical-intensive operations in the world.

And here an observation equally as simple as Marshall's suggests that *share relations, by blunting incentives, can enhance social efficiency* even absent the usual type of risk-sharing arguments that have been made.[7] If the marginal cost of a tenant's private input is less than the social marginal cost, the tenant facing full marginal returns from his or her effort will overutilize (in social terms) that input. Specific examples of such inputs, which play an important role in U.S. agriculture, are those whose use imposes a negative environmental externality on nonusers. For example, it is commonly believed that nitrogen fertilizers, which ultimately leach into groundwater sources, have market prices that do not reflect social costs.

In what follows, we investigate this issue using a reformulation of the usual production-under-uncertainty and moral hazard models, as suggested by Chambers and Quiggin.[8] We do not mean to imply, however, that the existence of externalities is the best explanation of the prevalence of share contracts in agriculture. Indeed, in preparing this paper our hardest task was to decide which of several alternative explanations (economies of scale, incomplete contracts, transaction costs, and so on) would be pursued. Our choice of topic reflects two facts: First, clear empirical evidence exists to support the initiation of research along these lines. Second, to our knowledge previous researchers have not followed this trail.

First, we offer some empirical evidence on the coincidence of share leasing and the use of potentially environmentally damaging inputs, and we represent the relationship with a simple, stylized version of the economic problem that we wish to study. We then model farmer behavior under share leasing in a state-contingent production framework, and we use that model to investigate contractual relations.

Some Empirical Evidence and the Economic Problem

Studies on externalities (e.g., soil erosion, groundwater contamination) caused by the use of chemical inputs have increasingly been attracting interest among agricultural economists. Few such studies, however, consider the possibility that tenure choice may alter the use of inputs, particularly inputs whose use imposes negative externalities. Why may tenancy produce such a distortion in incentives? To put this issue in perspective, we first examine some actual data.

Our data are from the U.S. Department of Agriculture's 1984 National Special Crop Survey, which involved over 529 major rice-producing farms.[9] In the data base, land tenure is classified as ownership, cash rental, share rental, or combination of methods (see Table 7.1). In the table, *pure holding* refers to accessing land by one method, and *mixed holding* refers to a combination of methods, with and without share renting. The distribution of sample farms in the table indicates that share tenancy is widely practiced: Fifty-three percent of the farmers surveyed used the share lease exclusively or in combination with other types of tenancy.

Table 7.1 also presents the mean value of input use per acre (by landlord and tenant) in value terms. A definite input-use pattern emerges for the four representative inputs examined (fertilizers, pesticides, drying inputs, and hired labor). With the exception of fertilizer, input levels are lower for share tenants than for owner-operators and cash tenants. In particular, owner-operators use pesticides and drying inputs much more intensively than do share tenants.

Several observations are pertinent: First, pesticides are often considered risk-reducing inputs, and a recognized advantage of share arrangements is risk sharing.[10] Thus, a share tenant likely would use relatively fewer risk-reducing inputs (pesticides) because his or her incentives to use such inputs are blunted by the risk-sharing aspects of the contract. As our theoretical results show (see the discussion following Equation 17), the use of risk-reducing inputs allows the farmer's share to be higher. As the farmer's share rises, the risk-sharing advantages of share leasing diminish. Second, and the main conjecture of this paper, recognizing the potential negative environmental impacts of pesticides, even absent risk considerations, the perceived allocative inefficiency of share leasing may induce share tenants to use pesticides more efficiently (in a social sense) than owner-operators.

Table 7.1 suggests the question addressed in this paper: Can share contracting of land be more socially efficient than cash contracting given environmental externalities to agricultural production? As our opening discussion and the theory of the second-best illustrate, the answer obviously is yes. But that said, one is still left with an imperfect understanding of the role various factors (e.g., risk considerations, moral hazard, contract incompleteness) play in determining when and to what extent yes is the correct answer. Thus, the reasons why share leasing emerges as socially efficient must be isolated. A starting point for developing this understanding is the specification of a model that approximates the interface among environmental externalities, agricultural production, and the land market.

Share leasing can be a "best" response (or an element of a best response) only in a world in which some imperfection other than the production externality exists. Because share leasing distorts all marginal price relations and not just those specific to the externality, a better

TABLE 7.1 Sample Distribution and Average Characteristics of Farms by Landholding Status

| | Tenure Status | | | | |
| | Pure Holding | | Share Rent | Mixed Holding Share-Rented Land | |
Characteristics	Owned	Cash Rent		No	Yes
Sample distribution (percent of farms)	104 (20%)	106 (20%)	178 (33%)	37 (7%)	104 (20%)
Inputs per acre*					
Pesticides	42 (53)	40 (45)	33 (34)	37 (31)	35 (28)
Fertilizer	31 (32)	39 (32)	32 (34)	35 (24)	32 (30)
Hired labor	27 (25)	15 (11)	18 (26)	23 (21)	22 (19)
Drying	38 (45)	34 (12)	34 (18)	35 (30)	34 (38)
Land improvement and conservation	29 (101)	5 (21)	7 (27)	9 (21)	8 (25)

*Numbers in parentheses are standard deviations.
Source: U.S. Department of Agriculture, 1984 National Special Crop Survey (Washington, D.C., unpublished).

response (in a purely theoretical sense) is to intervene at the source of the externality and make individuals face the social marginal cost of the externality through a tax or subsidy or input regulation. Presumably, this could be achieved by some omniscient government. Several reasons exist why such omniscience is not possible, however. Most important, unless the social marginal cost of the externality is invariant to the level at which agricultural production operates (e.g., the social marginal cost of nitrogen pollution is not related to the amount of nitrogen pollution), achievement through taxation or subsidization of a first-best requires exact knowledge of production behavior in order to set the appropriate tax.

This, then, raises the important issue of information asymmetries. Clearly, if accurately setting a tax or subsidy requires full knowledge of production practices, that knowledge must come from somewhere.[11] And unless all production practices are fully observable, that knowledge must be elicited from the farmers. But just as obviously, if farmers know that they will be taxed on the basis of what they divulge, they have the incentive to report falsely on their activities. This is the classic moral hazard problem. Thus in what follows, we start from the basic presumption that there is an inherent information asymmetry. And to crystallize the economic issues as well as to simplify the analysis, we presume that this information asymmetry takes the extreme form of a farmer's actions being observable (or less stringently verifiable) only to himself or herself. Any contract must be based, therefore, solely on something that is observable after the fact. And that something is taken to be agricultural output.

Having said this, it remains for us to detail the existing institutions within which these decisions are made. To streamline the analysis, we have kept things as simple as possible. Most important, we restricted our attention to linear contracts in which a single landlord interacts with a single farmer over the rental terms on a single piece of land in a world of uncertain production. The farmer's actions are not observable to the landlord, but his or her actions affect the landlord's welfare in a matter separate and apart from the landlord's dependence on the output of the agricultural production process. In other words, we consider the landlord as a proxy for society at large. We do so in the hope of approximating the type of equilibrium contract that might emerge from an evolutionary process between actual landlords and tenants when the tenant's behavior involves externalities.

Implicit in our analysis is the presumption that such persistent institutions like share leasing arise for a reason: They deal with a "problem" in such a manner that individuals who would gain from using alternative solutions are not able to convince those who would lose from the alternative arrangements to make the change. Our principal-agent analysis is only meant to be suggestive of this process.

It is important to recognize the inherently risky nature of agricultural production and the role that risk plays in the formation of equilibrium contracts. Considering the riskiness of production and farmers' risk attitudes is particularly important given the role that risk-increasing and risk-reducing inputs are usually thought to play in environmental damage.[12] In particular, the landlord and tenant's attitude toward risk, as well as the physical characteristics of some inputs in reducing risk, turn out to be important. This remains true even when tenants are risk neutral. In the next section we consider a relatively new approach to modeling these relationships.

Tenant Behavior with a Generalized Share Contract

Our starting point is a reformulation of the usual production-under-uncertainty model. The standard approach is to specify a production function that depends on physical inputs being committed prior to the resolution of uncertainty and on some random variable that indexes the "state of nature." Letting $x \in \mathbb{R}^n_+$ denote the vector of inputs, $\theta \in \mathbb{R}_+$ denote the random variable, and $f : \mathbb{R}^{n+1}_+ \to \mathbb{R}$ denote the production function, random output y is then defined by

$$y = f(x,\theta).$$

Our approach follows Arrow and Debreu by dealing in state-contingent commodities.[13] The primary notion, therefore, is that of a state space Ω, which is taken to be a finite set of the form $\{1,2,3, ..., S\}$, where S denotes the number of different states of nature. The production relations are governed by a production set $Y \subseteq \mathbb{R}^S_+$ defined by

$$Y(x) = \{y \in \mathbb{R}^S_+: \text{an input of } x \text{ results in an output } y_i \in \mathbb{R}_+ \text{ if state } i \text{ occurs}\}.$$

In words, $Y(x)$ gives the vector of state-contingent outputs that are consistent with a prior committal of the input vector x. (Here we follow the traditional approach and assume that all inputs are committed prior to the resolution of uncertainty; the extension to the case of sequential resolution of uncertainty is straightforward.)

The advantage of this approach is that it allows one to develop a theory of production under uncertainty that, on the technological side, is exactly equivalent to standard multiproduct production models and, therefore, well understood.[14] In what follows, we assume that $Y(x)$ represents the state-contingent production possibilities set for a single acre of land that the landlord is renting to a single tenant. We also assume that Y is nonempty, closed, bounded from above, and convex and that it possesses free disposability of output and input.

Following Holmstrom,[15] we assume that the tenant's utility structure is separable in returns (y) and effort, that is,

$$W(y_i,x) = u(y_i) - g(x),$$

where $W(y_i,x)$ is strictly concave in both arguments, $u(\ )$ is strictly increasing, $g(x)$ is strictly increasing, and both $u(\ )$ and $g(x)$ satisfy the von Neumann-Morgenstern postulates.[16]

As mentioned above, we restricted our attention to linear contract structures. Thus, the landlord is assumed to lease the land to the tenant in return for a percentage of the crop and a fixed cash rent—both payable at the end of the production period. Denoting a as the cash rent (which we allow to be either positive or negative) and b $(1 \geq b \geq 0)$ as the tenant's share of the crop, the tenant's expected utility is

$$u(by_i - a) - g(x).$$

This contract represents a mixed form of share leasing and cash rental payments that has pure share leasing $(a = 0)$ and pure cash rents $(b = 1)$ as special cases.

By the von Neumann-Morgenstern postulates, the tenant seeks to maximize his or her expected utility subject to the technological constraints defined by $Y(x)$. That is, the tenant solves

$$\underset{x,y}{\text{Max}} \left\{ \sum_{i=1}^{s} \pi_i u(by_i - a) - g(x) : y \in Y(x), \sum_{i=1}^{s} \pi_i = 1, \pi_i \geq 0 \right\}, \quad (1)$$

where π_i represents the tenant's subjective probability of state i occurring. Using a more compact notation (dropping the domain of the π_i), it is easy to show, however, that Equation 1 is equivalent to

$$\underset{y}{\text{Max}} \left\{ \sum_{i=1}^{s} \pi_i u(by_i - a) - c(y) \right\}, \quad (2)$$

where $c(y)$ is the nondecreasing and convex function defined by

$$c(y) = \underset{x}{\text{Min}} \{ g(x) : y \in Y(x) \}.$$

Defining the indirect utility function $V(\pi,b,a)$ as the solution to Equations 1 and 2, it follows that

$$c(y) \geq \sum \pi_i u(by_i - a) - V(\pi,b,a). \tag{3}$$

Hence, $c(y)$ and $V(\pi,b,a)$ define a dual pair. That is, under the regularity conditions of Y,

$$c(y) = \underset{\pi}{\text{Max}} \left\{ \sum \pi_i u(by_1 - a) - V(\pi,b,a) : \sum \pi_i = 1, \pi_1 \geq 0 \right\}. \tag{4}$$

The envelope theorem applied to Equation 2 implies

$$V_i(\pi,b,a) = u(by_i(b,a,\pi) - a), \tag{5}$$

where subscript i denotes the partial derivative with respect to π_i. Equation 5 therefore offers a modified version of the Hotelling-Shephard lemma,[17] that is,

$$by_i(b,a,\pi) - a = u^{-1}(V_i(\pi,b,a)), \tag{6}$$

where $u^{-1}(V_i(\pi,b,a))$ represents the inverse image of $u(by_i(b,a,\pi) - a)$, and $y_i(b,a,\pi)$ is the utility-maximizing yield in state i. Applying the envelope theorem to Equation 2 again yields

$$V_b(\pi,b,a) = \sum \pi_i u'(by_i(b,a,\pi) - a)y_i(b,a,\pi), \tag{7}$$
$$V_a(\pi,b,a) = -\sum \pi_i u'(by_i(b,a,\pi) - a),$$

where subscripts on V denote partial derivatives. Hence, $V_a(\pi,b,a)$ is minus the marginal utility of wealth, and $V_b(\pi,b,a)$ is the expected value of the product of marginal utility and yield. Together, Equations 5-7 imply

$$\text{ov}(u'(by_i(b,a,\pi) - a), y_i(b,a,\pi)) \equiv \sigma$$
$$= V_b(\pi,b,a) + V_a(\pi,b,a) \sum_{i=1}^{s} \pi_i y_i(b,a,\pi). \tag{8}$$

For a risk-averse (risk-neutral) individual, σ is negative (zero).

Our last task before the formal analysis of contract structure is to define notions of risk-increasing and risk-reducing inputs. An input j is said to be risk reducing if $x_j(\bar{y}) \geq x_j(y)$, where

$$x(y) = \text{argmin} \{g(x) : y \in Y(x)\}$$

and

$$\bar{y} = \left\{ \frac{1}{S} \sum_{i=1}^{S} y_i, \ \frac{1}{S} \sum_{i=1}^{S} y_i, \ \ldots, \ \frac{1}{S} \sum_{i=1}^{S} y_i \right\}.$$

An input j is risk increasing if the inequality is reversed, $x_j(\bar{y}) \leq x_j(y)$. The notions of risk-increasing and risk-reducing inputs are local or relative notions because they require examination of the input utilization required to produce $\bar{y}$ in each state compared with y. Risk-reducing inputs are those that are used more heavily in producing $\bar{y}$, which a risk-averse individual would prefer, than in producing y.

Without loss of generality, one would choose indexes so that as i increases yield falls. Thus, if input k is to be risk reducing, one naturally expects that for low values of the state index, $x_{ki}(\hat{y})$ will be negative and that for high values of the state index, $x_{ki}(\hat{y})$ will be positive, where $x_{ki}(\hat{y})$ represents the partial derivative with respect to the i state yield. Following this intuition, input j is quasi risk reducing at $\hat{y}$ if

$$x_{j1}(\hat{y}) \leq x_{j2}(\hat{y}) \leq \ldots \leq x_{jk}(\hat{y}) \leq 0 \leq x_{jk+1}(\hat{y}) \leq \ldots \leq x_{jS}(\hat{y}).$$

An input j is quasi risk increasing at $\hat{y}$ if the inequalities are reversed.

Contract Design

To model the possible environmental externalities associated with agricultural production, we assumed that there exists an input to the agricultural production process whose social cost is not captured by $g(x)$. For simplicity, we restricted our attention to the case of one such input. (The principles established below extend to the multiple-input case.) Let the total social cost associated with producing the state-contingent yield vector y using the input bundle x be $g(x) + d(x_j) + \epsilon$, where $d(x_j) + \epsilon$ represents an environmental externality associated with utilizing x_j. The function $d(\ )$ is strictly increasing and convex, and ϵ is an unobservable random variable with a mean of zero. Ex post, only the total externality and not the expected externality, $d(x_j)$, associated with using x_j is observable.[18]

Our interest is in studying socially "efficient" contracts, which we envisage as emerging from an evolutionary process of interaction among tenants, landlords, and society at large. We attempted to approximate the equilibrium of this process with a simple principal-agent model. The crude rationale for this model is that in such a process society and landlords are affected by farmers' actions, and they will seek to enhance their position using any economic means (including contract terms) available. Logically, any time they incur a cost that results in a tenant's taking certain actions that enhance their position beyond the cost, they should willingly incur that cost. Assuming that the landlords have title to the land and that they are risk neutral, the problem (remember the existence of the information asymmetry) is to choose a rental share and a cash payment according to

$$\text{Max}_{b,a} \left\{ (1-b)S^{-1}\sum y_i(b,a,\pi) + a - d(x_j(y(b,z,\pi))) : V(\pi,b,a) \geq \bar{W} \right\}. \quad (9)$$

The Lagrangean expression for Equation 9 is

$$L = (1-b)S^{-1}\sum_i y_i(b,a,\pi) + a - d(x_j(y(b,a,\pi))) + \mu V(\pi,b,a),$$

where μ is a Lagrangean multiplier (for simplicity we ignored the upper boundary conditions on b).[19] First-order conditions for an interior solution are

$$(1-b)S^{-1}\sum y_{ia} + 1 - d'\sum_i (x_{ji}y_{ia}) + \mu V_a = 0,$$

$$-S^{-1}\sum y_i + (1-b)S^{-1}\sum y_{ib} - d'\sum (x_{ji}y_{ib}) + \mu V_b = 0, \quad (10)$$

$$V(\pi, b, a) = \bar{W},$$

where the arguments of the functions have been dropped for notational simplicity. From the first two expressions in Equation 10, it is obvious that the rules for setting the cash payment and the rental share have natural interpretations in terms of Ramsey prices and the "inverse elasticity rule."[20] By the second expression in Equation 10, the departure of the rental share from unity will tend to vary inversely with the b-elasticity of expected supply. So all else constant, the more elastic the expected supply with respect to the rental share (assuming the elasticity is positive) the closer the rental share should be to one. For commodities that are relatively price elastic, one would expect higher rental shares, and one would expect the converse for commodities that are relatively price insensitive.

The first expression in Equation 10 also says that the divergence of the rental share from unity should vary inversely, again all else constant, with the absolute value of the reciprocal of the elasticity of expected supply with respect to the cash rental payment. This elasticity is directly reflective of the tenant's risk preferences. If the tenant is risk neutral, this elasticity is zero; if the tenant is risk averse, one generally expects the elasticity to be positive. Thus, roughly speaking, the rental share should be close to one when the tenant is relatively risk neutral, and it should be close to zero when the tenant is very risk averse. Given the risk-sharing properties of share contracts, the latter result is very intuitive. For when the share equals unity, the tenant must bear all the risk from production. When the share equals zero, the tenant bears none of the risk.

After some tedious manipulation that requires making use of Equations 7 and 8, the expressions in Equation 10 reduce to (again dropping function arguments)

$$\sigma = b^{-1} \sum [(1 - b) S^{-1} - d' x_{ji}][y_{ib} V_a - y_{ia} V_b]$$

$$V(\pi, b, a) = \bar{W}.$$

(11)

Differentiating the second expression in this equation shows that in equilibrium any increase in the cash rent must be associated with an increase in the farmer's share of the crop. Moreover, the farmer's crop share should increase at an increasing rate as the cash rent rises. The first expression in Equation 11 is the basis of our further investigations, in which we consider three separate special cases.

No Externality, Risk-Averse Tenant

Mainly for comparative purposes, the first special case is the standard moral hazard problem without the presence of an externality. Equation 11 reduces to

$$\sigma = b^{-1}(1 - b) S^{-1} \sum [y_{ib} V_b].$$

(12)

For a risk-averse individual, $\sigma < 0$. Hence, for the rental share to be positive but less than unity, the following expression also must be negative:

$$\sum [y_{ib} V_a - y_{ia} V_b].$$

(13)

Although exceptions exist, an increase in either cash rent or the crop share to the landlord is expected to increase state-contingent supply. To see the former, note that increasing the cash rent, *ceteris paribus*, decreases the ending wealth for the tenant. If the tenant is risk averse this, in turn, increases the ex post marginal utility that a tenant will realize from any increment to any state-contingent yield. (A risk-neutral tenant does not experience this effect.) Hence, there is a natural tendency for each state-contingent yield to rise. However, increasing any single state-contingent yield also increases the marginal cost of any other state-contingent yield that is substitutable for the state-contingent yield being increased. If increasing state-contingent yields raises the marginal cost of substitutable state-contingent yields sufficiently, the marginal-cost increase can overwhelm the incentive effect associated with increasing the cash payment.

If the state-contingent yield in question is complementary with other state-contingent yields, that is, it lowers their marginal costs, the latter effect is reversed and both effects push toward greater state-contingent yield. If the technology is input-nonjoint,[21] increasing the cash rent will lead to an increase in each state-contingent yield.

The other expression in Equation 13 represents the responsiveness of state-contingent yield to changes in the crop share. Generally, one expects this to be positive, too. However, state-contingent yields can fall in response to an increase in the crop share if the tenant exhibits a sufficiently high degree of relative risk aversion. To see why, note that increasing the crop share does two things simultaneously. First, it increases the tenant's return from each extra unit of state-contingent yield. This encourages the tenant to produce more. Second, because the tenant is risk averse, raising the crop share also decreases the ex post marginal utility that an individual realizes from each increment in state-contingent yield. If the tenant's relative risk aversion is large, his or her incentive to increase state-contingent yield might actually fall. Given that risk aversion is decreasing in state-contingent yields, this latter phenomenon should be expected to be a problem only in the worst states, that is, those with the largest indexes. In what follows, however, we always presume that Equation 13 is negative.

Several other facts are apparent from Equation 12. First, giving farmers a pure cash rental contract is only optimal when the tenant is risk neutral. This well-known result is a manifestation of the Harris and Raviv finding that risk neutrality on the part of the agent eradicates the moral hazard problem.[22] What is then optimal is simply to have the agent maximize social surplus. In the current case, this is equivalent to a pure cash rental contract. This result follows immediately by noting that Equation 11 is satisfied with the tenant's share set at unity only if σ equals zero. But this implies that the tenant's marginal utility of income is a constant-risk neutrality.

From Equation 11, all else held constant, the more the tenant's marginal utility varies with income, the more concave the utility structure;

and loosely, the more risk averse the tenant, the more the tenant's share will tend to depart from unity. Intuitively, this result manifests the fact that under moral hazard, production inefficiency is traded off against the gains from sharing risk. As the tenant becomes more risk averse in this sense, the more it pays to isolate him or her from production risk by setting the tenant share close to zero.

Externality, Risk-Neutral Tenant

In the second special case, a production externality exists but the tenant is risk neutral. As mentioned above, the standard result from the principal-agent literature is that a risk-neutral tenant removes the moral hazard problem. One then naturally expects that the optimal contract form would be pure cash rental. That expectation is erroneous because

$$(1 - b)S^{-1} \sum y_{ib} = \sum d' \, x_{ji} y_{ib}. \tag{14}$$

Equation 14 is not generally satisfied by setting the share to one. Setting the share to unity does not provide the tenant with the appropriate marginal incentives to control the use of the potentially polluting input. Rather, setting the share at unity provides the tenant with the maximum marginal incentive to produce, which exacerbates the externality problem. As it turns out, the magnitude of the optimal share depends on whether the input producing the externality is risk increasing or risk reducing.[23]

In examining Equation 14, note first that under risk neutrality, changes in the cash rental payment have no effect on state-contingent yield. (Profit maximizers ignore fixed costs.) Note also that each state-contingent yield is increasing in the crop share. (Profit maximizers have upward-sloping supply curves.) Equation 14 implies that the level of the optimal crop share depends on three factors: the direct marginal cost of the externality d', the elasticity of expected supply, and how the input in question responds to changes in state-contingent yields. We consider the last effect first.

For the sake of illustration compare two situations. Both situations are identical from the tenant's perspective. The only difference lies with the landlord: In the first the externality is caused by an input $\hat{x}_j$, which is risk reducing, and in the second the externality is caused by an input x'_j, which is risk increasing.

In the first case the optimal crop share (denoted by $\hat{b}$) satisfies

$$(1 - \hat{b})S^{-1} \sum y_{ib} = \sum d' \, \hat{x}_{ji} y_{ib},$$

and in the second,

$$(1 - b')S^{-1} \sum y_{ib} = \sum d'x'_{ji}y_{ib}.$$

Also assume for illustrative purposes that both the expected externality and state-contingent supplies are linear functions. Then,

$$b' - \hat{b} = S \sum d' \, (\hat{x}_{ji} - x'_{ji})y_{ib} / \sum y_{ib} \leq 0. \tag{15}$$

Under these circumstances, the optimal crop share is higher for the quasi-risk-reducing case than the quasi-risk-increasing case.

Although Equation 15 only applies exactly for the linear case, the general tendency it illustrates is both intuitive and important. A risk-reducing input that produces an externality should lead to higher crop shares (more nearly marginal-cost pricing) than a risk-increasing input producing an externality. Input use depends critically on the state-contingent yields that the tenant chooses. When the tenant is risk neutral, he or she tries to pick state-contingent yields that will maximize the expected return and pays no attention to the dispersion of the return across states of nature. In such instances, a risk-reducing input is unattractive to the tenant because its strength (smoothing state-contingent yields) is not prized by the tenant. Hence, the tenant uses relatively little of the input. The externality can be addressed by a minor departure from marginal-cost pricing. But if the input is risk increasing, it may be quite attractive to the tenant as a means of increasing expected yield. Therefore, the input externality can be expected to be quite significant, and the departure from marginal-cost pricing may have to be large.

The second major determinant of the crop share is the size of the marginal externality, that is, $d'(x_j)$. The greater the marginal externality, the smaller should be the crop share. For as noted earlier, share leasing leads to an underuse (compared with marginal-cost pricing) of inputs. And the greater the marginal externality, the larger should be the deviation from what would be obtained under marginal-cost pricing. In a crude sense, therefore, situations in which the externality problem is relatively severe should be positively correlated with relatively low crop shares.

The final determinant of the magnitude of the crop share is the responsiveness of expected yield to changes in the crop share (its own price responsiveness). Under risk neutrality, an increase in the share leads to higher state-contingent yields in all states and thus greater input use. All else constant, if the crop is very responsive to its own price, a small cut in the crop share will lead to a relatively large cut in state-contingent yields and, hence, to a relatively rapid diminution of the externality. One then expects the crop share to be relatively close to one. On the other hand, if the state-contingent yields are relatively unresponsive to changes in their own price, a cut in the crop share brings only relatively small declines in state-contingent yields and a persistent externality problem. Thus, one would expect the crop share to be closer to zero. Again, this last effect is a manifestation of the "inverse-elasticity" pricing rule.

The General Case

In preceding sections we demonstrated that, under the appropriate circumstances, the tenant's degree of risk aversion, the role that the polluting input plays in increasing or reducing production risk, the price responsiveness of state-contingent yields to changes in the crop share and the cash rent, and the marginal externality can all play an important role in determining the magnitude of the farmer's share of yield. In some instances, we have spoken as if each of the factors was a separate phenomenon, which is not the case. As just one example, the tenant's risk aversion and the state-contingent yield's responsiveness to changes in the cash rent are integrally linked.

In this section we consider how different (but not distinct) factors interact in determining the optimal crop share. We start with the simplest: the marginal externality. All else constant, one expects that the larger the marginal externality, the larger the crop share. This, indeed, is borne out by Equation 12, which we repeat for convenience:

$$\sigma = b^{-1} \sum [(1 - b)S^{-1} - d'x_{ji}] [y_{ib}V_a - y_{ia} V_b].$$

For a fixed level of σ, any increase in the marginal externality must be counterbalanced by an increase in the landlord's share of the yield— hence b drops.

With regard to the tenant's degree of risk aversion, it follows as before that, all else constant, the more risk averse (as measured by σ) the tenant, the smaller the tenant's share should be. Again, this happens because as b approaches one the tenant bears an increasing degree of production risk. The more risk averse the tenant, the less desirable that is. However, because of the presence of the externality and moral hazard, it will not generally be optimal to have the landlord (society at large) absorb all the risk for the tenant. We solve Equation 12 to get

$$(1 - b)S^{-1} = [b\sigma + d' \sum x_{ji}(y_{ib}V_a - y_{ia}V_b)] / \sum (y_bV_a - y_{ia}V_b). \quad (16)$$

Suppose that input x_j is severely quasi risk reducing in the sense that x_{ji} is negative for all but the very lowest states. The term

$$d' \sum x_{ji}(y_{ib}V_a - y_{ia}V_b)$$

is expected to be positive, which suggests that the crop share would be higher than if input x_j was severely quasi risk increasing. Increasing b does two things to the tenant: It exposes the tenant to more risk and it raises the tenant's ex post marginal returns in all states. On the other hand, increasing b does two things to the landlord or society at large: It lowers the returns from the production of the crop, thus forcing the landlord to rely more on cash rents, and by increasing the incentives for most state-contingent yields, it potentially exacerbates the externality problem.

When the input is risk reducing (especially in the extreme form noted above), the input provides self-insurance (by the tenant) against the worst states of nature. By providing self-insurance a risk-reducing input thus removes some of the need to shift risks from the farmer to society at large through the crop share. Hence, b can be larger than otherwise, because the risk-reducing nature of the input compensates for some increased risk that the tenant must face. Moreover, if the input is severely quasi risk reducing, raising b *may actually lead to a fall in its use* and, therefore, a gain (not a loss) on the externality front. Increasing b stimulates all state-contingent yields, but only the stimulus to the worst states raises the use of the polluting input—all other states push in the opposite direction. Use may actually fall. In any case, the incremental stimulus to use more b is relatively smaller than if the input was quasi risk increasing.

Equation 16 also shows that the earlier finding that the crop share tends to vary directly with the b-elasticity of expected supply still holds, but it must be tempered by considerations relating to the role that the polluting input plays in increasing or reducing the farmer's production risk. A similar statement applies to the a-elasticity of expected supply.

Conclusion

We have considered the potential interfaces between share leasing and production-based externalities. Share contracts are often criticized as being economically inefficient because they blunt economic incentives by only providing the tenant with a portion of the marginal returns from farming effort. However, if farm production involves the creation of undesirable externalities (for example, polluting runoff), social efficiency may require blunting the farmer's production incentives. Share contracts, as a consequence, may be socially desirable.

Evaluating the potential for share contracts to improve social efficiency in this context requires analyzing how share contracts simultaneously affect production incentives, risk sharing, and externality abatement. What is gained in terms of risk sharing and pollution control by the use of share contracts must be balanced against the production inefficiencies associated with share contracts. We have conducted a preliminary analysis of those trade-offs. Our principal findings include the following: Optimal share contracts obey a form of the inverse-elasticity rule. Other things being equal, the more price elastic is agricultural supply the closer the rental share should be set to one; and whether the inputs producing the externality are risk reducing or risk increasing plays an important role in determining the optimal share even if the farmer is risk neutral. Generally, if the input producing the externality is risk reducing, the crop share should be higher than if the input producing the externality is risk increasing. The final determinant of the optimal crop share is the sensitivity of the environment to the polluting input. Again, other things being equal, the more sensitive the environment is to changes in the polluting input, the lower should be the farmer's share of the crop.

Notes

Robert G. Chambers is professor, Department of Agricultural and Resource Economics, University of Maryland. His research was supported by Cooperative Agreement 43-3AEM-1-80066 between the Resources and Technology Division, Economic Research Service, U.S. Department of Agriculture, and the University of Maryland. Hyunok Lee is an economist, Office of Energy, U.S. Department of Agriculture. John Quiggin is associate professor, Department of Agricultural and Resource Economics, University of Maryland. The views expressed are those of the authors' and do not necessarily represent policies or views of the U.S. Department of Agriculture.

1. For an excellent survey, see N. Singh, "Theories of Sharecropping," in P. Bardhan, ed., *The Economic Theory of Agrarian Institutions* (Oxford: Clarendon Press, 1989).

2. Many historical studies do exist. See, for example, R. Day, "The Economics of Technological Change and the Demise of the Share Cropper," *American Economic Review* 57 (1967):427-449; and J. Reid, "Sharecropping and Tenancy in American History," in J. Roumasset, J.-M. Boussard, and I. Singh, eds., *Risk, Uncertainty, and Agricultural Development* (New York: Agricultural Development Council, 1979).

3. E. Nielsen and M. Moreheart, *Farm Operating and Financial Characteristics, 1986,* Statistical Bulletin 772, Economic Research Service (Washington, D.C.: U.S. Department of Agriculture, 1989).

4. E. Heady, "Marginal Resource Productivity and Imputation of Shares for a Sample of Rental Farms," *Journal of Political Economy* 63 (1955): 500-511.

5. R. Coase, *The Firm, The Market, and the Law* (Chicago: University of Chicago Press, 1987).

6. D. Johnson, "Resource Allocation under Share Contracts," *Journal of Political Economy* 58 (1950):111-123.

7. A.W. Marshall and I. Olkin, *Inequalities: Theory of Majorization and Its Applications* (New York: Academic Press, 1979).

8. R.G. Chambers and J. Quiggin, "Another Look at Moral Hazard," Australian National University, Research School of the Social Sciences, 1991.

9. The primary purpose of the survey was to obtain information on costs and returns in rice production and not on sharecropping. Thus, the data on individual farms contain limited information on share farming. U.S. Department of Agriculture, *1984* National Special Crop Survey (Washington, D.C., unpublished).

8. E. Lichtenberg and D. Zilberman, "Efficient Regulation of Environmental Health Risks," *Quarterly Journal of Economics* 49 (1988):167-178; and S.N.S. Cheung, *The Theory of Share Tenancy* (Chicago: University of Chicago Press, 1969).

11. Some may wonder why this information is not readily available to all. For example, in the nitrogen-pollution example cited earlier, one might suggest that nitrogen purchases are easily observable, and hence, an appropriate tax should be easy to set. Not surprisingly, this trivializes the problem. But it is trivialized at the cost of reality and believability, for the extent of nitrogen pollution depends on far more than just the amount of nitrogen purchased. Among other things, it depends on the care with which the nitrogen is applied, how the farmer makes use of other inputs or activities that might control nitrogen pollution, and the risk attitudes of different farmers, all of which are inherently unobservable except at the most extreme cost.

12. See Lichtenberg and Zilberman, "Efficient Regulation of Environmental Health Risks."

13. See J.J. Laffont, *The Economics of Uncertainty and Information* (Cambridge, Mass.: MIT Press, 1990).

14. The case may be extended to multiple outputs; see Chambers and Quiggin, "Another Look at Moral Hazard."

15. B. Holmstrom, "Moral Hazard and Observability," *Bell Journal of Economics* 10 (1979):74-91.

16. See Laffont, *The Economics of Uncertainty and Information.*

17. R.G. Chambers, *Applied Production Analysis: A Dual Approach* (New York: Cambridge University Press, 1988).

18. The random component is required because lacking it the landlord, given knowledge of the total externality (e.g., total nitrogen pollution), could always determine the amount of x_j that was used. And assuming that this information is verifiable to a third party responsible for enforcing contracts, contracts could always be made contingent on the level of x_j thus mitigating, but not removing, the moral hazard problem. In the case in which the externality depends on more than one component of x, the random component would not be necessary.

19. M. Intriligator, *Mathematical Optimization and Economic Theory* (New York: Prentice-Hall, 1970).

20. The "inverse-elasticity rule" requires departures from marginal cost or marginal value to be inversely related to the relevant elasticity. For example, in a taxation context, the inverse-elasticity rule implies that in taxing to raise revenues commodities with the lowest demand elasticity should be assigned the highest marginal tax. This correspondence between the sharecropping design

problem and the Ramsey-Boiteux-Samuelson-Baumol pricing problem does not appear to have been noted.

21. R.G. Chambers, *Applied Production Analysis.*

22. M. Harris and A. Raviv, "Optimal Incentive Contracts with Imperfect Information," *Journal of Economic Theory* 20 (1979):231-259.

23. A class of inputs can be risk increasing/reducing/neutral depending on conditions subsequent to the decision to use.

8

The Sources of Value
in Agricultural Land

Paul W. Barkley

Land *value* is of both conceptual and practical concern. Economists have been tireless in their attempts to ascertain the relative strengths of the various attributes that give land its value. Landowners and potential owners are perennially interested in the value of land as an asset and as a factor that provides a flow of productive services. Tax collectors are concerned because land's value—either as an asset or a factor—is the source of public revenue. In this paper I attempt to define and measure some of the attributes that give land its value. In doing so, I report some results of a land value study done in Washington State and speculate on why traditional land value studies have often been inadequate or flawed.

Rent

Of all the concepts explored and defined by economists, none is more venerable or more perplexing than rent. While the ancients had a reasonably well-developed concept of *surplus value*, it was the seventeenth-century mercantilist economist William Petty who brought several lines of thought together into a statement that provides a cogent and reasonably satisfactory definition of *rent*. Writing in 1662, Petty said,

> Suppose a man could with his own hands plant a certain scope of Land with Corn ... and had withal Seed wherewith to sow the same. I say, that when this man hath subducted his seed out of the proceed of his Harvest, and also what himself hath both eaten and given to others in exchange for Clothes, and other Natural necessaries; that the remainder of Corn, is the

natural and true Rent of the Land for that year; and the *medium* of seven years, or rather of so many years as make up the Cycle, within which Dearths and Plenties make their revolution, doth give the ordinary Rent of the Land in Corn.[1]

While Petty's definition rests on the notion of a surplus, it offers no help in separating or allocating "the ordinary Rent" into shares generated by the force of the underlying infrastructure, the capital imbedded in the land, and Ricardo's "original and indestructible powers of the soil."[2] Although Adam Smith mentioned rent in numerous places, he, like Petty before him, did not make an incisive distinction among the possible sources of the surplus. That has become the domain and the riddle facing later observers.

The end of the Napoleonic wars and the institution of the Corn Laws provided the great leap forward in developing the theoretical and practical (as well as political) importance of rent. Although Ricardo appears in the books as the progenitor of the theory of rent, West, Torrens, and Malthus all published treatises on the same subject in the winter of 1815, thus coinciding almost to the day with the publication of Ricardo's work.[3] The four works are very similar in their arguments. Ricardo emerged as the historical victor because of the clarity of his exposition and his notion that rents could be earned as a result of activity at either the intensive or extensive margin. Ricardo gave us *differential rent* whereas the others, especially Malthus, are more often associated with the more limited notion of *scarcity rent*. Ricardo reached his conclusions by examining the movement of the farming population onto land of lower and lower quality. The cultivated land of lowest quality defined the margin of cultivation. By noting the price of "corn" required to bring that land into production, Ricardo was able to define the rent accruing to all lands of higher quality.

Ricardo deserves credit for making rent one of the tools used by economists in their attempts to understand the functional shares of income and the effects of various forms of taxation on resource allocation and public revenues. Looking back from the vantage of the contemporary era, scholars sometimes puzzle over the way Ricardo used the language. By not distinguishing carefully and consistently between the modern notion of contract rent and the older notion of economic rent, he opened the door for a vast and still growing literature generally recognizable under the heading, "what Ricardo really meant was...." This controversy is certain to continue into the next century.

Despite the confusion over words, it is clear that Ricardo and his followers needed a surplus before rent could appear. This surplus materializes whenever there is a factor for which there is a positive derived demand but which has no (or an infinite) supply price, has zero (or a relatively low) opportunity cost, or can be increased in quantity only after at least the current production cycle has been completed.[4]

The surplus (rent)—or even the mere thought of a surplus (rent)—causes great anguish. Anglo-American economics deplores a surplus. The source of this disapprobation is obscure, but it is likely related to the Protestant work ethic or the Physiocrats' notion of sterile employment, a by-product of the Enclosures that finally said an individual's work could and should be rewarded, the common Marxian definition of exploitation, or the solemn fear that someone else might get the surplus. Regardless of the source, surpluses—and hence rents—purportedly breed sloth unless they are carefully directed into productive activity.[5] There is no guarantee, however, that the latter will happen, so no chance may be taken: Surpluses are likely targets for confiscation or at least heavy taxation.[6]

A comprehensive and modern neoclassical explanation of rent did not appear until Joan Robinson digressed from the main theme in her classic work on monopolistic competition.[7] Robinson provided tight logic as well as examples of factors other than those in perfectly inelastic supply that could and would receive rents. She added to our understanding by expanding the concept of transfer rents and the intramarginal uses of some factors. In doing so, she allowed for a greatly expanded source of rents, but she did not change any of the previously held ideas about the base nature of surpluses or the use of taxes to increase or decrease the intensity of use of a particular factor. The result of her intellectual excursions was the identification of many objects other than and in addition to the original and indestructible powers of the soil that could be taxed without serious injury to the productive base of the industrial world.[8] The practical result is the necessity of finding ways of identifying separable qualities of fixed assets that might be earning taxable rents.[9]

Rent and Value

The relationship between rent and value is well understood. Since rent is a net or residual return that is assumed to continue in perpetuity, it is capitalized to ascertain the value of the asset that produced it. This ostensibly simple process is always made difficult by the problems associated with determining the correct capitalization rate, measuring the correct perpetual residual to be capitalized, determining what to do with contract rents, and several other problems. Abstracting from these problems, a land parcel that reliably returns a net rent of $100 per year will have a capitalized value of $1,000 if the appropriate capitalization rate is on the order of 10 percent.[10]

The story now becomes difficult. Assume there exists an un-
improved land parcel that is used for crop production.[11] Assume further
that the parcel is not under any extraordinary pressure for conversion to
more intensive or less intensive use. If the land parcel is farmed by an
owner-operator, it is correctly regarded as a factor of production that
earns rents. The rents can be used for consumption, plowed into the
land as further development (improvement) costs, or taxed away
without changing the allocation of factors among uses. If the parcel is
sold, any untaxed rents accruing to the seller are capitalized into the
value (sale price) of the land. They then become a return to invested
capital for the new owner: a factor payment rather than a surplus. If the
parcel is farmed by a new owner, there is little matter. The new owner
counts as income some combination of imputed wages and returns on
invested capital. If, however, the land becomes an asset leased to a
tenant, some negotiating must take place to determine the division of
the rents and perhaps even the division of the returns on the investment.[12] The recent shift of much U.S. agricultural land from land-as-
factor to land-as-asset makes this a nontrivial problem for land-as-asset
owners, prospective tenants, assessors, and budget-dependent public
officials.

Embodied Improvements

The problem of distribution alluded to above becomes more severe
when one considers that most land in agriculture is not "just land."
The original farmer-owner usually makes a minimum investment to develop the land for agricultural purposes. Many of the investments (improvements) are permanent in that either they cannot be physically
separated from the land once they are installed, such as leveling or
terracing, or the mere fact of their *installation* drives the opportunity cost
of the investment to zero, as in the case of water wells or concrete
driveways.

Even though practicality insists that the ownership of permanent improvements runs with the land, frequently tenants or renters actually
install the improvements and earn any rents derived from them before
the lease runs out or the property is transferred. For this reason, it seems
increasingly important to attempt to learn the value of permanent improvements or to ask what contribution permanent improvements make
to the sale value of a parcel. A recent study in Washington State was
devoted to this problem.

The study centered on agricultural parcels transferred between 1980
and 1987. It involved 24 of the state's 39 counties, and those counties
were further arranged into six reasonably homogenous agricultural

regions. Data came from 908 new owners (buyers) who responded to a telephone survey. Each cooperating respondent provided over 350 pieces of information. An inquiry of this size produces an immense amount of information, which can be worked into answers to a variety of questions. Here, I omit a detailed elaboration of the modeling efforts and concentrate on some of the results from two of the six regions in the study.[13]

Feng Xu, the researcher, used a research method that was an adaptation of the Rosen hedonic regression approach to ascertaining the implicit value of attributes contained in varying intensities in a complex good, in this case a land parcel.[14] The method is in contrast to older methods that rely on demand shifters in a bid-curve/offer-curve context.

One of the two areas discussed here is the Yakima Valley, a diverse and productive agricultural area in the south-central part of Washington State. It is given over to the production of fruits, wines, and high-value vegetable crops. Farms are generally small by state averages. The other area is adjacent to the east and includes much of the vast region irrigated by the Columbia Basin Irrigation Project. It is a crop-growing area with large acreages of potatoes, corn, wheat, root crops, and hay crops. Farms are large and much of the region is quite remote.

Table 8.1 gives the means of several variables in the model. The dependent variable was sale price per acre. Several variables require explanation. *Time* is a count of the months from the beginning of the study period. Thus, January 1980 has a value of 1, February 1980 a value of 2, and so on. The average of the counts for each parcel indicates that the "average time of sale" was the spring of 1984 in the Yakima Valley, summer of the same year in the Columbia Basin.

Land-capability class is based on the Soil Conservation Service's long-standing scheme of eight classes wherein Class I soil is land of the

TABLE 8.1 Means of Selected Variables for Each Region

Variable	Yakima Valley ($N = 225$)	Columbia Basin ($N = 184$)
Size of parcel (acres)	56.27	210.86
Time (months from Jan. 1980)	51.38	55.09
Distance to town (miles)	4.3	7.4
Land-capability class (I-VIII)	3.9	3.2
Estimated gross income per acre (dollars)	747.64	417.71
Sale price per acre	$2,802	$1,519

Source: F. Xu, "An Economic Study of Contributions of Parcel Characteristics to Agricultural Land Values in Washington: A Hedonic Approach," Ph.D. dissertation, Department of Agricultural Economics, Washington State University, Pullman, 1990.

highest quality for agricultural purposes and Class VIII soil is not generally suitable for farming. These classifications are made with land in its natural state. The addition of irrigation water can make seemingly desert land that has been unfit for farming—perhaps Class VI or VII— become very productive, but the original land-capability classification does not change. That is what has happened in both regions. Landowners have made capital improvements to enhance the original and indestructible powers of the soil, but the land-capability class has remained the same. The average land-capability class, then, appears to bias land quality downward.

Gross income is a proxy for the net returns to agricultural enterprise. Survey data included crop acreage and yield by parcel. Where possible, Xu calculated the total yield from these data and then multiplied it by the average state price to obtain a measure of gross income for the parcel. If the information was incomplete, he derived gross income from secondary data sources.[15]

Table 8.2 shows the implicit value of various land characteristics. The characteristics are qualities similar to Ricardo's original and indestructible powers of the soil. Subject to the aforementioned problem with land-capability classifications, the values of these characteristics were not created by the installation and use of capital appurtenances and they will travel freely with transfer of the land. Any rents they generate are an appropriate object for dispute among the landowner, the tenant (if one exists), and the tax collector.

An increase of one mile in distance from town was accompanied by a decrease of $42.55 per acre in the value of land parcels in the Yakima Valley and by a decrease of $23.01 per acre in the Columbia Basin. An increase in the land-capability class was similarly accompanied by a decrease in per-acre value. A $1 increase in gross income was, however, accompanied by an increase of $0.76 per acre in per-acre value of the parcels in both regions so long as the values of other variables were held constant at their mean levels.

Table 8.3 shows the implicit value of selected capital fixtures designed to improve productivity and increase the value of land.

TABLE 8.2 Implicit Value of Selected Land Characteristics at Mean Values of Other Variables ($ per acre)

Characteristic	Yakima Valley	Columbia Basin
Distance to town (miles)	−42.55	−23.01
Land capability (at Class III)	−448.71	−63.07
Gross income per acre	-0.76	0.76

Source: Xu, "An Economic Study of Contributions of Parcel Characteristics."

TABLE 8.3 Implicit Values of Selected Capital (Embodied) Improvements at Mean Value of Other Variables ($ per acre)

Improvement	Yakima Valley	Columbia Basin
Windbreaks (in feet of length)	$ 5.32	$ 8.29
Irrigation systems		
Center pivot	NA	254.89
Sprinkler	391.54	228.88
Rill	303.57	205.27
Barns (at average size and age)	210.86	15.43
House (at average size and age)	372.57	105.41
Machinery (measured by assessed valuation)	1.34	0.85

Source: Xu, "An Economic Study of Contributions of Parcel Characteristics."

Irrigation equipment made a large contribution, but windbreaks (rows of closely planted trees used to protect crops more than to prevent soil erosion) made a small contribution. Buildings (barns and houses) made positive contributions larger in magnitude than one would expect. Close examination of the study results reveals that the contribution increases with the size of the structure and decreases with its age—exactly what one would expect.[16]

A critical early observer of these results commented that they are "interesting but not surprising," a clear endorsement of the efficacy of the study. The fact that results are of interest means that headway is being made in disaggregating the value of land into its constituent parts. The lack of surprises says even more; it implies that the theory, and perhaps even the method, is on target. The main task in completing the job relies almost solely on the availability of time and money to gather more comprehensive information.

The study shows that rents appear when capital fixtures are applied to land. Under very restricted assumptions, the per-acre rent for a sprinkler irrigation system in the Yakima Valley would be about $40 per year when a 10 percent capitalization rate is used and when the parcel to which the irrigation is applied has all the mean characteristics shown in Table 8.1. A house in the Columbia Basin would produce a per-acre rent of about $10 per year under similar assumptions.

If the parcel of land is operated by an unencumbered owner, the rents can be taxed away entirely without resource allocation being affected. An owner could extract the same total as contract rent with the same result. The problem arises when rents are capitalized and the parcel is transferred. Rent then becomes a return to invested capital, and the opportunity to tax without affecting use is reduced significantly. If the transfer is consummated using borrowed funds, the return to the capital owner (the person or institution to whom interest is paid) flees agriculture as a real rather than an opportunity cost. This burden, the terms of which do not usually honor short-run changes in yields or prices, is precisely what caused the financial crisis in agriculture in the early and mid-1980s.

The evidence presented here is solid but sketchy. The study in Washington State indicates that land value can be disaggregated. Such studies, however, will have to be combined with much more complete information sets before they can be used to shed light on tax policy, allocative efficiency, or simply the distribution of factor shares in agriculture.

Looking Ahead

The observations and results presented above are based on conventional theories and methods. The most blatant weakness in the underlying theory is the assumption of perfect competition in the land market. Granted, many observers allude to the fact that a market for agricultural land parcels is a local market and may not attract attention from outside buyers or other potential sellers from the inside. Despite this, the conventional analysis, like so many others, proceeds as if a land transfer was conducted within the constricting assumptions of perfect competition. Even Rosen's hedonics, for all the power the method provides, still assumes that homogeneous units of an attribute are bought and sold in a perfect market—one with so many buyers and sellers that no one can significantly affect either the buyer or the seller side of the market. This assumption does not hold in agricultural land markets, where only about 3.7 percent of all land is transferred in any year and only a few local buyers vie for a parcel that comes up for sale.[17]

Land markets are peculiar because parcels do not flow evenly onto the market. Parcels for sale come at infrequent and unpredictable intervals determined by economic, social, cultural, and environmental factors. Analysts are beginning to understand the economic factors. Numerous studies have shown that changes in factor or product prices will alter the return to land and, consequently, the implicit price of permanent improvements as well as the implicit price of the original and indestructible powers of the soil. Other factors, however, get in the way. Among the most important is the current owner's reservation price.

Reservation prices creep into the trading of any good sold in an imperfect market.[18] Sellers set reservation prices in the market for agricultural land parcels. Additionally, sellers (or potential sellers) set different reservation prices for different potential purchasers. A seller may sell to a neighbor at a realistic price, one that reflects the capitalization of all rents appropriate to the parcel. The same parcel may be available for purchase by the neighbor's ne'er-do-well son only if the price is somewhat higher, and if a non-Caucasian female buyer from a far away place should appear, the lowest acceptable price for the same land parcel may take a sudden jump.

The differential among reservation prices is not often examined. Cast in traditional terms related to demand and supply, the supply curve in a situation in which differential reservation prices come into play takes on curious characteristics—not just a curious shape. In most instances the parcel would be indivisible, that is, only the whole parcel would be for sale. The result is a supply curve that starts at a point such as Point A in Figure 8.1. Point A acquires distance from the horizontal axis to show the minimum reservation price at which the parcel will be sold to the "most desired" buyer. Point B is directly above Point A, which indicates that the quantity of land for sale cannot change (the parcel is indivisible), but the second most acceptable buyer will have to pay more to even enter the bargaining process. Several points may be stacked one above the other in price/quantity space. The perplexing attribute is that, as the price rises, more and more potential buyers become eligible to purchase the parcel—a situation quite in contrast to the usual formulation of supply. A more formal statement of this phenomenon is that the *buyers determine supply*. Conventional models based on perfect competition do not incorporate this peculiarity. Nor, I suspect, do the traditional models of bilateral monopoly.

Assuming that one parcel at a time comes onto the market, the situation depicted has a monopolistic seller facing an oligopsonistic cadre

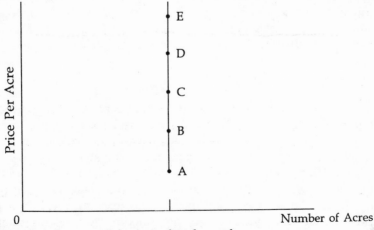

FIGURE 8.1 "Supply curves" for agricultural parcels.

of buyers, who may or may not share the same price or the same information as they begin and continue the bargaining process. Certainly situations of this kind arise in the market for agricultural land parcels. Future research efforts aimed at determining the value of land should take this reservation price/bargaining process into account, for understanding it may help observers and analysts distribute the value now gathered into the constant term in ordinary regression analysis. Put another way, researchers should be as cognizant of changes in the alphas as they are of changes in the betas in land value studies.

A second land-market problem arises in cases in which either environmental or amenity motives exist for purchasing agricultural land. Environmental motives differ from amenity motives insofar as amenity seekers are private parties purchasing land in order to consume some of the amenities it affords—a view, a riverfront location, bucolic surroundings, and the like. The environmental motive is a public, or at least a group, effort aimed at preserving some public or quasi-public environmental good associated with open space or agriculture. The rapid increase in the number and activity of land trusts is propelled by the environmental motive.

In either case, the transfer price of agricultural parcels cannot be traced to productivity, original powers, permanent improvements, or conventional rents. In such cases value arises from subjective rents the buyer is expecting to receive. Some studies have attempted to place values on these rents, but few have been successful in "valuing" the private amenities or public environmental goods associated with a particular parcel.[19]

A final problem in ascertaining value is the existence of speculation in the market for agricultural land. Although this motive is likely not as dominant in the 1990s as it was in the 1970s, it is still a venerable attribute of the market for agricultural land. Speculation distorts value, and in doing so, it also affects ownership and allocation: The former in turn affects distribution and the latter affects efficiency.

Conclusion

The question that prompted this paper seems as insistent now as in the beginning. The theory, which once seemed so precise, now seems only to hint at some of the broad applications while missing practical applications and nuances affecting the ownership, transfer, and value of agricultural land parcels. The analytic methods, which are improving each day, seem more demanding of data and more reckless with the assumptions necessary to make them relevant. More than this, one can suspect that a full century of sometimes intensive inquiry about landownership and land value should have yielded more definitive and more durable results.

The problem stems in part from the fact that the role of land changes through time, and the hypotheses that guide inquiries cannot keep pace with the role(s). We as a nation (or perhaps we as a civilization) expect more from land than ever before, and our expectations appear to be growing. There was a time when land meant little more than our daily bread. Now, among other things, it means our bread, our individual small claims to space on the planet, a place to recreate, and a last vestige of wilderness. And all this is in addition to our expectation that land will provide a flow of income as well as a store of wealth—land as factor as well as land as asset—for us and for those who will come later.

The most formidable problem regards the lack of specific knowledge of the market for individual land parcels. The market is where the various forces work themselves out. It is where bargains are struck, bargains that affect both efficiency and distribution. The market is where rents may be transformed into other types of factor rewards. It is where the assessor and the tax collector make their decisions on rates and the distribution of payments. And the market is where the investigator/scientist/researcher can find the evidence needed to take the next analytic step regarding rent, ownership, value, and other aspects of land.

So the message has been turned on end: rents, then determinants, then markets. The work on determinants will continue and perhaps yield additional insights as the current data set is exploited. The theory of rent will stay in place, although there is room for comparative analyses of who gets what. It is the markets, market motivations, and market imperfections that may well stand as a limit to where this work can go. That limit should be explored in the next century of work on land, landownership, and land value.

Notes

Paul W. Barkley is professor, Department of Agricultural Economics, Washington State University.

1. This quotation, or parts of it, appears in the writings of many classical and neoclassical economists. The original is found in Petty's *A Treatise of Taxes and Contributions*, written in 1662. The fact that Petty comes so quickly to the explicit notion of rent implies that the term was already well established in the economics literature of the mid-seventeenth century. The quotation here is taken from A. Marshall, *Principles of Economics*, 8th ed. (New York: Macmillan, 1948), Book VI, Ch. IX:635, where it appears in a footnote.

2. This omission is understandable. At the time Petty was writing, little more than labor and seed were used to make a crop. The extensive use of capital in

British agriculture was some decades away. This being the case, land became the claimant of all surplus value.

3. Ricardo's earliest work on rent was *Essays on the Influence of a Low Price of Corn on the Profits of Stock; Shewing the Inexpediency of Restrictions of Importations*. The work was published in 1815, but it is most easily found in P. Sraffa, ed., *The Works and Correspondence of David Ricardo*, Vol. IV (Cambridge: Cambridge University Press, 1951-1973). Torrens' work is the most like Ricardo's since he, too, worked with the law of diminishing returns. R. Torrens, *An Essay on the External Corn Trade* (London: Longman, Rees, Orme, Brown, and Green, 1815). The West essay was originally published in London as *Essay on the Application of Capital to Land, With Observations Shewing the Impolicy of any Great Restriction on the Importation of Corn, and That the Bounty of 1688 Did Not Lower the Price of It*. The essay is most easily found as a reprint in J.H. Hollander, ed., *Sir Edmond West on the Application of Capital to Land, 1815* (Baltimore: Hollander, 1903). Malthus' contribution is in T.R. Malthus, *An Inquiry into the Nature and Progress of Rent* (London: John Murray, 1815).

4. Marshall described the rents accruing to factors that are temporarily fixed in supply as *quasi-rents*.

5. This has always seemed a curious inconsistency in economic theory, practice, and policy. A surplus *qua surplus* draws harsh condemnation and even harsher treatment from the tax collector. At the same time, the surplus is known to be absolutely necessary before investment can take place, a position frequently used to justify an unequal distribution of income in developing nations and special tax advantages for the wealthy in advanced nations.

6. Henry George was the nineteenth-century champion of this view. A California journalist, he (no less than Petty, Smith, Ricardo, and the others!) drew conclusions from what he saw around him. Land speculators in California were appropriating federal lands and making huge fortunes. George suggested the fortunes were not the result of any socially useful activity, so the "rents" earned through speculation should be taxed away. The speculators responded by suggesting that their buying and selling permitted the land to come into production long before the usual homesteading process would have. The truth in this case is moot. Much has been written about Henry George's position. For a mildly pro-speculator article, see G.D. Nash, "Henry George Reexamined: William S. Chapman's Views on Land Speculation in Nineteenth Century California," *Agricultural History* (July 1959):133-137.

7. J. Robinson, *The Economics of Imperfect Competition* (London: Macmillan, 1933):Ch. 8.

8. This discussion is not specific to the industrial economies. The same effects obtain in any society in which surpluses are taxed.

9. An excellent discussion of the various classifications of rent is F. Dovring, *Land Economics* (Boston: Breton, 1987). See especially Ch. 8 and 12. A slightly different, but very useful discussion of returns to land and rent is C.C. Mabbs-Zeno, "Taxonomy of Land Value Concepts," in G. Wunderlich, ed., *Land—Something of Value*, Part 1: "Price and Market Issues" (Cambridge, Mass.: Lincoln Institute of Land Policy, 1982).

10. There is much dispute about the correct rate at which to capitalize returns to agriculture of agricultural land. For the moment, it is assumed the opportunity cost of capital in ventures of similar risk is ascertainable and is the appropriate rate.

11. The assumption is, of course, unrealistic. For all land in crop production or in any other kind of economic activity, some "development costs" have been incurred to improve some aspects of the parcel before it can be put to use. Many of the costs—such as for roads, property boundaries, water rights, and protection—are borne by the public before settlement. Other costs, including a minimal amount of fencing and the first breaking of the soil, are private in character but may be one-time costs.

12. The latter case, in which owners and renters negotiate over the division of interest payments, is most likely to happen in situations in which land is purchased for speculative reasons.

13. Method and results in their complete detail can be found in F. Xu, "An Econometric Study of Contributions of Parcel Characteristics to Agricultural Land Values in Washington: A Hedonic Approach," Ph.D. dissertation, Department of Agricultural Economics, Washington State University, Pullman, 1990.

14. Rosen's approach has been used in a number of studies relating to land value. The original work is S. Rosen, "Hedonic Prices and Implicit Markets: Product Differentiation in Perfect Competition," *Journal of Political Economy* 82(1974):34-55.

15. In some cases, Xu had partial information. When this was so, he took as much data as possible from the questionnaire response then augmented it with state and county data from the Census of Agriculture. In the worst possible case, he used county averages for cropping patterns, yields, and prices to make the parcel estimates.

16. In Region A, barns cease to make any contribution to value when they reach 72.7 years of age. In Region B, the threshold comes at 54 years. Houses in Region A are completely depreciated at 91.5 years. In Region B, their contribution drops to zero at age 78.0 years.

17. The market for urban residential real estate may come closer to meeting the hypothetical ideal. This alone may explain why the literature on urban real estate values is so much larger than that for agricultural land.

18. Consumers' attempts to bargain down the price of an automobile are nothing more than attempts to ascertain the dealer's reservation price for the vehicle. If buyers and dealers were to compare notes and be honest about their transactions, it would probably become evident that no consumer reaches a bargained price that is at or even near the dealer's reservation price.

19. For an interesting attempt to learn the effects these values have on market prices of agricultural land, see M. Blakeley, "An Economic Analysis of the Effects of Development Rights Purchases on Land Values in King County, Washington," M.A. thesis, Department of Agricultural Economics, Washington State University, Pullman, 1991.

9

Market Price of Land as a Measure of Welfare

Patrick N. Canning

The application of hedonic price theory in the real estate market is widespread. Hedonic analysis can be used, for example, as an input into welfare- and policy-impact studies and to estimate implicit prices or costs for nonmarket goods or externalities. Many of the hedonic studies since the 1970s have focused on developing a specification that would make the hedonic real estate price model consistent with the paradigmatic model first developed by Rosen.[1] Little attention has been given, however, to how the output of the analysis should be interpreted within the framework of economic welfare theory and capital theory.

In this paper I explain the distinction between a land parcel's productive value within an industry and its value on the open market. I show why the distinction is important when developing estimates of producer surplus, producer welfare, and rent to land as an input in production. Finally, I show how the hedonic land model should be used when conducting industrywide welfare analyses. The emphasis of the last discussion is on the importance of using data on an industry's land rents in conducting welfare analyses.

Here, *welfare* is narrowly defined to be the net present market value of characteristics and amenities associated with land in the context of a profit-maximizing industry. The focus of this paper is industry analysis, so issues of consumer surplus and the validity of money measures of social welfare are not critical. Rent will be defined by the annual residual income to land after nonland annual expenses are deducted. In equilibrium, this value will be equal to the rental rate for land used as an industry input. This is graphically represented as the area above the *annual* market price for land and below the derived demand for land. In this paper, references to an industry's market rental rate are assumed to be equal to the industry rent.

Economists often claim that land values are the present value of expected rents. Many empirical studies show, however, that the market value of land and the annual rent earned from employing land as an industry input can have a weak statistical relationship. Analysts have demonstrated this point empirically in the market for agricultural real estate.[2] Factors other than agricultural rents may determine agricultural land values. Land price can be driven by a consumptive value (e.g., the prestige of owning a large farm or ranch) and by a productive value arising from several unrelated industries (e.g., leasing farmland for sport hunting). Below, I present illustrations that show the distinction between a parcel's market value and its productive value within a given industry. The illustrations are intended to illuminate the process of asset pricing in the real estate market when the land has more than one source of value.

Industrywide producer welfare can be measured by the area above price and below the derived demand curve for a necessary input, when utility is derived from maximization of profit. Land is a necessary input to many industries, such as agriculture, and the annual cost of land is equal to the rent. The significance of this fact is that rent has been regarded as an effective measure of producer welfare in much of the economics literature since Marshall's *Principles of Economics* appeared in 1930.[3] Below, I present illustrations that depict producer welfare within an industry and show how it is represented by rent.

The real estate market has been a popular and well-suited area for the application of welfare and implicit price analysis. With a properly designed functional form, and conditions that satisfy the rules for applying the hedonic model, analysts can use market real estate data to conduct meaningful welfare analysis. Below, I show how to derive the reduced-form hedonic equation using land with rent as the dependent variable. In this form, the hedonic results have a direct welfare interpretation for analysis.

Background

The theory of hedonics is more aptly described as the theory of implicit prices. It has been widely applied in conjunction with real estate market data. In such applications, real estate is depicted as a differentiable product that has a unique market value based on the sum of all the parcel's characteristics. The real estate market has a great deal in common with Rosen's model of the implicit price market.[4]

Welfare measurements, ex post and ex ante policy analysis, and ex post decomposition of component values of a real estate parcel are popular outputs of hedonic analyses of real estate markets. Much of this literature focuses on market-level estimates of inverse supply and/or demand functions for those characteristics. The dominant empirical approach employed in this body of literature is to model the price of a real estate parcel as a function of parcel characteristics, buyer and seller characteristics, and industry characteristics (e.g., input and output prices, demand and supply shifters).

It is often of interest to policy analysts and policymakers to distinguish between recipients of welfare impacts that occur within an industry and owners of industry resources. For example, a statewide ban on use of a certain pesticide in Texas could have a significant impact on the agricultural industry in the state. However, Pope has demonstrated that most of rural land value in Texas is a consumptive value and is not based on returns from agriculture.[5] It is possible, then, that a ban on the pesticide could enhance rural land's consumptive value in the state through its enhancement as a wildlife habitat. The enhancement of consumptive value could be sufficient to offset the lost agricultural revenues. If an impact study was conducted to measure the effects of the pesticide ban on the agricultural sector, analyzing the effect of the pesticide policy on the price of land might show that it would have no impact at all. If, instead, agricultural rents were analyzed, negative impacts would most likely be found.

Factor rents are the residual returns after all costs not associated with a factor are deducted. If one considers the value of land in a utility maximization framework, land not only produces rents from productive uses such as agriculture, it also may provide rents (in the form of a positive utility) from consumptive uses after consumptive costs are deducted. So a consideration of rents to land that are generated solely by its use as a factor of production ignores those rents that may result from land's use as a factor of consumption.

The distinction between resource values and rents is important. Although land price is the capitalized value of economic rents to land, the source of each rent may come from several industries and from non-market origins. In qualifying gainers and losers in any welfare analysis that treats land as a differentiated factor of production, changes in the price of land can provide a misleading measure of an industry's welfare impacts. Landowner welfare impacts are important in many economic analyses and land price is an important information source in welfare analysis. However, for industry analysis, when land is used as a factor of production, an industry's rent-to-land schedule is more meaningful for measuring welfare impacts across the industry.

A focus on industry rent represents a more narrow approach to market analysis than does parcel price. One consequence of a more narrow focus is that resource adjustments into and out of the industry being analyzed are not fully captured by adjustments in industry rents, while a parcel's market price will reflect such adjustments. However, the nature of the real estate market and the role of land as an argument in, for example, a household utility function are difficult problems to address when analyzing a parcel's market price. In many instances, it is sufficient to conduct an industry-specific impact analysis and then determine to what extent these results capture general equilibrium impacts. In any case, a consideration of the trade-offs between analysis of market land price versus industry rents to land as a factor of production should be carefully considered when planning a research agenda.

The current use of hedonic models in the real estate market is summed up well in Palmquist's 1989 *Land Economics* article.[6] Palmquist emphasizes the importance of identifying (1) an underlying structural model on which reduced-form equations are based and (2) the guidelines for interpreting the empirical results from applying the model to market data. His latter emphasis adds to a long list of articles on how to interpret the output of market hedonic equation estimates.[7] His emphasis on model development includes a derivation of a "variable profit function" that produces both bid and offer functions for land parcels. The dependent variable in the bid/offer equations is equivalent to rent.

Palmquist, however, does not emphasize the connection between rent and producer welfare. In this respect, he reveals a shortcoming of the body of empirical hedonic studies that use their results to make inferences about welfare effects for specific markets, industries, interest groups, and so on. In particular, such studies do not directly address how the choice of a dependent variable ties in with true market measures of economic welfare. As if to confirm this lack of emphasis, concurrently with his *Land Economics* article, Palmquist coauthored an article in the *American Journal of Agricultural Economics* and switched the dependent variable in his model from rent to market value of real estate for data convenience, but he did not discuss the implications of the change.[8]

Land Has Productive and Consumptive Values

Consider a parcel that is used strictly as a factor of production within a single industry and that has no other productive or consumptive use. The market value of this parcel would be determined by factor rents and the perceived discount rate. Under the simplifying assumptions usually employed in capital theory—no expected real growth in rent, nondepreciation of land, and a constant discount rate over time the market price of this land is,

$$P = V_{I1} = \frac{Q \times R_{I1}}{\sigma}, \tag{1}$$

where P is the market price of a parcel, V_{I1} is the discounted value of rents to land in a single industry over the life of the asset, Q is parcel size (in acres), R_{I1} is the average expected rent per acre earned in industry $I1$ in the current time period, and σ is the discount rate.

Figure 9.1 depicts a plausible market representation of Equation 1. In Figure 9.1a, total price is represented by the line $0\text{-}V_{I1}$ as a concave function in parcel size. The depiction of a concave rent function in Figure 9.1b (R_{I1}) necessarily follows from Figure 9.1a and the assumptions underlying Equation 1.

Aside from its productive value, land can also be an argument in an individual's utility function.[9] In this context, ownership of land can entail an additional consumptive value. For agricultural land, Pope gives such examples as a desire to own a rural home, a place to hunt and fish, and so on.[10] In most of his examples, the consumptive value could be alternatively thought of as a complementary productive value. For example, owner-operated farmland can be thought of as an owner renting out his land to himself. This same owner may also incorporate the market value of hunting on his land in deriving the value of parcel ownership. He chooses to pay the hunting fee to himself instead of hunting on someone else's land.

Modifying Equation 1 to depict a parcel of farmland that also generates income from hunting fees (and/or other complementary consumptive uses),

$$P = V_{I1} + V_{I2} = Q \times \frac{[R_{I1}(a, ..., k) + R_{I2}(h, ..., m)]}{\sigma}, \tag{2}$$

where R_{I1} and R_{I2} are rents per acre from industries 1 and 2 and $a\text{-}m$ are arguments that affect the level of rents in those industries. Equation 2 represents a land parcel that generates income from two industries. With this specification the industries are independent. In the example above of farmland that is also used for hunting, Equation 2 is a plausible market representation. Note that the two industries' rent functions share several common arguments ($h\text{-}k$). Those arguments may affect the two industries' rents similarly, or they may have opposite effects.

In Figure 9.1a, Equation 2 is depicted by the solid curve $0\text{-}P$. The curve $0\text{-}P$ is the solution to Equation 2 at different levels of Q, and it represents the market price for land across different parcel sizes. The

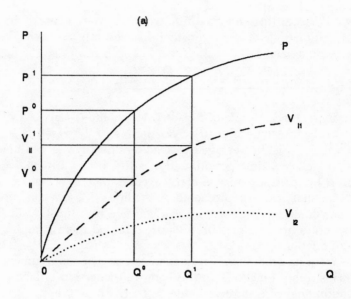

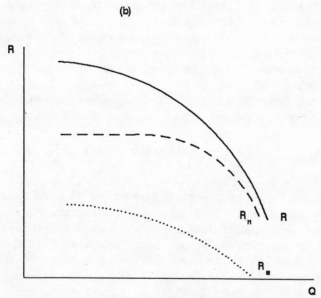

FIGURE 9.1 Total and annual price of land.

curves 0-V_{I1} and 0-V_{I2} are the value of land in industries 1 and 2, respectively, at different levels of Q. In this depiction, the marginal rental income from the second industry (V_{I2}) falls to zero at some small parcel size. As in the single-industry case, there is a concave rent function for both industries (R_{I1} and R_{I2}) and for the combined industry curve (R). Note that the average per unit rental rate in industry 2 quickly falls to zero as Q increases. The concavity of the total price function around its mean parcel size (Q^0, Q^1) implies that the average unit price declines as parcel size increases. A concave total parcel price function in the area of the mean parcel size can come about from a combination of the parcel's several use values. For example, a linear total price function in the area of the mean parcel size for the parcel's primary productive use (i.e., cropland) and a concave function for the parcel's primary consumptive use (i.e., as private recreation grounds) would be consistent with the depiction of the curve 0-P in Figure 9.1a. In the example of a parcel owner who uses the land for hunting, parcel size may become irrelevant after a certain amount of land is acquired. However, that need not be the case, and R_{I2} could also have been drawn in any number of other ways.

Real estate prices in many sectors of the economy are driven by the rent from a single dominant industry. However, even in regions where a single industry dominates the land market, secondary industries and consumptive uses of land can play a significant role in price formation. Figure 9.1a demonstrates this point. Take the market price of P^0 for a land parcel of size Q^0. The value of this parcel to its primary industry (V_{I1}) is V^0_{I1}. The difference ($P^0 - V^0_{I1}$) represents the value of land in the secondary industry. If a policy is implemented that has the effect of shifting the optimal parcel size from Q^0 to Q^1 (Figure 9.1a) without changing the total price curves, the observed change in the market value of land is $P^1 - P^0$. However, the change in the value of land in industry 1 due to the new policy is $V^1_{I1} - V^0_{I1}$. The two changes are not necessarily equal. Conducting welfare analysis for a specific industry, such as $I1$, using data on market land prices can yield misleading estimates of welfare impacts.

The problem with conducting welfare analysis within a specific industry using land values is that only the market price (0-P) is observed. On the other hand, data on the rent of industry factors can often be obtained. Using data on rents to land is a more relevant approach in welfare analysis than using data on the observed market prices of land.

Real Estate Market Data Can Be Used in Welfare Analyses

In a profit-maximizing industry, *producer surplus* is the area above the industry's output supply curve and below the market price. In a competitive market, many small price-taking firms must be aggregated to derive a market supply curve. Also, a single industry may produce multiple outputs. For example, a regional agricultural industry may produce a wide variety of outputs. Even single crops (such as cotton) can have more than one output product (cotton lint and cotton seed). In such cases, measures of industrywide producer surplus, or changes in producer surplus, can be difficult to obtain.

Total producer surplus for an industry is equivalent to total rent for any industry input that is necessary to produce nonzero levels of output for any single product or combination of products.[11] Such inputs are considered as necessary, and land typically falls into that category. As a necessary input, land has an annual market price, $\hat{R}$, that is just high enough to cause the derived demand for land to fall to zero. At that point the industry is forced to shut down.

With the concept of a shut-down price, producer surplus (S) in the output markets equals the rent to a necessary factor input, such as land (R_l).[12] Producer surplus equals total profit plus total fixed factor costs. First-order conditions can be derived from the profit function, and the optimal output supply and factor demand levels (conditioned on fixed input and output prices) can be plugged back into the producer surplus function, as follows:

$$\text{Max } S(P,W) = S(Q(P^*,W^*),X(P^*,W^*)), \qquad (3)$$

where P is the vector of output prices, W is the vector of input prices, Q is the vector of output quantities, X is the vector of input quantities, and $*$ is a flag that signifies an optimal price vector for profit maximization.

From the envelope theorem,

$$\frac{\partial S^*}{\partial p_i} = \tilde{q}_i\,(P,W) = \text{product supply for output } q_i\,, \qquad (4)$$

and,

$$\frac{\partial S^*}{\partial w_j} = \tilde{x}_j\,(P,W) = \text{derived demand for input } x_j\,. \qquad (5)$$

The shut-down price for each output i is $\hat{P}_i$. By definition, the solution for total producer surplus is

$$\sum_{i=1}^{n} \int_{p_i=\hat{p}_i}^{p_i^*} \tilde{q}_i(P(p_i),W^*)dp_i = \sum_{i=1}^{n} S_i\,(P(p_i^*),W^*) = S(P^*,W^*), \qquad (6)$$

where P equals $(P^*_1,P^*_2, \dots ,P_i, \dots P^*_n)$.

Equation 6 represents the total area above the supply curve and below the market price for each of the n industry outputs. This is the definition of an industry's producer surplus.

A result identical to that of Equation 6 can be derived by analysis of a necessary input:

$$\int_{w_j^*}^{\hat{w}_j} x_j \, (P^*, w_i^*, w_j) \, dw_j \;=\; -\int_{w_j^*}^{\hat{w}_j} \frac{\partial S}{\partial w_j} \;=\; S\,(P^*, W^*). \tag{7}$$

By replacing the w_j in Equation 7 with R_l, land can be treated as a necessary input. Integrating the derived demand for land from the market price (R^*_l) and the shut-down price ($\hat{R}_l$) gives the total rent to land. Thus, the existence of an industry's shut-down price for land guarantees that rent to land as an industry input is equivalent to the industry's total producer surplus. In a profit-maximizing industry, this yields a measure of producer welfare. Figure 9.2 illustrates how this result leads to estimates of welfare impacts. Although a single output and a single input are depicted, similar graphical interpretations could be presented using multiple inputs and/or outputs.

Consider a simultaneous input and output price change as follows: $R^0 - R^1$, $P^0 - P^1$. The change is measured in the output market (Figure 9.2a) by a change in producer surplus from area c at prices P^0 and R^0_l, to area $a + b + c + d$ at prices P^1 and R^1_l, for a net gain of area $a + b + d$. Alternatively, rent to land is measured by area w (Figure 9.2b), at prices P^0 and R^0_l, and the area $w + x + y + z$ at prices P^1 and R^1_l, for a net gain of area $x + y + z$. From Equation 7, the change in rent ($x + y + z$) is equal to the change in producer surplus ($a + b + d$).

In many instances it is difficult to obtain estimates of an industry's supply curve, especially if the industry produces multiple outputs. On the other hand, data on an industry's rent to land are often available on the basis of, for example, an average per acre market rental rate. Taking the product of that average value and the total quantity produces an estimate of total rent to land.

Observed changes in rent to land are general equilibrium effects and are difficult to attribute to any single factor or series of factors. This fact precludes conducting meaningful welfare analysis by simply observing market rent data before and after a particular policy has been implemented. However, meaningful welfare analysis can be obtained from market rent data using hedonic analysis when certain conditions are met. In the next section I demonstrate how to derive a hedonic model for land rents. The model provides a direct means of conducting welfare analysis.

112

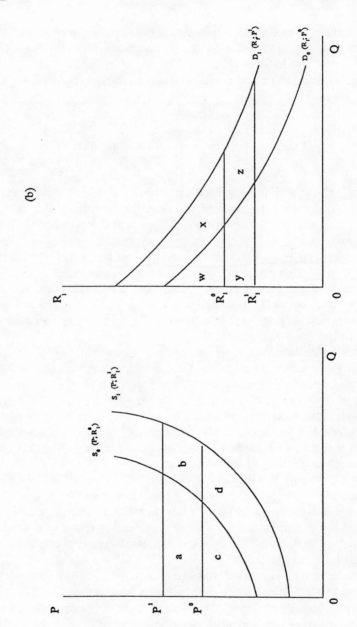

FIGURE 9.2 Output supply and input demand curves.

Hedonic Study of Land Rents Facilitates Welfare Analysis

A decomposition of rents to land can be obtained from a hedonic land model. Palmquist, as noted, derived such a model for a profit-maximizing industry. In practice, however, most empirical hedonic land model studies use real estate price as a proxy for rents. In the previous two sections I demonstrated the potential problems associated with using market price data to make assertions regarding impacts on an industry's welfare. The Palmquist model does not justify using market price in place of rents.

The spirit of the Palmquist model is that of a profit-maximizing industry facing exogenous input and output market prices. Each producer seeks to maximize variable profits, which is the difference between the total value of output and nonland inputs. Production is a function of input (exclusive of land) and output prices (W,P), a vector of characteristics of the real estate parcel (Z), and a vector of firm characteristics (α).[13]

The profit-maximization problem can be solved for output supply and nonland input demand functions, which can be substituted back into the variable profit function (π^v),

$$\pi^{v*}(P,W,Z,\alpha) \;=\; \sum_{i=1}^{n} P_i \tilde{q}_i\,(P,W,Z,\alpha) \;-\; \sum_{j=1}^{m-1} w_j \tilde{x}_i\,(P,W,Z,\alpha), \qquad (8)$$

where W is a $1 \times (m-1)$ nonland input price vector, and all other variables are as previously defined.

Each firm must decide on its reservation level of net profits (π^d). The difference between variable profits and reservation net profits is the firm's bid function,

$$\theta\,(P,W,Z,\alpha,\pi^d) \;=\; \pi^{v*} - \pi^d . \qquad (9)$$

This represents the maximum bid a firm will make for renting a parcel of land with characteristics Z, given its desired profit level.

A similar derivation for a seller's offer function is made, and an equilibrium rent schedule is defined by the locus of all market intersections of bid and offer functions. In equilibrium, the increase in a firm's bid for characteristic z_i is equal to the increase in the rent of land,

$$\theta_{z_i} \;=\; \frac{\partial R_1}{\partial z_i}, \qquad (10)$$

where R_1 is the rent to land.

The essence of the hedonic land model is that each parcel of land is a unique collection of characteristics. Each characteristic affects the productivity of the parcel within a specific industry. The interaction of land characteristics, factor and output prices, and owner characteristics determines the equilibrium rent schedule. If the estimated hedonic function is properly specified, the hedonic land model will decompose the market rent function, thereby providing a basis for conducting meaningful welfare analysis.

Under certain conditions, the hedonic price model can be used to obtain estimates of the derived demand functions for the characteristics of the land and the different factors of production, which lead to direct estimates of producer welfare. More often, however, the model is used to estimate implicit prices for each of the arguments of a hedonic function. The prices can usually be identified as upper or lower bound estimates of an underlying demand function. In such instances, meaningful welfare analysis is still obtained, but it is limited to rough estimates for impact analysis.[14]

Land Rent Data Can Provide Information
That Land Price Data May Disguise

To summarize the previous three sections,

- Real estate prices may represent the capitalized value of rents from several industries, as well as consumptive uses.
- An analysis of welfare impacts within a specified industry, or series of industries, can be conducted using industry's rent to land. Using data on real estate values can capture welfare impacts from unrelated industries, as well as the effects on the personal resource owner's utility level.
- Using a hedonic rent model for land facilitates the decomposition of land rents and, thus, provides a basis for the analyses of welfare impacts.

To understand the relevance of these three related points, consider an analysis of the welfare impact of two unrelated policy instruments—a pesticide use ban and tougher gun control laws. For the purpose of illustration, assume the real estate market has only two industries—cropland and sport hunting.

If a state government outlaws application of a widely used pesticide in crop production, some marginal cropland that would not be cost effective to farm without a pesticide application would be taken out of production. A plausible scenario regarding the effect in a state with tough pesticide-application laws is for the wildlife population to increase. This, in turn, may benefit the state's sport hunting industry. Assume rent in the sport hunting industry increases by an amount that is equal, but opposite, to the loss in cropland rent due to the pesticide ban.

Total rent to land, and hence the market price of land, would be unaffected by the pesticide ban. Yet, the total productive value of cropland will decline. This effect in the cropland market can only be discerned from data on market land rents.

Figure 9.3a depicts the pesticide example when assuming a fixed supply of land. Total welfare in the cropland industry, measured by the area beneath the demand for cropland (D_{f1}) between shut-down price $(Q = 0)$ and the market rental price for cropland, before (R^0_{f1}) and after (R^1_{f1}) the pesticide ban, changes by area $b + e - f$. Since total rent for land in all uses is unchanged, the welfare effect of this policy for landowners is zero.

Figure 9.3b depicts the gun control example, assuming a fixed supply of land and using the same market scenario as in the pesticide case. If a new law is enacted that makes it more difficult to own firearms, Figure 9.3b depicts a plausible market outcome. The new gun control law will cause the cost of sport hunting to increase. The demand for land for hunting purposes falls, which causes the total welfare to landowners to change by the area $m - p - q$. The gun control law has no effect on the cropland industry, so the cropland industry's rent is unchanged. Total welfare in the cropland industry is unchanged.

In both examples the market price of farmland would provide misleading results in an analysis of the cropland industry. In other instances, the market price can provide good estimates for the analysis of welfare impacts. However, even when it appears that the conditions are met for the proper use of market price data, one cannot always be certain that effects in other industries, and consumptive value effects, are not being included.

Most applied economic research is conducted by economists who specialize in specific industries. Such analysts make a career out of knowing what arguments belong inside the brackets of an implicit industry rent function $(R\{a, \dots ,n\})$. But the arguments that belong in an implicit market price function for real estate may span several industries and include arguments from personal utility functions. Thus, even if real estate price data are an attractive proxy for an industry's rents due to data availability, secondary rent data can still prove to be more valuable. The potential for an underspecified hedonic land price equation is greater than for an underspecified rent equation for an industry.

Conclusion

A parcel of land represents many things to many people. To a farmer, land represents an input in the farm operation that provides him the

116

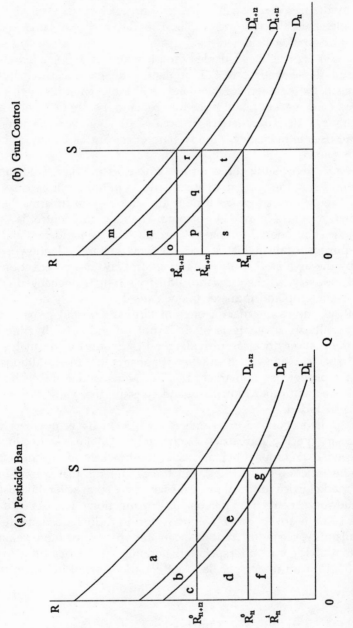

FIGURE 9.3 Welfare impacts of market intervention.

opportunity to secure rents. This same farmer may also consider the land to be a source of personal welfare that enables him to fulfill a desire to cultivate the land and provide food for many people. To many urban dwellers, that same parcel may represent an amenity to be enjoyed through weekend rides through rural farm country. Developers may see this farm as an ideal location for a new residential community, while an industrial firm may find it an ideal location to build a processing plant. Environmentalists may view a large segment of this farm as a wetland refuge for migratory birds.

These, and many other interests, compete for the use of land. Since land is a scarce resource, all of the competing interests contribute to the determination of current market price. Farmers compete with each other by bidding up the rental rates on rented land, and they compete with all potential owners in bidding up the ownership price. Both the urban dwellers and environmentalists contribute to the ownership price also. Policies such as tax abatement programs that reduce the tax burden to farmland owners who agree to keep their land in farming, and wetland protection legislation that rewards protection and penalizes destruction of wetlands, can affect market price.

This is far from an exhaustive discussion of the interests that contribute to determining the market price for land. But it brings to bear the complexities involved in constructing a hedonic model of the real estate market. In many instances a hedonic model of industry rents to land is a more realistic goal.

Notes

Patrick N. Canning is an agricultural economist, Economic Research Service, U.S. Department of Agriculture. The views expressed are the author's and do not necessarily represent policies or views of the U.S. Department of Agriculture. The author appreciates the valuable comments of Daniel Hellerstein, John Reilly, and Gene Wunderlich.

1. S. Rosen, "Hedonic Prices and Implicit Markets: Product Differentiation in Pure Competition," *Journal of Political Economy* 82, no. 1 (1974):35-55.

2. K. Gertel and F. Llacuna, "What Low Rent-to-Value Ratios on Cash Rented Farmland Tell Us," in *Agricultural Land Values and Markets: Situation and Outlook Report*, Economic Research Service AR-18 (Washington, D.C.: U.S. Department of Agriculture, 1990):39-43; C.A. Pope, "Agricultural Productive and Consumptive Use Components of Rural Land Values in Texas," *American Journal of Agricultural Economics* 67, no. 1 (1985):81-86.

3. A. Marshall, *Principles of Economics* (London: Macmillan, 1930).

4. Rosen, "Hedonic Prices and Implicit Markets."

5. Pope, "Agricultural Productive and Consumptive Use Components."

6. R.B. Palmquist, "Land as a Differentiated Factor of Production: A Hedonic Model and Its Implications for Welfare Measurement," *Land Economics* 65, no. 1 (1989):23-28.

7. See J.N. Brown and H.S. Rosen, "On the Estimation of Structural Hedonic Price Models," *Econometrica* 50, no.3 (1982):765-768; D. Epple, "Hedonic Prices and Implicit Markets: Estimating Demand and Supply Functions for Differentiated Products," *Journal of Political Economy* 96, no.1 (1987):59-80; F. Xu, "An Econometric Study of Contributions of Parcel Characteristics to Agricultural Land Values in Washington: A Hedonic Approach," Ph.D. dissertation, Washington State University, Pullman, 1990, as well as other papers cited in these endnotes.

8. R.B. Palmquist and L.E. Danielson, "A Hedonic Study of the Effects of Erosion Control and Drainage on Farmland Values," *American Journal of Agricultural Economics* 71, no. 1 (1989):55-62.

9. Pope, "Agricultural Productive and Consumptive Use Components."

10. Ibid., 81.

11. See R.E. Just, D.L. Hueth and A. Schmitz, *Applied Welfare Economics and Public Policy* (New York: Prentice-Hall, 1982):Ch. 4.

12. For a vigorous proof of this result, see Appendix A in Just et al., *Applied Welfare Economics and Public Policy*.

13. See Rosen, "Hedonic Prices and Implicit Markets," for a justification of including the characteristics of the firm vector.

14. Palmquist, "Land As a Differentiated Factor of Production," provides a discussion of the conditions that dictate how to interpret the output of a hedonic land model.

10

Rising Inequality and Falling Property Tax Rates

Mason Gaffney

It is a common belief that property tax relief is "good for farmers." It certainly raises the private share of economic rent. That in turn raises the investment grade of farmland and encourages its purchase as a store of value, a place to park slack money. This may be at odds, however, with using it as a vehicle for enterprise and an outlet for workmanship. Lower farm property taxes are associated with lower ratios of capital to land, and labor to land, both over time and among states. They are also associated with larger mean farm size and less equal distribution of farm sizes.

In the sections that follow, I first document the rise of inequality in the distribution of farmland that followed a sharp drop in farm property tax rates after 1930. Then I show, by cross-sectional analysis, a positive relationship between higher property tax rates and more intensive use of farmland, which in turn is associated with more equal distribution of farmland. Conversely, I find property tax relief associated with underuse and underimprovement of land.

A priori, a tax on buildings works to suppress building and to penalize smaller farmers, whose building to land ratio is higher than that of bigger farmers. The findings seem to show, therefore, a stronger countereffect, proincentive and prosubdivision, of the other part of the property tax, the part based on land value.

Property Tax Relief and the March of Concentration

The national average of farm property tax rates peaked in 1930 at 1.32 percent. It fell to 0.77 percent in 1945, and stabilized at about that level—

it was 0.85 percent in 1987.[1] Sales and income taxes, which bear heavier on urban activities, replaced the missing property taxes as sources of revenue.

Vanishing Farmers and Unaffordable Farms

Mean acres per farm had remained fairly constant for 65 years (1870-1935), at about 155 acres, despite two major industrial merger movements. After 1935 the mean took off and had tripled to 462 acres by 1987. As the number of farms was falling, national population was on the rise. In 1900 there was one farm per 11 Americans; in 1987 only one per 113. Farms became unaffordable. Real wage rates have not risen as fast as real land prices since 1955, and not at all since about 1975,[2] which has raised the labor-price of land. Coupling this with rising acres per farm, the labor-price of a farm roughly tripled, from about 6 years' wages (before payroll deductions) in 1954 to about 17 years' wages in 1987.[3]

The Vanishing Middle Class

In 1900 the Census Bureau began publishing farm data ranked by acres per farm. Using those data, the Gini ratio (GR)[4] was .58 in 1900, and it rose only slowly, to .63 in 1930. After that it rose faster, to .70 by 1950, plateaued there for 15 years, then rose again to .76 by 1987.[5] (By comparison, GRs for personal income are much lower, about .40, and are much more stable over decades.) The accelerated rise since 1930 coincided with the rise of mean acres per farm, and both followed the fall of property tax rates.

As a measure, GR deals only with concentration among existing farms. Industrial economists fault it for not reflecting the loss of farms. Acknowledging the critics, GR can be modified to combine both effects: Simply add the ghosts of 4.5 million farms that died between 1935 and 1988 to the lowest bracket, as farms with zero acres in 1988. This raises GR for 1988 from .76 to .92, a radical rise of inequality since 1930 (.63). Calculating the GR this way gives one a better sense of how concentration shot up after 1930-1935. In the Great Depression (1930-1941), millions of small farms provided a refuge for the jobless and homeless. Today, that refuge is closed, with explosive social consequences in urban slums.

The Rise of Land Quality in Vast Farms

The concentration of the *value* of farm real estate is growing faster than that of farm *acres*. The value of land and buildings ($L+B) per acre in the top bracket (farms of 1,000 acres and over) has risen relative to that of all farms. For easy recall and reference, I label this ratio *Gamma*. Gamma is the top bracket's acre value divided by the mean acre value. In 1910, Gamma for $L+B was .35. By 1930 it had dropped to .29, after 20 years of high farm property tax rates.[6] By 1987, after 57 years of low property tax rates, it had doubled to .61.[7]

Accordingly, the share of $L+B in farms of 1,000 acres and over rose faster than the share of acreage from 1930-1987. The share of acreage rose from .28 to .62, a rise of 123 percent. The share of $L+B rose from .08 to .38, a rise of 375 percent.

The land share of real estate value (LSREV) in the top bracket (1,000 acres and over) has probably risen faster than overall. LSREV is an acronym for $L/($L+B), that is, the value of land as a fraction of the value of land and buildings together. Gamma for $L alone always stood higher than that for $L+B during the years 1900-1940, when the census published separate data on $L and $B for all farms. There is no comparable later data published to test directly whether Gamma for $L has risen even higher over Gamma for $L+B (for 1988, the Agricultural Economics and Land Ownership Survey, AELOS, separates $L and $B only for owner-occupied farms, not for all farms). There is indirect evidence, however, that LSREV in the top bracket may have risen faster than overall.

One indicator is the share of harvested cropland, by size of farm. This share in the top bracket has risen relative to the share for all farms. This ratio in 1925 was 8.5 percent/37.3 percent, or .23. It rose to .37 in 1950 and to .69 by 1987.[8]

Another confirming indicator is the rising concentration of irrigated land. When irrigation was young in Anglo-America (1890-1914), it was the recourse of small farmers struggling for land against bonanza wheat farmers and ranchers (the familiar grist of horse operas). Then, vast spreads were subdivided to create small irrigated farms. There was drastic subdivision and intensification (1900-1930).[9] Land in farms of 1,000 acres and over actually dropped (nationally) by 15 percent from 1900 to 1910, the only drop on record. Now, however, 34 percent of all irrigated land is in the top bracket, farms of 2,000 acres and over.[10] Control of irrigated land means control over water. Control of water gives control over arid lands roundabout. Ownership and control based on water have become highly concentrated. For farms with irrigated land, GR = .82,[11] substantially higher than the GR of .76 for all farms.

An independent study by Villarejo illustrates the trend from 1940 to 1982 in a specific area intensively studied by Wilson and Clawson in 1940. The study area was the irrigable and irrigated land in Kern and Tulare counties, California. Replicating the study in 1982, Villarejo found that GR = .71 and that "land ownership has become more concentrated as more land has been placed in irrigated farms."[12]

A last confirming indicator is concentration by sales. Data for this are available from 1950. From 1950-1987, GR for farms ranked by sales rose faster from 1950-1987 (.67 to .80) than GR for farms ranked by acres (.70 to .76). Sales were less concentrated than acres; now they are more concentrated. That is consistent with the hypothesis that land quality in large holdings is rising.[13]

Rising Land Share and Rising Ratio of Price to Cash Flow

The LSREV almost certainly rose from 1940, when land prices were depressed, to 1987. By splicing disparate tables to get comparable data, I estimate that LSREV for all farms rose from .69 to about .80.[14] Higher LSREV means a higher price to cash flow (P/C) ratio. That is because cash flow (C) from buildings and other capital includes allowance for depreciation (D). Depreciation is part of cash flow, but not part of earnings; price is capitalized only from earnings (C-D). Thus, the price of capital is capitalized from less than its cash flow. The price of land, oppositely, is capitalized from more than its cash flow. It is from cash flow plus the current appreciation (C+A).[15] Land price also captures expectations of cash and service flows from various nonfarm elements, many of which are deferred and speculative.

High ratios of farm price to cash flow are another barrier to farm entry. Direct data on farmland P/C ratios are not available, but a rough surrogate (to show trend, not value) is the ratio of farm real estate values to gross farm revenues. This ratio was low (2.56) in 1945, when a gloomy market looked for another postwar farm depression and land buyers got lucky. It rose to 4.0 in 1954, and to 5.9 in 1982. Farmland prices dropped sharply in the mid-1980s, but still left the ratio at 4.35 in 1987, much higher than for 1945-1950.[16]

A high P/C ratio shows a higher share of $L in farm wealth. A common belief is that high capital costs of machinery and equipment ($M&E) are peculiar to modern farm technology and are the main barrier to farm entry. That belief doesn't wash, however.[17] Cyrus McCormick was mass marketing mechanical reapers before the Civil War. Today, $M&E is about 10 percent of all farm assets, much smaller than $L+B.[18] In addition, loans invested in $M&E are usually self-liquidating from the excess of cash flow over interest, but loans for buying land mean *negative* cash flow for several years. Meeting a negative cash flow requires pumping in still more outside capital, an added barrier to entry.

To sum up, rising acreages mean there are fewer farms overall. Rising labor prices per farm mean aspiring farmers who lack prior wealth can no longer buy in. Rising GRs mean acreage is less equally shared among a given number of farms. Rising Gamma factors mean the higher quality land is moving into bigger farms. The Gamma data are confirmed by rising shares of cropland and irrigated land in vast farms. Rising P/C ratios reflect a higher LSREV, and they mean it is harder for a newcomer to acquire any farm acres. The combination means the agricultural ladder has been pulled up. Entry is nearly impossible for farmers lacking outside finance; exit and latifundiazation proceed apace. These changes accompanied and followed a 40 percent drop in farm property tax rates.

The Lesser Improvement of Larger Farms

A result of rising concentration is the separation of land from capital. With some exaggeration, American *latifundia* are now lands without buildings, but buildings are clustered on smaller farms, many without enough land. This implies at least three points. First, building wealth is more equally distributed than land wealth. Second, the property tax would be more progressive if changed to a pure land tax, exempting buildings. Third, many *latifundia* are not being used to their potential, and capital on some small farms is undercomplemented with land. I support the case first using national data, and then by comparing states.

It is awkward that the 1987 Census of Agriculture defines "farm size," and ranks farms, only by acres rather than value. I used the acreage rankings above for intertemporal comparison because they are comparable with each other over time and are all that is available over time. Data on value per acre are available by acreage brackets, but a proper data set to test my thesis cross-sectionally would *rank* farms by land value ($L), rather than acres. This would reshuffle and rerank individual farms.[19] For example, in the brackets from 260 acres to 1,999 acres, there are now more farms worth $1 million and over than there are in the top bracket (2,000 acres and over).[20] Half the farms in the top bracket are worth less than $1 million each. If all farms were properly reranked by value, the degree of inequality and the effect of "size" on factor proportions would change. In what follows, I use available data to simulate what those changes might be. One available data set, although partial, *is* ranked by value, and it confirms my thesis with startling force.

National Data

Concentration of Irrigated Land. The yield per acre of most crops stays level or rises with harvested acres per farm. At the same time, sales per dollar of real estate fall somewhat.[21] The most likely reason is that the quality of harvested land rises with quantity. There is, to be sure, a trade-off between quality and quantity, but there is also a bond. Whoever can afford more can afford better. Which effect is stronger? The question must be resolved by data.

The 1987 Census of Agriculture does not provide overall land-value data (separate from $B), but it does provide one surrogate for land quality: land irrigated. Irrigated land is generally flatter, lower, and warmer; in addition, the water supply itself is an easement over more land (the watershed, whose acreage is not counted with acres per farm). Farms of 2,000 acres and over have 34 percent of all irrigated land, but only 24 percent of $L+B.[22] That indicates higher land quality coupled with lesser improvement.

The 1987 census ranks farms by "acres harvested," not in the aggregate, but crop by crop. For almost all crops, the share irrigated rises steeply with acres per farm.[23] Alfalfa is an example. Sixty-seven percent of acres in the top bracket are irrigated, compared with 23 percent for all farms producing alfalfa. The ratio of those percentages forms an index, *Zeta* (share of land irrigated on vast acreages, relative to all farms).[24] For example, for alfalfa Zeta = .67/.23 = 2.9. (The Zetas for other crops are given in the endnote.[25]) This finding is very strong because it runs against the ranking bias. These farms are ranked by all acres harvested; this bias alone would make Zeta < 1 if the scatter of points was perfectly symmetrical about both axes. If the census ranked these same data by acres irrigated, instead of acres harvested, the Zetas would be much higher.

Comparing different crops, high values of GR go with crops that are mostly irrigated. For example, 85 percent of tomato acres and 14 percent of silage corn are irrigated. For tomatoes, GR = .91; for silage corn, GR = .52.[26]

It is easy to presume that in a state of extremes, like California, high GRs result simply from consolidating high-priced irrigated land with vast arid ranches, "the cattle on a thousand hills." Several of the older Wright Act[27] irrigation districts are strikingly egalitarian, it is true, with small mean farm sizes.[28] These older districts have become, however, exceptional. An intensive study of the huge Westlands Water District, 100 percent irrigated with cheap, subsidized federal water, shows GR = .77.[29] Villarejo consolidated data from 10 districts receiving among them 48 percent of all Central Valley Project water, for GR = .69.[30] These high GR values come from 100 percent irrigated lands.[31] These and other data[32] on irrigated acres support the thesis that quantity and quality of cropland are mates more than alternatives. The vaster farms also get more water per acre.

Land Concentration for Farms Ranked by Sales. The Census of Agriculture now also ranks farms by sales per farm. This yields higher GR values: .80 in 1987, compared with .76 by acres. Sales are a measure of dollar values. This suggests, without proving, that GR-by-$L > GR-by-acres.

In 1950, the top class (at that time, farms with sales > $25,000 per year) comprised 1.9 percent of all farms, 26 percent of the sales, and 41 percent of the irrigated land.[33] Again, this finding is very strong because it runs against the ranking bias, which is to put a higher share of sales in the top bracket.

I used 1950 above because the current census does not consolidate this information. It does, however, show it on a crop-by-crop basis.[34] For example, for cash-grain corn, in the top group (highest sales per farm), 37 percent of the acres are irrigated versus 14 percent for all groups. It goes on like that for all crops (except rice, all of which is irrigated). This finding is unaffected by ranking bias, pro or con.[35]

Lack of Buildings on Latifundia. The 1940 Census of Agriculture, as noted, was the last to separate $L from $B, overall. In 1940 the building share of real estate ($B/[$L+B], or BSREV) was .69 in the lowest acreage bracket, .31 for all farms, and .12 for farms of 1,000 acres and over.[36]

AELOS (1988) gives no comparable comprehensive data, but it does give two series that test the point and have the advantage of disaggregation. One is for "owner-operators" and one for "landlords with debt." For the owner-operators, ranked by acres per farm, BSREV was .63 for farms under 10 acres; .29 for all farms; and .12 for farms of 2,000 acres and over.[37] Building values are much more equally distributed among these farms than land values.

For "landlords with debt,"[38] the BSREVs are lower overall (.11) than for owner-operators (.29), but the immediate interest here is how the shares fall with size of holding. Ranking by acres per farm, BSREV is .11 overall, and falls gently to .07 in the top bracket. These data, however, are also ranked by $L+B. Ranking thus, BSREV is still .11 overall, but— here is the shocker—BSREV falls to an astonishingly low .01 in the top bracket.[39]

A share of .01 is breathtaking in any such scatter, but more so here because the ranking variable includes $B. When a scatter of points is loose, the choice of ranking variable (i.e., the definition of "size") biases the findings to show the share of the ranking variable rising with size. However, the current data are ranked by $L+B, which is neutral between $L and $B. Thus, BSREV = .01 in the top bracket is free of ranking bias and fully significant without adjustment. This is an uncommonly strong relationship. *The biggest landlord holdings, in dollar value, are 99 percent pure land.*

Lack of Family Labor on Latifundia. Lack of buildings reveals lack of family labor, because so many farm buildings are operator dwellings, whose economic function is to house operator labor near the job site. The Census of Agriculture no longer publishes data on family labor.[40] As a surrogate, one can assume that operator labor inputs are roughly in proportion to operator housing, which the census reports separately. In 1988 operator dwellings were 48 percent of farm real estate assets in the smallest acreage bracket, 16.4 percent for all farms, and falling steadily, 4.4 percent on farms 2,000 acres and over.[41] For family-held corporate farms (of all sizes), the share is 6.3 percent; for other corporate farms, 3.2 percent. These data support the common impression that smaller and unincorporated farms are better supplied with operator family labor.[42]

In 1950 the census reported more detail than it does now on inputs used by farms ranked by sales. Class I farms (the largest) had 22 percent of the land in farms and 7 percent of the farm labor (at that time, family labor was included). Class VI farms (the smallest) had 5 percent of the land in farms and 11 percent of the farm labor.[43] This contrast would be much greater if farms were ranked by acres or $L+B because sales reflect the presence of labor inputs, as well as feeder livestock and purchased feed. These contrasts of people to land ratios were brought out in many studies in that more socially conscious era.[44]

To sum up what national data show, there is evidence that land quality rises with acreage harvested, using irrigated acres as a surrogate for quality, and that BSREV falls. Ranking farms by sales, the same rule holds. For all owner-operated farms, ranked by acres, BSREV falls steeply with size. For landlords with debt, ranked by $L+B, BSREV falls even more steeply with size, nearly to zero. The last point distills my thesis to its essence in one datum.

Comparisons Among States

AELOS provides a third set of separate land and building values. These are aggregates by state.[45] Grouping data by areal units, as Reid did in her study of housing and income, is one way to overcome regression fallacy.[46] The idea is to group data on some basis other than the variables being studied and then to compare those variables among the groups. States serve the purpose, just as neighborhoods served Reid in her housing studies.

Lesser Improvement of Land in States with Larger Farms. One method of testing how $B grows with $L is to compare their dispersions. The result is unbiased because the two variables are treated the same—neither ranking is given priority over the other. The egg-shaped envelope of scatter points is standing on its end if the y variable is more dispersed, and leaning on its side if the x variable is more dispersed. Any standard measure of dispersion is acceptable.[47] I use two. One is the mean deviation, dividing each by its respective mean to standardize it for comparison with others. I also calculated coefficients of variation (CV), which are standard deviations divided by the respective means.

My results support the hypothesis that farmland values are much more concentrated than farm building values. The CVs are .44 for land value, and .24 for building value. (See Table 10.1 for details.)

TABLE 10.1 Dispersion of Farm Sizes, U.S. and States, by Type

Group	LSREV	$L/A	A/Fm	L/Fm ($k)	B/Fm ($k)	L+B/FM ($k)
50 states	.71	537	299	161	64.7	225
Mean deviation (MD)	—	—	177	70.9	15.7	—
MD/mean	—	—	.59	.44	.24	—
Std. deviation	—	—	319	102	23.2	—
CV	—	—	1.07	.63	.36	—
34 Rural-urban states	.70	708	213	151	64.4	215
Mean deviation (MD)	—	—	67.5	66.9	13.9	—
MD/mean	—	—	.32	.44	.22	—
Std. deviation	—	—	97.1	101	20.8	—
CV	—	—	.46	.67	.32	—
7 small urban states	.70	3186	106	337	143	480
Mean deviation (MD)	—	—	13.5	128	18.5	—
MD/mean	—	—	.127	.38	.129	—
Std. deviation	—	—	15.1	140	22.7	—
CV	—	—	.143	.415	.159	—
9 arid ranching states	.78	201	879	201	56.3	258
Mean deviation (MD)	—	—	423	57.0	13.2	—
MD/mean	—	—	.48	.283	.234	—
Std. deviation	—	—	567	64.4	16.6	—
CV	—	—	.645	.320	.295	—

Notes: The nine arid ranching states are North Dakota, South Dakota, Nebraska, Kansas, Montana, Wyoming, Nevada, Colorado, and New Mexico. (Arizona is surprisingly missing, because of its high $L/acre.)

The seven small urban states are Massachusetts, Rhode Island, Connecticut, New Jersey, Delaware, Maryland, and New Hampshire. (New Hampshire is surprisingly included, because of its small area and high $L/acre. Ideally, northern New Hampshire would be treated separately as rural, but then many other states should be split as well.)

The 34 "regular" states are all the others.

LSREV = land share of real estate value, i.e., $L/($L+B); $L/A = land value per acre; A/Fm = acres per farm; L/Fm = land value per farm; B/Fm = buildings value per farm; L+B/Fm = land+buildings value per farm.

My overall findings are displayed in Figure 10.1, a scatter plotting of LSREV against $L per farm, by states. Land value per farm ranges from $71,000 (West Virginia) to $630,000 (Arizona). Arizona and other big-farm states have higher LSREVs than West Virginia and other small-farm states. Overall, the scatter displays a strong positive relationship between $L per farm and LSREV, state to state.[48] This supports the basic finding, which is, otherwise put, that land is much more concentrated than buildings among farms.[49]

Urban Influence. Data by states also provide new insights into inter-state and interregional differences. I divide states into three groups: 9 small urban states, 7 arid ranching states, and 34 rural and rural-urban states (see Table 10.1). For the small urban states, the CV values for $L and $B are .42 and .16; for the arid ranching states, .32 and .29; and for the 34 rural states, .67 and .32.[50] Thus, $L is more concentrated than $B among the states within each of the three groups, but the difference is greatest among the small urban states, where farm values are most af-fected by urban speculation. This suggests that the effect of urban land speculation is toward higher concentration of landholdings, a point made earlier by Gray, and by Goldenweiser and Truesdell,[51] and obser-vable today around growing cities.[52]

Association of Property Taxation and Land Improvement. The spe-cific contrast of two states, Wisconsin and Florida, illustrates and ex-emplifies my general findings. In Table 10.2, I rank the 50 states by LSREV. The complement of LSREV is BSREV. Wisconsin has the highest BSREV, .47; Florida has the lowest, .15. Yet, Wisconsin's farm property tax rate (PTR) exceeds Florida's 4 to 1. Wisconsin, the high-tax state, leads Florida 3 to 1 in farm output per dollar of farmland value, 5 to 1 in farm buildings per dollar of farmland value, and (surprisingly) 7 to 3 in machinery/livestock. Florida, the low-tax state, leads Wisconsin in GR (2 to 1), in $L per farm (5.5 to 1), in acres per farm (3 to 2), in $L per acre (4 to 1), and in real estate/all assets (11 to 8) (Table 10.2).[53]

Florida and Wisconsin are not exceptions or outliers, but bellwethers. Extending the data to eight states below Florida, and eight above Wisconsin, the differences persist and accumulate consistently. The "Florida 9" are Florida, Arizona, New Mexico, Hawaii, Montana, North Dakota, Wyoming, California, and Texas. The "Wisconsin 9" are Wisconsin, Delaware, Maine, Pennsylvania, New York, New Hampshire, North Carolina, Oklahoma, and Ohio. There are two con-trasting Gestalts along the lines shown.

The Wisconsin 9 have higher PTRs overall than the Florida 9. To the extent that the PTR is a cause of the effects with which it is associated, its effect is not so much to abort farm capital, as expected. It is associ-ated with high BSREV. High PTR is also associated with small farms

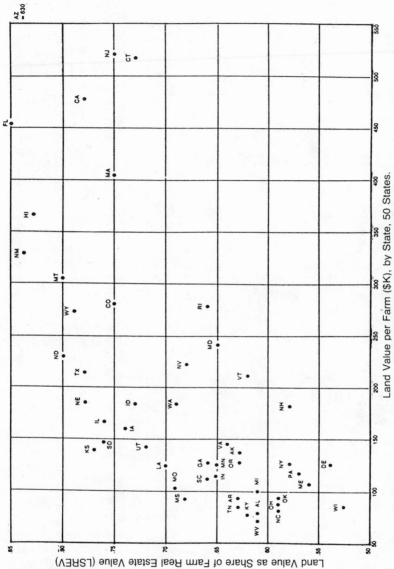

Land Value per Farm ($K), by State, 50 States.

FIGURE 10.1 LSREV plotted against $L per farm, by state, 1988. *Source:* Calculated from Bureau of the Census, *1987 Census of Agriculture,* Vol. 3, *Related Surveys,* Pt. 2, *Agricultural Economics and Land Ownership Survey* (Washington, D.C., 1990):Table 71.

TABLE 10.2. States Ranked by LSREV, Top and Bottom Nine

State	LSREV	L/Fm	L/A	GR	PTR	L+B/AFA	M&E/LS	A/Fm	L/AFA	Leased Share	Sales/L
FL	.85	452	1686	.847	.54	.88	.75	306	.75	.26	.23
AZ	.84	630	542	.870	.44	.86	.55	4752	.72	.77	.31
NM	.84	329	137	.782	.37	.84	.52	3230	.71	.48	.32
HI	.83	366	1726	.962	.35	.85	4.57	353	.71	.51	.25
MT	.80	304	180	.617	.85	.79	1.59	2451	.63	.32	.18
ND	.80	229	279	.467	.96	.73	4.02	818	.58	.51	.23
WY	.78	274	118	.682	.81	.77	.70	2314	.60	.42	.24
CA	.78	476	2318	.875	.55	.86	1.11	368	.67	.58	.31
TX	.78	215	570	.782	.56	.84	1.19	376	.66	.51	.22
OH	.59	91	702	.556	.95	.78	2.56	130	.46	.42	.33
OK	.59	92	361	.649	.60	.79	.97	255	.47	.46	.43
NC	.59	89	943	.621	.47	.81	2.94	95	.48	.49	.59
NH	.58	183	1370	.547	.97	.86	1.85	134	.50	.14	.15
NY	.58	126	704	.506	1.58	.75	1.52	223	.43	.22	.40
PA	.57	118	945	.490	.80	.76	1.41	153	.43	.33	.40
ME	.56	106	520	.528	1.17	.74	2.27	214	.41	.15	.70
DE	.54	126	1299	.679*	.44	.82	3.75	205	.44	.57	.85
WI	.53	84	444	.436	2.13	.64	1.32	221	.34	.28	.72

* 1982 data used; 1987 data for Delaware not available.

Notes: LSREV = land share of real estate value, i.e., $L/($L+B$)$; L/Fm = land value per farm; L/A = land value per acre; GR = Gini ratio, intrastate, by acres; PTR = property tax rate on real estate, de facto; $L+B/AFA$ = land+buildings as share of all farm assets; M&E/LS = machinery and equipment divided by livestock, dollar values; A/Fm = acres per farm; L/AFA = land value as share of all farm assets; leased share = fraction of acres in state under lease; and sales/L = sales (of farm output) per dollar of land value (est.).

Sources: Data are from Bureau of the Census, *1987 Census of Agriculture*, Vol. 3, Pt. 2, as follows: separate land and building values, p. 229, Table 70; other asset values, p. 61, Table 28; Gini ratios calculated from data in Table 5, (p. 179); tax rates, p. 181, Table 51; leased land, p. 5, Table 2; sales, p. 20, Table 8; $L+B, p. 61, Table 28. $L+B was converted to $L using the LSREV factor in Column 1. This is an estimate because the LSREV factor applies to owner-occupied farms, but the sales and $L+B data are for all farms. This approximation is necessary because fully coordinated published data are lacking.

(low \$L per farm, low \$L per acre), low GR values, high ratios of M&E to livestock and to real estate, low shares of leased land,[54] and fuller land usage, as measured by sales per \$L.

The inverse relationship between PTR and GR is particularly consistent and noteworthy. In this respect North Dakota and Delaware, otherwise nonconforming members of their respective groups, fall into line. Delaware has a low PTR and a high GR; North Dakota, the opposite. The egalitarian effects of a high PTR seem stronger than its negative incentive effects, even though buildings are part of the tax base. These egalitarian effects would be stronger if the tax base was limited to naked land value, because LSREV rises steeply with size of farm. Untaxing buildings would also eliminate negative incentive effects.

Conclusion

One may at least firmly conclude that large farm units are less improved and less peopled than small and medium-sized farms. There are two possible interpretations. One is that big farms are more efficient, getting more from less, but that is refuted by their getting less output per \$L. The other is that Veblen was right, many of them are oversized stores of value, held first to park slack money and only secondarily to produce food and fiber and complement the owner's workmanship.[55] The Florida 9 may represent a home grown rural "third world" of large, underutilized landholdings that preempt the best land and force median farmers onto small farms on low-grade land.

The issue cannot be settled in a few words, but the implications for tax policy are the same either way. If large units are more efficient, they can bear heavier taxes. If they are less efficient, heavier PTRs will induce them to release surplus land for others, which will tend at the margins to equalize factor proportions, moving more states from the Florida toward the Wisconsin model.

Notes

Mason Gaffney is professor, Department of Economics, University of California-Riverside.

1. The rates for 1930 and 1945 are from U.S. Department of Agriculture, *The Economic Almanac* (New York, 1960):33. The 1988 rate is from Bureau of the Census, *1987 Census of Agriculture*, Vol. 3, *Related Surveys*, Pt. 2, *Agricultural Economics and Land Ownership Survey* (Washington, D.C., 1990):179, Table 50. Earlier information is fuzzy, but before 1930 there were no state sales taxes and few state income taxes. In 1920, half of all *state* government revenues were from property taxes, as well as 90 percent of local revenues (particularly counties and school districts). The levies of special improvement districts, e.g., for irrigation

and drainage, are not legally "taxes," but "benefit assessments," and were in addition to the numbers given.

2. In constant dollars, average hourly earnings of nonsupervisory production labor in U.S. manufacturing peaked in 1975 and had dropped about 7 percent by 1988. Bureau of Labor Statistics, *Handbook of Labor Statistics*, Bulletin 2340 (Washington, D.C., 1991):312, Table 80.

3. Average hourly earnings (before tax) of nonsupervisory production workers were $1.71 in 1955 and $8.57 in 1985. The value of land and buildings per farm was $20,400 in 1954 and $289,000 in 1987. Using 2,000 as the number of working hours per year yields the labor-cost of a farm in yearly wages. I have understated both the rise and the years by using "earnings" instead of disposable pay after payroll taxes, which have risen sharply. Also, I did not allow for layoffs, sickness, injury, unemployment, etc.

4. The GR is a measure of unequal distribution. It is a pure index that sums and standardizes large amounts of disparate data in one number. A rise in GR means the big got bigger and/or the small got smaller. It ranges from .00 (complete equality) to 1.00 (complete inequality). Its essence is explained in many basic texts on industrial organization. See, e.g., D. Needham, *The Economics of Industrial Structure and Performance* (New York: St. Martin's Press, 1978):424.

5. Calculated from the Census of Agriculture for various years. The full set of GRs is: 1900 = .58; 1910 = .57; 1920 = .60; 1925 = .62; 1930 = .63; 1935 = .65; 1940 = .67; 1945 = .70; 1950 = .70; 1959 = .71; 1969 = .71; 1982 = .75; 1987 = .76.

6. Calculated from Bureau of the Census, *1940 Census of Agriculture* (Washington, D.C., 1941), Vol. 3:78-79, 82; and *1950 Census of Agriculture* (Washington, D.C., 1951), Vol. 2:776.

7. Calculated from Bureau of the Census, *1987 Census of Agriculture*, 93, Table 51; *1940 Census of Agriculture*, Vol. 3:78-79, 82; and *1950 Census of Agriculture*, Vol. 2:776. In 1940 and 1950 the top bracket was 1,000 acres and over; in 1987 it was 2,000 acres and over. I adjusted for this by combining the top two brackets in 1987.

8. Data for 1925-1950 are from Bureau of the Census, *1950 Census of Agriculture*, Vol. 2:780-782; and for 1987, the *1987 Census of Agriculture*, 90-91, Table 51. To maintain comparability it was necessary to consolidate the top two brackets in 1987.

9. For example, the number of farms in Stanislaus County, California, quintupled from 1900 to 1920. Subdivision for more intensive culture by small farmers was the dominating trend there then. Heavy land taxes were levied there (by irrigation districts) to finance public irrigation works. See B.F. Rhodes, "The Thirsty Land," Ph.D. dissertation, University of California, Berkeley, 1943; available from the university's Main Library and on microfilm, HD1740, M6R4. See also A. Henley, 1969, "Land-value Taxation by California Irrigation Districts," in A. Becker, ed., *Land and Building Taxes* (Madison: University of Wisconsin Press, 1969).

10. From Bureau of the Census, *1987 Census of Agriculture*, 16, Table 8, and 84, Table 51. The movement in California is separately studied by R. Fellmeth, *Politics of Land* (New York: Grossman Publishers, 1973); M. Goodall, "Property and Water Institutions in California," draft, Claremont Graduate School,

1991:1-18; P. Roberts, "Power and Land in California," a summary of the Nader report, chaired by R. Fellmeth, 1971 (available from California State Library, Sacramento, and various University of California campus libraries); P.S. Taylor, *Essays on Land, Water and the Law in California* (New York: Arno Press, 1979); D. Villarejo and J. Redmond, *Missed Opportunities—Squandered Resources* (Davis: California Institute for Rural Studies, 1988). Re: concentrated control of water in Hawaii, see P. Philipp, *The Diversified Agriculture of Hawaii* (Honolulu: University of Hawaii Press, 1953):18-20.

11. Calculated from Bureau of the Census, *1987 Census of Agriculture*, 16, Table 8. Because of the peculiar arrangement of data, this figure needs cautious interpretation. For other confirmation, however, see below.

12. D. Villarejo, *How Much is Enough?* (Davis: California Institute for Rural Studies, 1986):101, 108.

13. Data on sales for 1930 are not available, but going back to 1900, GR by sales was .50, and GR by acres was .58.

14. In 1940, the last year in which the Census of Agriculture separated $L and $B, LSREV was .69 overall. In AELOS (1988) LSREV is reported for owner-operators (.71), and for "landlords with debt" (.89), but not for overall LSREV. From that, I "ballpark" LSREV at .80 for 1988.

15. The standard capitalization formula (omitting the property tax rate) is $P = CF/[i\text{-}g]$, where P is land price, CF is current cash flow, i is interest rate, and g is annual growth rate of CF. Rearranging terms, $P = [CF+Pg]/i$. Pg is the current annual increment to land price. The formula is simplified, but in the market, brokers have been capitalizing and selling Pg for ages using this basic theme and variations.

16. From Bureau of the Census, *1987 Census of Agriculture*, 7, Table 1, for 1954-1987 data; *1950 Census of Agriculture*, Vol. 2, Pt. 10:775-76 and Vol. 2, Pt. 9:753, Table 1, for 1945. The data for earlier years require some piecing out, but are roughly as follows: 1900 = 4.55; 1910 = 5.56; 1920 = 3.85; 1930 = 4.17; 1940 = 4.17. Within those spare numbers lie the stories, follies, hopes, heartbreaks, delusions, labors, savings, and lives of millions of Americans.

17. Historians would not expect it to: *latifundia perdidere Italiam* two millenniums before modern technology. Veblen, supposedly a technocrat, did not buy the farm technology story either. A farm boy and historian, he saw farm machinery conforming to the Procrustean bed of speculative landholdings, rather than the other way around. T. Veblen, "The Independent Farmer," in T. Veblen, *Absentee Ownership* (New York: B.W. Huebsch, 1923):129-142. In 1916, after many giant farms had been divided, Fordson came out with a new, smaller tractor.

18. Bureau of the Census, *1987 Census of Agriculture*, Vol. 3, Pt. 2:58, Table 27.

19. Failure to observe this point is "regression fallacy." See A.E. Waugh, *Elements of Statistical Method* (New York: McGraw-Hill, 1943):387-389.

20. I.e., 56,355 farms versus 35,484 farms over 2,000 acres; Bureau of the Census, *1987 Census of Agriculture*, 93, Table 51.

21. Ibid., 36, Table 44, and 84, Table 51. This means sales per dollar of land fall with size of farm since LSREV rises with size of farm.

22. Ibid., 16, Table 8, and 84, Table 51.

23. Ibid., 36, Table 44. G. Wunderlich has made the same point in a brilliant (but, ruefully, unpublished) note, "Wetter is Better," Economic Research Service, U.S. Department of Agriculture, 1985.

24. This is the counterpart of Gamma, used above.

25. Zeta values by crop, calculated from Bureau of the Census, *1987 Census of Agriculture*, 36, Table 44. Cash corn = 2.1; silage corn = 3.3; sorghum = 0.8; wheat = 1.0; barley = 1.3; oats = 3.2; cotton = 1.4; tobacco = 1.8; soybeans = 2.0; dry edible beans = 1.5; potatoes = 1.1; sugar beets = 1.5; peanuts = 1.8; alfalfa hay etc. = 3.3; other hay = 7.5; seeds = 1.4; vegetables = 1.3; tomatoes = 1.2; sweet corn = 1.6; berries = 0.9; orchards = 1.2; rice = 1.0.

26. Those who find GR index numbers too abstract will find more meaning in these raw data. For tomatoes, the top acreage bracket contains 1.1 percent of the farms, 45 percent of the harvested acres, and 52 percent of the irrigated acres in tomatoes. For silage corn, the top bracket contains 1.0 percent of the farms, 11.3 percent of the harvested acres, and 26 percent of the irrigated acres in silage corn.

27. Wright Act irrigation districts in California are special improvement districts whose governing boards are democratically elected (in most others, voting is by property value). Wright Act districts were the major vehicle of rapid settlement and subdivision, 1902-1930, before there were any outside subsidies. During this period, tax assessments on land in several districts were extremely high. These districts levy exclusively on land, exempting buildings.

28. Series of *Factual Reports* on specific irrigation districts (I.D.), U.S. Bureau of Reclamation, Sacramento office, ca. 1947. The reports give data for calculating the following GRs: Lindsay-Strathmore I.D., .31; Ivanhoe I.D., .46; Madera I.D., .45. These data are from 1947, before the districts began getting political rent from federally subsidized (Central Valley Project) water. They are less egalitarian today.

29. Calculated from data in D. Villarejo and J. Redmond, *Missed Opportunities—Squandered Resources*, 45.

30. Calculated from Villarejo, *How Much is Enough?* 28.

31. These lands are also subject to a "160-acre limitation" that nominally accompanies federal water. Enforcement is toothless, but sporadic attempts have some effect. Other vast districts, not in these data, get *state*-subsidized water free of any acreage limitation, and their GRs run higher.

32. A good general source for California is Department of Water Resources, Bulletin 23 (Sacramento, series).

33. Bureau of the Census, *1950 Census of Agriculture*, 1118, Table 1.

34. Bureau of the Census, *1987 Census of Agriculture*, 120, Table 52.

35. There is no ranking bias because neither acres nor irrigated acres is the ranking variable. Sales is the ranking variable, and gross acres are compared with irrigated acres.

36. Bureau of the Census, *1940 Census of Agriculture*, Vol. 3:80. An earlier insightful article on the subject is D. Weeks, "Factors Affecting Selling Prices of Land in the 11th Federal Farm Loan District," *Hilgardia* 3, no. 17 (1929):459-542.

37. Bureau of the Census, *1987 Census of Agriculture*, Vol. 3, Pt. 2:229, Table 70.

38. Ibid., 219, Table 64.

39. As $L+B per farm rises, $B per farm actually falls, which is astounding. Like most extreme findings, this one results from several concurrent factors: (1) these data are for ownership, not operation; (2) these are all rented lands; and (3) these data are ranked by value, not acres. Thus, they are ideal to test my thesis in its purest form. They show, technically, how very sensitive concentration data are to the choice of ranking variable. Above all, they show substantively that the largest holdings of farm wealth consist of land without buildings.

40. It is a wry commentary on modern attitudes that a farm family's own work is no longer counted as labor.

41. Bureau of the Census, *1987 Census of Agriculture*, Vol. 3, Pt. 2:229, Table 70.

42. This also implies that land in smaller farms is more productive in terms of supplying the service flow of shelter, plus the amenities of rural life, to families. To appreciate the weight of this factor, consider that the 1990 census shows 40 percent of American households pay more than 30 percent of their income for housing. As discussed above and again below, land in small farms is also more productive in purely cash terms (sales per $L). The two kinds of productivity are additive.

43. Bureau of the Census, *1950 Census of Agriculture*, Vol. 5, Pt. 6:51, cited in M. Gaffney, "Land Speculation," Ph.D. dissertation, University of California, Berkeley, 1956, 207.

44. See Gaffney, ibid., 203-209. Cited there are supporting data from studies by C. Goodrich, J.A. Baker, L. Nelson, C. Hammar and J.H. Muntzell, W.J. Cash, A.O. Craven, A. Raper, T.J. Woofter et al., J.V. Rogers, D.G. Miley, H. Weaver, W.W. Wilcox and W.E. Hendrix, S. Hamilton and D. Parker, D. Weeks, H.L. Roberts, L. Gay, Jr., E. Jacoby, and R. Hardie.

45. Bureau of the Census, *1987 Census of Agriculture*, Vol. 3, Pt. 2:230, Table 71. These data are just for owner-operators. More coverage would be better, and is stored, but this is all that is released in AELOS.

46. Margaret Reid, *Housing and Income* (Chicago: University of Chicago Press, 1962). Discussion is in R. Muth, "Permanent Income, Instrumental Variables, and the Income-Elasticity of Housing Demand," unpublished manuscript, ca. 1971, 1-40. Reid's studies were in conjunction with developing the "permanent income hypothesis," which was an extended exercise in offsetting regression fallacy. See also the discussion in M. Gaffney, 1971, "The Property Tax Is a Progressive Tax," *Proceedings*, National Tax Association, 64th Annual Conference, Kansas City (Columbus, Ohio: National Tax Association):421-424.

47. A. Wallis and H. Roberts, *Statistics* (Glencoe, Ill.: Free Press, 1956):263 and preceding.

48. Using $L to rank the states would reintroduce an element of ranking bias if grouped data were not being used. Lumping data causes extreme understatement of the relationship displayed, so no net exaggeration is perpetrated by Figure 10.1.

49. If that is not clear, think of it in extreme terms. It is as though buildings were all of equal value, from farm to farm, and farms differed only in their lands.

50. To sharpen these differentials, I have experimented with dividing states synthetically into regions. Thus, it is reasonable to impute the characteristics of Iowa to the northern third of Missouri and the southern third of Minnesota, leaving the residuals to the other two-thirds of each state. The result is a steep jump in the mean deviation of $L per farm, and a small rise in that of acres per farm and $B per farm. County-by-county data processed in this way would make the points even sharper. Several prior researchers have used county data to good effect.

51. L.C. Gray, "Land Speculation," In E.R.A. Seligman, ed., *Encyclopedia of the Social Sciences* (New York: Macmillan, 1931); E.A. Goldenweiser and L. Truesdell, *Farm Tenancy in the United States*, Bureau of the Census Monograph No. 4 (Washington, D.C.: Government Printing Office, 1924).

52. Florida, singled out below as a "bellwether" state, is not a "small" urban state, but ranks high in urban sprawl, which spreads urban price influence over farmland: 7.4 percent of Florida is "urban and built-up" compared with less in other states of comparable area and population—5.1 percent in Illinois, 5.2 percent in Michigan, and 5.8 percent in New York (U.S. Department of Commerce, *Statistical Abstract of the United States 1988* (Washington, D.C.: Government Printing Office, 1989):187.) Florida ranks low in per capita income, but second among states in domestic travel spending. The Florida land boom of 1926 is history, but the dispersed settlement pattern that fostered it still stamps Florida, and helps explain its farmland characteristics, namely, high LSREV and high GR.

P. Raup points out that recreation-retirement uses, along with tax shelters, even dominate ranchland values in some arid states. See his statement in Subcommittee on Monopoly, Senate Small Business Committee, *Role of Giant Corporations* (Washington, D.C.: Government Printing Office, 1972), Pt. 3:3969.

53. Florida also outranks Wisconsin in many measures of social and civic morbidity. Florida leads the nation in violent crimes per 100,000 population, and it leads Wisconsin 5 to 1 (Federal Bureau of Investigation's Uniform Crime Rates, *1991 World Almanac and Book of Facts* (New York: World Almanac):848). That is the more significant considering its age distribution, which is short on the violence-prone youthful cohorts. Florida ranks 44th in voter turnout, to 4th for Wisconsin, even though Florida ranks first in share of population over age 65, the high-voting ages. Florida also leads Wisconsin in infant mortality rate, 12.8 to 9.5; divorce rate, 6.7 to 3.6; and prisoners per 100,000 people, 243 to 102. In a cultural factor like patents issued per million people, Wisconsin leads Florida 185 to 113. (Data from U.S. Department of Commerce, *Statistical Abstract of the United States 1990* (Washington, D.C.: Government Printing Office, 1991):xii-xxi, 535; U.S. Department of Commerce, *State and Metropolitan Area Data Book,1986*, Bureau of the Census (Washington, D.C.: Government Printing Office, 1986); U.S. Department of Commerce, Commissioner of Patents and Trademarks, *Annual Report* (Washington, D.C., selected years); Congressional Quarterly, *America Votes*, Vol. 19 (Washington, D.C., 1991). These data are only partial and exploratory: Many factors, including urban factors, contribute to such contrasts. A

much-discussed treatment is W. Goldschmidt, *As You Sow* (Glencoe, Ill.: The Free Press, 1948). Also worth consulting is M.R. Greenberg, G.W. Carey, and F.J. Popper, "Violent Death, Violent States, and American Youth," *The Public Interest* no. 87, Spring (1987):38-48.

54. Florida, my bellwether state, is an exception to this rule.

55. T. Veblen, "The Independent Farmer," 129-142.

11

Use-Value Assessment of Farmland

J. Fred Giertz

The political battle over the preferential treatment of farmland for property tax purposes is effectively over in the United States. It has ceased to be a controversial political issue, and perhaps for that reason, it now draws relatively little attention from researchers. By the late 1980s, every state had some type of use-value assessment or other preferential treatment for farmland. In terms of the political battle, the proponents of use-value assessment were clearly the winners. In terms of the intellectual debate over the impact of such assessment practices, the opponents have prevailed in their view that use-value assessment practices seem to have little impact on land-use decisions. To the extent the laws have had an impact, it has been in the area of distribution, not allocation, by shifting property tax burdens away from farmland or by preserving existing de facto preferences for farmland historically granted by assessors.

In this paper, I provide a general overview of the reasons for passing such laws as well as a discussion of their impacts. My description and analysis are not specific to any one state, but rather draw on common themes from many states.[1] In the concluding section, I suggest that the wealth of data that now exists be used in evaluative research on the allocative and distributive impacts of use-value assessments.

The Objectives of Use-Value Assessment

The traditional belief was that the appropriate way to assess property, including farmland, was at its fair market value. On equity and efficiency grounds, a strong case can be made for this approach. The least distorting land tax would be a site-value tax that excludes the value of improvements on the land. In practice, however, most states use the value of land and improvements on the land as the basis for taxation.

The perception that market value often does not reflect the current income generated by farmland gave rise to proposals to depart from the goal of assessing property at its fair market value. It was suggested, on allocative and distributive grounds, that agricultural land should be treated differently for property taxation purposes than other types of property. The major allocative arguments for special treatment were that taxing agricultural land at its market value led to (1) the conversion of land to urban uses, thus reducing open space and creating urban sprawl, and (2) on a broader level, the overall reduction of cropland and thus a reduction in food production capacity for the future. Critics also argued on equity grounds that the property tax paid on farmland was not closely related to the benefits received from government services and was therefore unfair.

Use-value assessment of farmland now is the most widely used device for providing preferential treatment of farmland under the property tax. The market value of property is determined by its current and possible future uses. In some cases, capitalized current returns do not explain the current market price of property, especially when land is in transition. For example, the income generated by farmland on an urban fringe often does not support the market price of the land because its value is determined by potential urban uses. Current use value may also diverge from market value for agricultural land with no alternative non-agricultural uses because of expectations about future developments in agricultural markets. This would occur if it is generally believed that agricultural prices will rise substantially in the future.

In actuality, much of the push by farmers for preferential assessments was defensive in nature. Historically, the practices employed by local assessors in many states had already led to de facto preferential assessment of farmland. Traditionally, farmland was often assessed at a lower percentage of market value compared with other types of property. Such practices, however, were subject to court challenge and thus unreliable. In many cases, use-value assessment laws simply ratified practices that were already in place.

The Impact of Use-Value Assessment

When use-value assessment proposals were considered for adoption, most of the debate focused on land-use questions. In retrospect, however, the issues were more often distributive, not allocative, in nature. The proponents of use-value assessment asserted that there was some type of market failure in regard to land use that had to be corrected, but their real purpose was simply to lower their tax liability.

Allocative Impacts

Advocates of agricultural preferences suggested that private market forces were channeling agricultural land into inefficient uses, most often urban uses rather than open space. They viewed preferential treatment of farmland as a subsidy that would promote an activity (farming) generating positive externalities. Few studies, either at that time or later, have supported this proposition. In fact, the urban development process is now viewed as a relatively efficient process of converting land from rural to urban uses. No basis was found for asserting that the preferences granted through use-value assessments are related in a close way to the external benefits provided by open space. An even weaker case was found for preferences as a means of preserving cropland to increase food production. Even though the arguments were weak on theoretical grounds, they had an important appeal to many citizens and certainly aided in the adoption of use-value laws.

It is now generally believed that the allocative goals of use-value assessment were not particularly compelling. Further, even if the goals were deemed worthy, use-value assessment practices are not sufficiently powerful to have any major impact on land-use decisions. The differences in return between urban and rural uses on the urban fringe are generally so large that preferential assessments are likely to have little or no impact on long-term decisions about land use.[2]

In addition, the highest and best use (now and in the foreseeable future) for most agricultural land is in agriculture. The value of only a small fraction of land in most states is affected by urban development. Nevertheless, most use-value techniques value land whose only conceivable use is in agriculture at lower levels than market value. This suggests that the use-value formulas that are enacted are seriously flawed in that they do not correctly measure what they purport to assess. There seems to be little concern, however, about refining the measures.

Distributive Impacts

The most important impact of use-value assessment practices is in the area of redistribution, although this is seldom emphasized in public discussion. Use-value assessment (as practiced in most states) redistributes income to the owners of farmland from taxpayers in general at the local and state level. Alternatively, it maintains the existing redistributive pattern in situations in which de facto underassessment of farmland was already being practiced. The precise distributive impact of the preferential treatment of farmland depends on the percentage reduction below market value resulting from use-value assessment, the proportion of total assessed value in a district that is given preferential treatment, and the effective tax rate on property. In addition, the determinants of state aid to local governments, especially schools, must be considered. Not surprisingly, the impact of use-value assessment varies considerably from district to district.

Take as an example a district that is predominantly composed of farmland. Preferential assessments may have relatively little impact on landowners in the district. If most of the property in the district is assessed at lower levels because of use-value practices, there will be a major reduction in the district's property tax base. Either overall property tax collections will decline markedly (along with the level of locally provided public services) if tax rates are kept the same, or the rates must be increased substantially to maintain the same level of tax collections and public services. Somewhat surprisingly, owners of farmland in this setting receive relatively little in the way of benefits through preferential assessment.[3] A large number of farmland owners will experience only a small decrease in taxes, and a few owners of other types of property will experience a large increase in taxes. Many rural districts have experienced problems of maintaining local government services with the advent of use-value assessment. Such districts may receive additional state aid, however, if aid is inversely related to property wealth, as is often the case with state educational aid formulas.

At the other end of the spectrum, owners of farmland in predominantly nonagricultural settings may receive major benefits from use-value assessment. First, agricultural use-values are likely to be substantially less than market value in this type of environment. In addition, lower assessment levels will result in relatively small decreases in the total property tax base since only a small fraction is in agricultural land. Thus, such jurisdictions are not likely to experience a major cutback in public services or increases in property tax rates. In contrast to the previous case, a small number of "winners" will experience major tax reductions (the owners of farmland), and a larger number of nonagricultural landowners will experience a small loss.

This analysis suggests the arbitrary and capricious nature of this type of preferential assessment whereby benefits vary from district to district based on relative land-use patterns. Further, most of the benefits of a newly enacted use-value assessment law are realized by current owners in terms of higher farmland prices. Lower property taxes mean a higher stream of future net returns, which will likely be capitalized directly into land values. Future owners of farmland will be forced to pay higher prices because of the lower levels of taxation and thus will realize few if any benefits of preferences afforded farmers.

It is interesting to reflect on the political popularity of use-value assessment programs. As noted above, every state has enacted some type of preferential treatment for the property taxation of farmland, even states in which rural interests are relatively weak. Several reasons account for this. First, most of the discussion is couched in terms of lofty issues, such as the preservation of farmland and open space and the avoidance of urban sprawl. Little mention is usually made of the distributive issues of who pays more and who pays less. In addition, in many states the drive for preferential assessments was actually to preserve the status quo (against possible court challenges) whereby farmland was already assessed at less than market value. In such states, the new laws did not create major redistributions of tax burdens. Finally, the success of use-value assessment laws is an example of the well-known political phenomenon wherein a small, but well-organized political coalition with much to gain can dominate a much larger, but weakly organized group whose losses in terms of higher taxes are diffuse and relatively small on a per person basis.

The Burden of Property Taxation on Agricultural Land

In the past 20 years, the relative property tax burden on agricultural land in the United States has been dramatically reduced. This can be demonstrated with a variety of measures. In this section, I discuss several measures, especially in relation to changes in farmland assessment practices.

As shown below, the share of property taxes generated by farmland in the United States has declined dramatically since World War II—from over 10 percent in 1950 to about 3 percent currently:[4]

Percentage of Total Property Tax Payments from Agricultural Land

1950	1955	1960	1965	1970	1975	1980	1985	1989
10.2	8.7	7.6	6.8	6.4	5.6	5.0	3.8	3.2

The decline has been due in large part to the rapid increase in the non-agricultural property tax base, not the decline in the value of farmland.

Figure 11.1 presents information concerning the property tax burden on farmland in the United States compared with the value of the land and the value of gross domestic product (GDP) in the farming sector. Property taxes per $100 of land value were relatively steady, at about 1 percent, from 1950 until the early 1970s. Then, the ratio rapidly declined

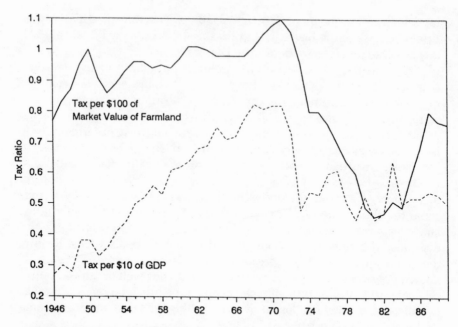

FIGURE 11.1 Tax per $100 of farmland value and farmland tax per $10 of gross domestic product, U.S., 1946-1989.

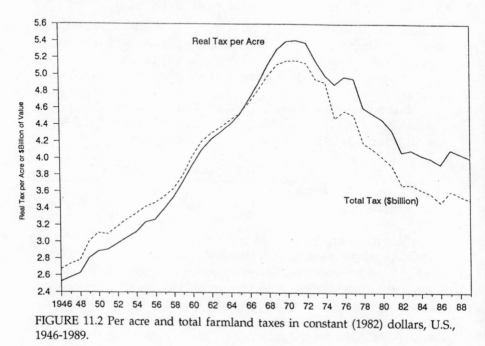

FIGURE 11.2 Per acre and total farmland taxes in constant (1982) dollars, U.S., 1946-1989.

(to less than 0.5 percent) until 1980, a reflection of the fact that property tax levies did not keep pace with increasing land values. Part of the declining relative tax levies is attributable to de facto underassessment, that is, assessors did not keep values current during periods of rapidly increasing land prices. Part of it may also be related to the advent of use-value assessment laws. Note that the trend of the declining tax-to-value ratio was established before most use-value assessment laws were in place. The decline in farmland prices in the early 1980s reversed this trend somewhat, and the tax-to-value ratio rose to about 0.7 percent in 1989.

The ratio of property taxes to farm GDP also decreased dramatically in about 1970. After World War II, property taxes on farmland rose from about 3 percent of GDP to about 7.5 percent in 1970. The ratio fell to about 5 percent after 1970 and has remained at about that level since.

Figure 11.2 presents information about real (inflation-adjusted 1982 dollars) property tax levels for farmland in the United States from 1946 to 1989. Taxes per acre and per $100 of land value rose steadily from the end of World War II until about 1970, after which the tax burden steadily declined.

It is difficult to evaluate precisely the impact of use-value assessment on the property tax burden on farmland. Clearly, the period when use-value assessment laws were enacted across the country coincides with a declining relative property tax burden (measured in a variety of ways) on farmland. Whether the use-value laws were the major cause of the decline is a difficult question to answer because many other changes were occurring simultaneously. Those other changes include major fluctuations in the value of farmland and farm incomes, the movement away from local (property tax) financing of education in many states, and the beginning of the so-called property tax revolt in the mid-1970s. A more detailed empirical study would be useful to attempt to determine the relative impact of these various factors on property tax burdens on farmland. A casual analysis of the data suggests that the importance of use-value assessment practices in limiting the property tax burden on agricultural land cannot be dismissed.

Conclusion

Research in the area of use-value assessment of farmland has declined in recent years. With laws in place in every state, there is relatively little policy debate on the basic issues relating to preferential treatment of agricultural land since relatively few new proposals are being considered for adoption. It is unfortunate, however, that more evaluative research is not being undertaken because a wealth of data now exists with which to evaluate the allocative and distributive impacts of use-value assessment practices. Evaluative research could be used to refine existing practices so as to target better the results to the goals of the programs while also preserving the property tax base, especially in rural areas.

Notes

J. **Fred Giertz** is professor, Institute of Government and Public Affairs, University of Illinois at Urbana-Champaign.

1. A good bibliography of use-value assessment research is contained in J.P. Michos, "The Literature of Use-Value Assessment," Economic Research Service, U.S. Department of Agriculture, Washington, D.C., 1991 (photocopy), bibliography presented at the Land Ownership, Tenure, and Taxation seminar, Washington, D.C., October 4, 1991. Also see, R.W. Dunford, D.L. Chicoine, and D. Ervin, "A Critical Review of the Income Capitalization Approach to Use-Value Assessment," in T.A. Majchrowicz and R.R. Almy, eds., *Property Tax Assessment: Processes, Records and Land Values,* Economic Research Service (Washington, D.C.: U.S. Department of Agriculture, 1985); and D.L. Chicoine and A.D. Hendricks, "Evidence on Farm Use-Value Assessment, Tax Shifts, and State School Aid," *American Journal of Agricultural Economics* 67, no. 2 (1985). This paper draws from material in J.F. Giertz, *An Analysis of Use-Value Assessment of Farmland and Its Application in Illinois,* Occasional Paper Number 3, Office of Real Estate Research (University of Illinois at Urbana-Champaign, 1982).

2. There are, however, some interesting perverse effects of use-value assessments in urban areas. In the suburban Chicago area of Illinois, many relatively small lots that are being held for developmental purposes are farmed for tax, not agricultural, reasons. Specialized farmers make their living farming small parcels (sometimes less than one acre) located in urban areas. Under Illinois law, keeping a parcel in cultivation can lower property taxes by as much as 90 percent, which often saves landowners tens of thousands of dollars. This practice has generated some unusual agreements between landowners and tenant farmers. For small parcels, the effective rent is often zero or even negative.

3. Owners of nonagricultural land in predominantly agricultural areas are likely to see large increases in their property tax liabilities, however.

4. Data concerning property taxation levels for farmland come from the Farm Real Estate Taxes (FRET) series maintained by the Economic Research Service of the U.S. Department of Agriculture (1991). Data for total property tax collections are from Advisory Commission on Intergovernmental Relations, *Significant Features of Fiscal Federalism,* Vol. II (Washington, D.C., 1991). Data for gross domestic production in the farm sector and the implicit gross national product deflator are from the *Economic Report of the President* (Washington, D.C.: Government Printing Office, 1991).

PART THREE

Options

We are by no means out of the woods in regard to social policy towards land and land rent. It remains a source of socially appropriable economic surplus, and the whole relation of the market in land to the needs of society, however these are defined, remains an unsolved one.

—K. Boulding, *Towards a New Economics*, 1992

12

Making Land-Settlement Policy in a Federalist System

Leonard Shabman

Why do we settle the nation's land as we do? Is an "unrestricted," "unfettered," or "free" market in land the signaling mechanism that determines the pattern of land uses and density of specific uses in that pattern? What, if any, public policy is warranted to restrict the operation of the land market? Questions such as these, which attribute land settlement and use to the prices dictated by the land market, foster a perceived conflict between market-determined prices of private property rights in land and the diminution of those prices by public policy. A so-called trade-off between the goals of "private property values" and "public health, safety, and welfare" frames the land-settlement policy debate. This is unfortunate. The land market, the prices created therein, and the settlement patterns that result are already an artifact of a collection of federal, state, and local government policies, even if no single policy is intended to alter the way we settle the land. Our national land policy is made by intent, and by accident, at all levels of government.

The nation's unintentional land policy is a source of concern for those who wish to retain the use of rural land in food and fiber production, but see it threatened by other uses. The aggregate data do not, however, support such a concern. In the United States the amount of acreage devoted to crops, pasture, and forestland has fallen only slightly through time, and land in a variety of other uses (mostly urban) has risen only slightly as a percentage of the total.[1]

There must, therefore, be more to the concern for national land-settlement policy, even if the concerns for food and fiber are the issues initially broached. The broader concern appears to be about the apparent creation of a new landscape in all areas, rural and urban. A windshield survey of the nation's urban areas and rural towns reveals commercial and residential activity relocating to the "edge" and then beyond the original city and town centers.[2] Such a survey also reveals the heavy reliance on automobile travel for even the most modest household or business errands. Often, the old centers seem to have spun off pockets of residences, shops, or employment, and those new areas, along with the old town centers, now exist as but one part of a populated area seemingly lacking any center. The creation of this new landscape requires that land provide a service, here termed *spatial separation*, but more commonly and pejoratively called *sprawl*. The demand for separation continues despite the conventional wisdom that the resulting sprawl brings adverse economic, fiscal, and environmental consequences. Concerns over the "costs of sprawl" have motivated intermittent proposals for public policies and programs to limit the use of land for separation. This *growth management* is expected to make cities and suburbs more livable and to preserve the character of rural areas. Growth management is based on the premise that more land is being used now than is needed for "urban uses" of residential, commercial, industrial, and transportation sites. Presumably, the remainder of the land is left for food, fiber, and other "rural" uses. Often, physical land-consumption requirements are created to establish how much land is needed for urban use, but the reliance on physical data confuses the measure of land as physical space with the service of separation the space provides. I discuss this argument in some detail in the section below. Following that discussion, I address the question, Why do we settle the land as we do? I conclude the paper with observations about the challenge of reforming the nation's land policy.

Land for Separation: How Much Land Do We Need?

Webster's New Collegiate Dictionary (1980) includes definitions of *sprawl*. One definition is "to spread the limbs in a relaxed, awkward or unnatural position." Another definition is "to spread awkwardly or without a regular pattern; to take up more space than is necessary, as handwriting, a line of men, etc." To call the use of land for separation "sprawl," then, is to suggest that something is wrong with the way the land is being settled. The term *sprawl* implies that more land is being used than is needed. But how much do people need?

One approach to defining land needs is to calculate physical "requirements." A sophisticated version of this argument acknowledges the value to people of at least some types of separation, and a prototypical landscape is usually described that includes varying densities and mixed land uses. For example, such a landscape is said to exist in areas such as Reston, Virginia, a planned suburban community developed about 20 years ago.[3] Reston includes a mix of land uses and residential housing styles, and within the project boundaries, 40 percent of the land is open space.

Rather than suggesting that people settle at particular average densities, Risse argues that desirable land settlement within a regional space should be described. In that area will be a variety of residential living options, but the average density of the settled areas might be quite high. Imagine dividing, say all of Fairfax County, Virginia, where Reston is, into Reston-sized geographic units and settling those areas at the average density of Reston (10 people per acre). In this case, two-thirds of the land area of Fairfax County would be vacant. There might be pockets of Restons, separated by open areas available for "rural," land-extensive economic activities. Risse defends his Reston vision by noting that, "Just about everyone who chooses to live in the suburbs would love Reston. The rest want to live in urbane downtowns or on a farm."[4]

Underlying such physical calculations of "need" (which are interesting and useful) is the premise that urban activities should be supported by a smaller physical land base than the current rate of land consumption is leading to. But the need for separation is a social one, and the willingness and ability to pay for separation determine urban land-consumption rates. Descriptions of how the land *could* be settled in accord with some ideal type are not all the evidence that is needed to make a case for how the land *should* be settled. Indeed, the "ideal type" is really a statement imposing an external judgment that the people who are in the current suburbs and beyond would be better off living in a spatial arrangement that brings their residences closer together on smaller lots and that brings them closer to their places of work and shopping. External judgments about modern suburban culture and design, which are associated with sprawl, are made on cultural and aesthetic grounds[5] but such judgments are not new. In his book *Crabgrass Frontier*, historian Kenneth Jackson[6] finds such judgments deeply rooted in our history. He begins his history by quoting Keats from "The Crack in the Picture Window":

> Even while you read this, whole square miles of identical boxes are spreading like gangrene ... developments conceived in error, nurtured by greed, corroding everything they touch.

Peter Schmitt, in describing the disappointments from the late nineteenth-century movement to the countryside could be writing a criticism for the 1990s:

Realists soon concluded that suburbs too often copied their mother cities. Urban gridirons destroyed the spirit of the country as new houses rose side by side on twenty-five foot lots in the midst of empty fields where there was no more of nature than straggling Chinese elms along a curbstone. Children might see the forest in a hedgerow and the prairie in a vacant lot, but to adults, life in the suburban countryside was sometimes less romantic. Even with rapid transit, factory and office workers left early and returned late, sleeping peacefully in the country air, but spending their waking hours in going and coming. "The suburban husband and father is almost entirely a Sunday institution," a writer in *Harper's Bazaar* concluded in 1900.[7]

Yet the sprawling settlement patterns have continued, even as the critics continue to question the need to use land in this way. An alternative framework for defining and understanding land-use needs—at least for an economic analysis—is required. The economic question is whether there are net social costs of the land-settlement pattern. The economic question focuses on the validity of two sub-questions. (1) Are there benefits to separation that should be considered before condemning this use of land? (2) Is there well-documented evidence of the costs of separation?

The Benefits of Separation

Historians have called the demand for separation the "suburbanization movement," although it is occurring today at the edge of cities as well as in the countryside. The suburbanization of America has a long history:

> Fredrick Law Olmsted and Calvert Vaux published their plan for Riverside, Chicago's first suburban development, in 1868. They noted the drawing power of the metropolis, but they also found a "counter-tide of migration, especially affecting the more intelligent and more fortunate classes." It seemed to Olmsted and Vaux that "the most attractive, the most refined, and the most soundly wholesome forms of domestic life" were to be found in residential suburbs.[8]

Many of the areas that were early suburban enclaves are today viewed as cities. For example, the Yonkers area near New York City and the Chevy Chase area north of Washington, D.C., were suburbs, but they used little land in their creation. The association of lower population-density settlement with suburbanization is a phenomenon of more recent decades. The trend toward more land-consuming suburbanization arose, according to Anthony Downs,[9] as a result of a particular vision of how U.S. metropolitan areas ought to be developed. This vision demands the dedication of more land to residential, transportation, commercial, and industrial uses and to separation among and between uses. For Downs, this idea was built on four pillars, each of which was an aspiration shared by nearly all American households:

- Ownership of detached, single-family homes on spacious lots.
- Ownership and use of a personal automobile.
- Workplaces consisting predominantly of low-rise office or industrial buildings or shopping centers, in attractively landscaped, park-like settings.
- Small communities with strong local self-governments that permit existing residents to have a strong voice in controlling their local environments.

Downs' description of this American vision applies in all regions, rural and urban. Thus, from the small town in central Virginia to the Virginia suburbs of Washington, D.C., patterns of land settlement are emerging that, at first analysis, provide evidence for the existence of benefits from separation. Land is being used to separate individual homes on large lots in the name of privacy. Land is being used to separate places of residence, places of work, and public facilities in the name of preserving neighborhoods. People separate themselves from the places where they spend their leisure time and call their residences first and second homes. Land is being used to separate racial and socioeconomic classes from each other as images of urban crime and congestion make the spatial separation of the suburbs appear as an escape from urban pathologies. Indeed, even if one discounts the power of the vision Downs described, it is difficult to deny the obvious pattern of flight from urban and close-in suburbs to the countryside.[10]

Clearly, *separation* is not another term for open space. *Open space* is a physical description of the result of the demand for the separation service. Separation by physical distance satisfies a number of social and cultural ends. People seek benefits from using land for separation, benefits that have been sought for a century and a half. And, separation is expected to protect private financial interests—the market prices of land. All other things equal, separation is distance that has a positive effect on land prices. Thus, separation distance is quite different from the negative effect that distance from a central place is expected to have on land prices in the standard economic models.

The Costs of Separation

The costs of separation (sprawl) have been described and used to support recommendations for changes in policy to alter land settlement. The evidence to support the claims made about those costs is not compelling, however. In the 1980s, an asserted cost of sprawl that captured public attention was that the physical loss of agricultural land to urbanization would compromise the nation's food-production capacity.[11] Professionals spilled a lot of blood over that issue,[12] and by a composite of agronomic, engineering, and economic insight the debate has reached the point that most analysts would agree that "informed opinion now discounts any threat to food and fiber production from continued urbanization."[13]

With the argument for preserving farmland in order to maintain food-production capacity set aside, the possible costs of sprawl have been described in other ways. But would the assertion that those costs are significant stand up to the same degree of critical scrutiny given the agricultural land preservation argument? Might the arguments for those other costs become equally questionable? Consider some of the typical arguments about the cost of sprawl.

Metropolitan Agriculture. Concern has been expressed about farm operators' ability to continue production in the face of urbanization because agricultural land uses are economically idled by the pressures of higher urban land prices and by challenges of the new suburban neighbors to the nuisances created by traditional farming practices.[14] Urbanization, however, may not be the critical factor in the decline of land dedicated to agricultural use in many areas. Up and down the East Coast at least, land-extensive feed grain production is rapidly declining, which could release millions of acres of land from row crops. This transition in the agricultural production sector is not being initiated by urbanization; rather, it is driven by shifts in national farm policy that are letting the comparative advantage of Midwestern agriculture in row-crop production take effect. Reversal of this trend may require development of new production technologies for existing crops and of alternative crops better suited to the land resources of the region. Meanwhile, the expansion of urban areas may support alternative agricultural enterprises, but they are unlikely to be land extensive. There is evidence of an increased economic product from agriculture in metropolitan areas.[15] And, Vesterby and Heimlich's analysis shows that nontraditional agricultural land use actually expanded in areas of rapid population growth between 1960 and 1980.[16] Currently, a credible working hypothesis about the relationship of a region's urbanization to the economic product earned in agriculture is that the net effect is neutral or perhaps slightly positive, even as land used in agricultural production declines.

Environment. Environmental concerns, mostly over nonpoint source water and air pollution, have also been used to focus attention on land settlement.[17] Water quality degradation has been attributed to the runoff from urbanized areas, runoff that is expected to exceed that from farm- and forestland. In almost all cases, such conclusions are based on engineering computations that assert a fixed pollution-loading coefficient for a variety of pollutants per dwelling unit or per automobile. Whether the pollutant loadings are based on sound information is not clear. For example, in Virginia no estimate is available of the use of chemicals on suburban lawns. Also, pollution-loading calculations do not account for the possible effectiveness of urban best-management practices to reduce pollutant loadings, such as sediment retention basins, street sweeping, and changed lawn fertilization practices. In short, no distinction has been drawn between land being in suburban landscapes and how the land in those landscapes is being managed or might be managed to mitigate environmental effects.

Local air quality problems have been linked in a conclusive way to automobile miles traveled. As land-settlement patterns increase the miles driven, an argument can be made that a more compact pattern and density of settlement might improve air quality. Much driving is discretionary, however, and total automobile miles traveled is only partly related to distances that must be traveled. Also, as automobile engine technologies change, or if relative costs for personal driving versus mass transit are altered, automobile use and the resulting air pollution might be reduced. In short, land settlement probably contributes to air quality problems, but the relative importance of land settlement in increasing miles driven versus the relative costs of alternative transportation or changes in automobile engine technology is not well established.

Economic Development. Another concern about separation has been the apparent loss in the competitiveness of the private economy in world markets. Fischel argues that, in part, this can be a result of scattered development, which causes a loss in the agglomeration economies that have long characterized the urban economy.[18] Perhaps there is a linkage among sprawl, high housing and labor costs, and loss of competitive advantage in a region. Such hypotheses suggest the need for research; they are far from established conclusions, however. Indeed, the validity of such hypotheses will be weakened by the opportunities for spreading out economic actors in response to the new electronic office and the telecommunications revolution.

Fiscal Impact. The current fiscal condition of many local governments has made controlling the costs of providing public services a matter of increased importance. Almost as a part of the conventional wisdom is the argument that separation—sprawl—raises the net cost of local government.[19] However, as in many other arguments about the costs of separation, what people think they know may not be well founded. A recent comprehensive review of the fiscal costs of urbanization concludes as follows:

While some generalizations can be gleaned from past research by craftily up-dating material and piecing together data from several places in an attempt to construct the whole cloth, the first unanswered question is whether the fabric would hold together against a comprehensive, contemporary study that is well controlled for the factors that appear to be important from previous efforts.[20]

Summing Up

From this brief review it appears that the costs of separation are un-certain and may not be as great as many suggest and that the individual benefits of separation are not often recognized. For example, the case for environmental effects rests on compelling deductive arguments that problems can arise, but rarely on empirical evidence. Further, the pos-sibility that public policies might be employed to change behaviors to reduce the environmental costs of the emerging density and pattern of land use is not acknowledged. Most troubling is that the costs of sprawl are often treated as established facts, even in the writings of those who are most analytic about the concern over the availability of farmland.[21] But the evidence to support these cost-of-sprawl assertions is meager, as Porter observed:

> Hypotheses and theories formulated in the 1950s and 1960s about the efficien-cies of alternative development patterns, relationships between land uses and public facilities, costs and benefits of growth, and the effects of regulatory policies and practices have not been adequately explored and evaluated, al-though they continue to be applied in the absence of alternative concepts.[22]

There is a need for better documentation of the consequences of the density and pattern of land settlement in order to inform the debate about land-settlement policy. Policy as it affects land settlement is the subject of the next section.

Why Do We Settle the Land As We Do?

The governance of urban growth has reemerged as a major policy issue in many communities across the United States. In such communities, the advent of rapid growth and change is perceived by many residents as the root of local problems with traffic congestion, overcrowded schools, water shortages and water quality degradation, loss of open space and environmental amenities and other urban ills....

Yet, after 20 years of experience with growth management, it must be said that we know very little about how to manage urban development.... We understand little about how urban growth occurs, how urban systems change in the process of growth, how urban development needs can be balanced with environmental or other concerns, or how specific techniques to manage change actually work.[23]

Porter, the author just quoted, is right, so any attempt to address the question posed in this section must be made with some hesitancy. What is offered here is a general economic-political model of the pattern and density of land settlement, which can be used to understand better the dynamics of land-use change and the considerations necessary for effective policy design.

Economic and Policy Influences on Land Settlement

Economic models of land settlement are typically derived from the Von Thünen-type rent-gradient models.[24] Originally, the models were used to predict farmland prices as a function of commodity value and total transportation costs to a central place. All other things equal, higher total transportation costs reduced annual land rents, which were then capitalized as lowered land prices. The Von Thünen model has been applied to urban land use by replacing commodity transportation costs with commuting costs to a central business district (CBD). Under a series of restrictive assumptions, the model predicts a decline in land prices and a change in land uses with increasing distance from the CBD. However, adding complex reality to these models compromises their predictive power regarding prices and use of specific parcels for large regions. Randall is quite explicit on this matter:

> More detailed models of urban land use and rents can, of course, be constructed. But the gain in descriptive reality is often accompanied by an offsetting loss of generality. If we allow preferences to vary among classes of consumer workers, the neat pattern we just predicted could become unraveled....
>
> Other considerations may be introduced—for example, multiple places of employment (the CBD, the docks, a manufacturing district, suburban shopping centers), topographical features (harbors, rivers, hills), differences in the age and quality of housing (in addition to differences in lot size), differences in neighborhood amenities (schools, parks, cultural facilities, crime protection)—that are helpful in specifying empirical models for particular applications but, again, produce few unexpected general results.[25]

One obvious modification to the simple model would be to make separation distance between a variety of uses a *positively* priced service of land. This valued service might include separation of residences from commercial centers or separation of residences from each other (large residential housing lots). For this discussion, consider an individual residential landowner's price for separation to be the cost of travel between her residence and commercial and employment sites, where separation of the sites has a positive value for the residential landowner. This price of separation includes both the out-of-pocket costs for travel and the opportunity cost of time. Following standard theory, the quantity demanded of the separation service would be inversely related to the cost of travel. There are several demand shifters in this framework: the price of the land parcel used for separation in its alternative use (perhaps as determined by agricultural returns); the price of complementary goods, such as charges for public services and property tax levels; and tastes and preferences for separation, perhaps as related to demographic factors.

One important lesson to be learned from the rent-gradient models, despite their poor predictive power, is that changes in policy that increase the price of separation may be differentially capitalized into prices of individual land parcels. For example, consider an existing pattern of employment, commercial, and residential land uses within a region. A rise in transportation costs imposed by taxing gasoline (or by road congestion) may cause prices of parcels located farther from existing employment or commercial centers to fall. Unless this encourages another land user to dedicate the lower priced land to an alternative (nonurban) use, some urban residents will trade off higher commuting costs for the lower land prices in outlying areas. This may result in fewer people (lower average density in the outlying areas) than would have been the case without the rise in transportation costs. Meanwhile, higher average density might be achieved nearer to commercial and employment centers. Of course, other adjustments may occur with time. The lower land prices and higher transportation costs might encourage the relocation of commercial and employment centers, which could result in a new pattern of such centers in the region. Or, perhaps, people will switch employment or shopping locations.[26]

The observation that the price of individual land parcels and land settlement may adjust to policy changes is as far as the economic model of land-price formation leads. More realism about land-settlement outcomes is gained by grafting a political component onto the economic model of land rents, which gives rise to the need to address speculative behavior. For some, speculation is of central importance.[27] One author finds that, "Spread and sprawl in forestry, cities and agriculture are common results of the dominant force driving American politics, the quest for unearned increments to land price."[28]

The definition of "unearned increments" might be debated, but the possibility that the increments can be created by policy decisions is unassailable. Above, I presented an example of how energy policy can *indirectly* affect land prices. But other types of policy actions are more obvious to owners of particular parcels. Decisions about highway location or zoning are expected to change *directly* the pattern and density of settlement and, therefore, the wealth of the owners of the parcels being affected. When wealth-creating possibilities are realized and can be directly attributed to a policy action, landowners who stand to gain or lose from changing land prices are motivated to political action to influence these obvious land-settlement policy decisions. Many refer to "speculation in land"; "speculation in land policy" may be a more accurate description of speculative behavior, however. The economic return to speculation is realized more from policy decisions that favorably influence the price of particular parcels of land than from a good guess on the land "market." As a result, those policies whose potential for wealth creation is easily recognized will generate intense opposition from some landowner/voters and intense support from others. This particular type of political activity over land settlement is most intense at the local level and will influence land settlement to some degree.

Wealth-Making Policy Is Pervasive

The scope of policies that may influence land settlement in the federal system is broad, and space does not permit a full description. What is striking, even from a brief consideration of policies, is that many potentially influential policies are not made with the intent of affecting the pattern and density of land settlement. Consider the following policy categories: expenditure policy (which includes tax forgiveness and direct spending), regulatory policy, and revenue policy. Tax expenditures are special exceptions from the payment of taxes that reduce the tax liability for an economic agent. Examples include agricultural use-value taxation, deductions for home mortgage interest payments in determining federal and state taxable income, and special tax treatment of capital gains and losses from real property transactions. The first two policies are intended to influence either agricultural land use or home ownership, often in order to influence land settlement. The capital gains provisions apply to any type of financial loss, but they provide a modest financial safety net for speculative behavior in land policy. Direct expenditures by a governmental unit may be made for land, capital items, or operating expenses, using the revenues from dedicated sources or general funds. Programs for the purchase of development rights are expressly for influencing land settlement. Expenditures for infrastructure have long been identified as policies that might influence land settlement, either by intent or by accident, but they are not all that is needed. Highway construction, in particular, by reducing the price of separation, can affect the density and pattern of land settlement. Governmental expenditures are intended to improve the quality of life in a community by providing such services as quality schools. Whether the pattern and density of land settlement within a community are affected by, for example, school spending is not clear, but population distribution across communities (e.g., central city versus suburbs) may well be influenced by such spending as people move to where they perceive the higher quality schools to be.

Regulatory policy includes restrictions that limit how land may be used or how some other activity may be conducted. The federal wetlands regulations under Section 404 of the Clean Water Act are an example of direct land-use regulation. Local zoning programs also fit this policy category, as might efforts to rearrange land-use rights, such as in a transferable development rights program. A complete list of nonland-directed regulatory programs would be quite extensive and would surely include policies that indirectly influence land use.

Revenue policy is typically for financing expenditures, but it may include user fees and taxes expressly for the purpose of altering economic decisions. Specifically, are fees, charges, or taxes intended to raise revenue or to reflect the marginal cost of providing a service and/or to internalize off-site costs? This is the question of marginal versus average-cost pricing often posed by economic analysts, who suggest that failure to charge marginal costs subsidizes the consumption of the separation service. The extent of the subsidy is extremely difficult to demonstrate empirically, but at a conceptual level the argument may have merit.[29]

The scope of policies that influence land settlement is vast. Not all policies influence land prices and land settlement in the same way, however. This can be easily recognized by dividing policies, not into the categories of expenditures, regulation, and revenues, but rather into two somewhat imprecise categories suggested by the political-economic model described earlier. The first category includes the policies that increase or decrease the demand of individual landowners and/or communities for land for separation, either by affecting the price of separation or shifting the demand for separation. (This implies that the community acts on behalf of the individual landowners within its jurisdiction.) Call these *separation demand-determining policies.* In the second category are policies that attempt to direct a particular density and pattern of development mostly by regulation, but also by use of fees and taxes. Call this second category *direct price-redistribution policies.* Price-redistribution policies will directly and obviously affect the prices of specific properties. Examples are federal wetlands regulations, zoning, transferable development rights, and other frequently suggested growth management measures. At times, other types of policies may have an obvious and direct effect on prices of specific properties, such as when low-income, racially mixed public housing is proposed in an area of expensive single-family homes. Of course, demand-determining policy is price redistributing but not directly and obviously so.

An excellent illustration of a demand-determining policy is national energy policy, which affects the price of, and hence demand for, separation. Consider the debate now under way in the Congress over whether to raise the corporate average fuel economy (CAFE) requirement to 40 miles per gallon by 2000. The CAFE concept seems sound. Congress passes a law requiring increased automobile fuel-use efficiency. If cars use less fuel per mile driven, there will be less need to import oil and less associated air pollution. But what of the price of separation?

In 1972, when the CAFE regulation was first put in place, the average automobile could travel about 13 miles per gallon of gas. By 1987 (the most recent year for which data are available), the average car on the road traveled about 19.2 miles per gallon; meanwhile, new cars added to the national fleet in 1987 traveled 31.2 miles per gallon. During the same time the nominal price of gasoline rose through the 1970s and then fell through the 1980s, and inflation-adjusted prices of gasoline fell consistently from 1973 to 1987.

The combination of better gas mileage and falling real gasoline prices lowered the cost of driving and thus the cost of separation. In the decade from 1978 to 1987, the real price (1972 base) of driving a mile for all cars on the road fell from 4.45 cents to 2.72 cents. Considering only the new cars added to the fleet in 1987, the cost per mile driven was only 1.67 cents. Falling inflation-adjusted gas prices, combined with CAFE-mandated increases in technical fuel efficiency, have decreased the real price of separation.

If the real cost of moving a mile in a new 1987 automobile was made equal to 1978 costs, a gasoline tax of 90 cents per gallon (letting $1.10/gallon be the current price) would be required. I am not suggesting this would reduce miles driven to the 1972 level because changes in preferences for separation and real income increases have also occurred. Still, recognizing how much the price of separation has fallen helps to explain the pressures increasing the demand for separation.

Another illustration of demand-determining policy is the reliance of local governments on the real property tax, often because the state government limits local governments' use of other revenue sources. This limitation, when combined with the conventional zoning power of local governments, will increase the community demand for separation. In many areas the perception (whether correct or not) is that property tax revenues from commercial and high-priced residential property exceed the local cost of providing services to those properties. Conversely, property tax revenues are expected to be less than the local cost of services for most other residential property. In areas where this belief is strongly held, there is every reason to expect that the poor will be zoned out of communities, for example, by zoning requirements for large lots. Indeed, there is reason to believe that residential development in general will be discouraged and that residential settlement will be displaced to an outlying political jurisdiction, where extensive travel to work and to commercial locations will be required. These exclusionary zoning practices will often be justified as environmental protection measures or ways to control services costs (no-growth ordinances or adequate-public-facility ordinances).[30] However, a central factor supporting the zoning decision is the fiscal policy environment. Changing the land-settlement effect of this policy interaction would require either expanding local governments' access to revenue sources other than the property tax or changing the financial responsibility for provision of some local services.

A list of demand-determining policies would be a long one. Changes in capital gains taxation rules can alter the investments made in real property. The rate at which highway improvements are made may affect congestion and alter the opportunity cost of separation. Racial, educational, or crime control policy failures and successes in the cities or close-in suburbs will shift the demand for separation from those places. Fischel is quite explicit on the importance of these kinds of policies. Near the end of his book, *The Economics of Zoning Laws*, after attempting to make the case that economic arguments can explain suburban zoning behavior, he concludes, "suburban exclusion of the poor is rooted in a larger social problem whose dimensions transcend the realm of land-use control."[31] That social problem is, in his view, the failure of national crime control policies.

All the possible demand-determining policy influences cannot be explored here, but it is important to recognize how policies that are quite removed from direct land-use controls determine the demand for land's service of separation. In turn, demand-determining policies increase the price of land dedicated to the separation service. Then, when regulatory controls on land use are proposed, the potential of those restrictions for reducing property prices—albeit prices created in part by demand-determining policies—is a real one. And, intense political opposition logically follows as prices in private property markets are threatened by regulation. Meanwhile, the speculation in land policy for a favorable rezoning, for example, continues. The political activity generated by direct price-redistribution policies can limit the ability of governments to execute programs to change, directly and obviously, the pattern and density of land use.

It now may be time to focus more directly on the way demand-determining policies dictate the pattern and density of settlement and on policies of growth management based on reform of those policies. But, most demand-determining policy is made for reasons other than land-settlement (energy policy, local revenue limitations, capital gains taxation, and so on). Indeed, land settlement is probably the unintended effect of such policies. Thus, it will be admittedly difficult to make the case for redesigning the potentially most significant demand-determining policies to make them more sensitive to land settlement because their primary policy purpose is elsewhere. Wholesale reform for the purpose of addressing land settlement is not likely, but marginal reforms in demand-determining policies might be possible. Precedents do exist. National agricultural and tax policies have been reformed so as to continue to support farm income but to reduce the policy incentive to farm erodible lands and drain wetlands. Differential rates of taxation on capital gains might be established, but without making real property eligible for those provisions. Much needs to be accomplished in order to make a more compelling case for building growth management around demand-determining policy. As a start, better information is needed. Indeed, "if there is one key to effective land-use policy, it is finding a means for lowering the costs of relevant information."[32] What information is needed?

On Advocating the Reform of Land-Settlement Policy

Reform advocates need far more valid (documented) descriptions of the land-use changes now occurring. Only then can any real problems of land settlement be adequately documented. A common assertion is that population growth is consuming agriculture and the natural world:

> Take, for example, 1500 acres of farm or forest, divide it into 300 lots, dig 300 wells, plant one septic tank on each plot, and add a home for three people. You will have accommodated just one day's worth of immigrants to Florida.[33]

Here, 1.67 acres of Florida's land is said to be allocated to each new person in Florida, just for residential housing. At this rate of land consumption, with 300,000 new people arriving in Florida each year, the state would rapidly be consumed by urban development. This type of calculation is offered to direct attention to population settlement and land use, but because of its obvious limitations, it is treated as hyperbole rather than cogent argument. A recent study by Vesterby and Heimlich illustrates what is needed.[34] Using aerial photography and satellite imagery of "fast growth" counties across the United States, they tracked the use of specific land areas through time for 1960-1970 and for 1970-1980. They defined fast-growth counties using a combination of the percentage increase in population and minimum initial population levels. The criteria were slightly different for the different study years. For the 1970-1980 period the study covered 135 counties, and for the 1960-1970 study, 53 counties.

By extrapolating from a sample of points to the counties as a whole, Vesterby and Heimlich described changes in land-use density in the fast-growth areas. They described categories of land use based on cover type; for example, residential home sites, commercial sites, and public facilities are "urban" land uses. By relating changes of land to urban uses to changes in household numbers, they computed "marginal urban land-use consumption" for the fast-growth counties. For both time periods, they found an unchanging marginal urban land consumption of .46 acres per household. However, because of reduced household sizes in the 1970s, the marginal per capita urban land consumption was a bit higher than it was for the 1960s. For the 1970s, given an average household size of 2.18 persons, marginal per capita land consumption was 0.22 acres per new person.

This study is evidence, based on a carefully constructed data base, that the kind of urban land consumption described in the assertion about Florida is not the situation in fast-growth areas. Indeed, Vesterby and Heimlich found that the more rapidly a county is growing, and the larger the original population, the lower is the marginal urban land-consumption coefficient. If these results are applied to "slow growth," low-population counties, which were not included in the Vesterby-Heimlich study, larger marginal per capita land consumption may be found, but it will be in isolated areas. The need to make this extrapolation points to a limitation of the Vesterby-Heimlich study. It covers only a few areas and is for only two time periods. Also, sample size limitations prohibit disaggregation to even the state level, and the data on individual counties are not at all statistically reliable. Thus, their work paints a useful general picture, but it may not describe the settlement pattern in rural areas in which farm- and forestland uses still represent a substantial part of the economic base.

A land-use pattern with pockets of urban uses, both high and low density, also may result from using the separation service of land. The separation service comes from spreading out land uses over an area with nonurban space remaining in between urban uses. The scattering of these pockets of use over the landscape is often visible to the casual observer, but no recent studies adequately document this occurrence. One piece of evidence in this regard can be established from census data on metropolitan areas.[35] The Bureau of the Census defines a metropolitan statistical area as a geographic area consisting of a large population nucleus (a census-defined urban area) together with adjacent areas that have a high degree of economic and social integration. Over the past three decades, the number of areas classified as metropolitan has increased, but the average density of all the areas decreased from 365 persons per square mile in 1960 to 315 persons per square mile in 1985. For there to be an increase in the number of metropolitan areas while average population densities decrease, the pattern of settlement in those areas must be spreading out if, as Vesterby and Heimlich suggest, there is no change in density where there are urban uses.

One tentative conclusion suggested by the preceding is that fears of being physically consumed by growth in density over large areas would seem unwarranted, although in the early stages of urbanization large residential consumption of land per capita may be occurring. Still, even if there is density of specific land uses, a new type of separation may be occurring as pockets of uses spread out from each other. This is a new image of sprawl and it must be better described and understood. The new imaging technologies and geographic information systems may, with adequate study resources, help shed light on this aspect of population settlement. Much more needs to be known about what is happening on the ground if land-use policymaking is to be well informed and if policy change is to be successfully advocated. Such studies will be expensive and time consuming, and determining how to get such work done will be a challenge. Advocates of reform also need better information about the benefits and costs of alternative development patterns. Efforts to design and implement growth management policies have not been well executed in many states and localities. At the same time, efforts to bring the federal government's attention to land settlement foundered in the 1960s, and federal actions have not been considered since. There are many complex reasons why land-settlement policy has been difficult to make, but it seems plausible that one constraint on new policy initiatives has been the inability to articulate a compelling argument about the net social gains of policy changes to manage whatever "sprawl" is documented. Policy reforms will occur only in relation to goals to be achieved, defined in relation to current and future problems. Sprawl development is said to degrade air and water quality, destroy wildlife habitats, threaten the food supply, raise tax burdens, diminish the quality of public services, increase the price of housing, and reduce the competitiveness of the economy. Reform of demand-determining policies may be advocated to address such problems. However, improved information on the validity of such claims is needed if there is to be a fruitful public debate on how to target and defend policy reform.

Conclusion

Success in making land-settlement policy will require a focus on those policies that raise the price of, and shift the demand for, the separation service of land. But is achieving demand-determining policy change an unreasonable objective? Despairing of making such changes, many authors suggest that a more limited perspective is all that is practical. Bjork observes, for example,

> Those who expect more sweeping proposals for the protection of our environmental and political heritage than are encompassed in recommendations for changes in [local] taxation, utility pricing, user fees, and zoning alterations may continue to search for comprehensive panaceas elsewhere than in the modification of property rights. They will not escape the necessity of making hard choices with real costs.[36]

Indeed, there will be hard choices, but effective, direct land-settlement controls may not be possible without attention to demand-determining policy. One can imagine that rigidly adhering to a local zoning policy will alter development patterns in the face of the demand-determining policy. But that is a wish based more on hope than on the hard lessons of zoning experience.[37] The policy forces that determine the price and demand for separation must be described, understood, and then addressed if there is to be any long-term prospect for a national land-settlement policy other than the accidental policy that now obtains. This is not a new or novel idea. In his 1979 book, *Room and Situation,* Hite observes,

> In any advanced society, land-use patterns are an inevitable result of government policies toward ... basic social institutions. If those patterns are economically wasteful or environmentally unwise, the remedy lies in institutional reform on a broad scale. Conventional land-use planning and zoning are merely symptomatic prescriptions that fail to correct the underlying institutional flaws responsible for the problem.[38]

In a recent review of the literature and experience with land-settlement policy, Meeks concludes that

> political economists of both the left and the right, with credible documentation, argue that land use and conservation are inextricably tied to American tax law and, in fact, the structure of our economy. Without addressing these fundamental areas, they reason, land use planning laws and regulations will not succeed and may even cause further resource degradation.[39]

A new approach to making land-settlement policy will only come with credible data, cogent research results, and articulate communication of the results to inform the political system about the current settlement pattern and the costs, benefits, and causes of that settlement. Perhaps land-settlement impact statements are needed as a route to reform. Developing such statements, however, will require far better theoretical understanding of the factors determining land settlement and better data to verify the insights from such theorizing than are currently available. And, because policy shifts are seldom made in response to mere speculation, such as that which often characterizes the arguments about the "cost of sprawl," still more analytic effort will be required. Finally, fundamental policy reform will proceed slowly, but reform is unlikely to occur at all without better understanding of the issues and choices.

Notes

Leonard Shabman is professor, Virginia Polytechnic Institute and State University.

1. C. Barnard and R. Hexem, *Major Statistical Series of the U.S. Department of Agriculture*, Vol. 6, *Land Values and Land Use*, Agriculture Handbook No. 671 (Washington, D.C.: U.S. Department of Agriculture, 1988).

2. J. Garreau, *Edge Cities: Life on the New Frontier* (New York: Doubleday, 1991).

3. E.M. Risse, "Some Facts About Growth in Virginia," in *Newsletter*, Piedmont Environmental Council (Warrenton, Va., 1989).

4. Ibid.

5. T. Hiss, *The Experience of Place* (New York: Knopf, 1990).

6. K. Jackson, *Crabgrass Frontier: The Suburbanization of the United States* (New York: Oxford University Press, 1985):3.

7. P. Schmitt, *Back to Nature: The Arcadian Myth in Urban America* (Baltimore: Johns Hopkins University Press, 1990):20.

8. Ibid., 20.

9. A. Downs, *The Need for a New Vision for the Development of Large U.S. Metropolitan Areas* (New York: Solomon Brothers, 1989).

10. N. Pierce, "Regional Governance: Why? Now? How?" in *Newsletter*, Center for Public Service, University of Virginia (Charlottesville, 1991).

11. Subcommittee on the City, Committee on Banking, Finance and Urban Affairs, House of Representatives, Committee Print 96-15 (Washington, D.C.: Government Printing Office, 1980).

12. F. Schnidman, "Discussion: The National Agricultural Lands Study and State and Local Concerns," in R. Heimlich, ed., *Land Use Transition in Urbanizing Areas*, Economic Research Service (Washington, D.C.: U.S. Department of Agriculture, 1989).

13. M. Vesterby and R. Heimlich, "Land Use and Demographic Change: Results from Fast Growth Counties," *Land Economics* 67(1991): 279.

14. W.A. Fischel, *The Economics of Zoning Laws: A Property Rights Approach to American Land Use Controls* (Baltimore: Johns Hopkins University Press, 1985).

15. R.E. Heimlich and D.H. Brooks, *Metropolitan Growth and Agriculture: Farming in the City's Shadow*, Economic Research Service, AER-619 (Washington, D.C.: U.S. Department of Agriculture, 1989).

16. Vesterby and Heimlich, "Land Use and Demographic Change."

17. Alliance for the Chesapeake Bay, *Managing Growth in the Chesapeake Region: A Policy Perspective*, Chesapeake White Paper (Annapolis, Md., 1989).

18. Fischel, *The Economics of Zoning Laws*.

19. Alliance for the Chesapeake Bay, *Managing Growth in the Chesapeake Region*.

20. J. Frank, *The Costs of Alternative Development Patterns: A Review of the Literature* (Washington, D.C.: Urban Land Institute, 1989):42.

21. See, for example, Fischel, *The Economics of Zoning Laws*; A. Randall, *Resource Economics* (New York: John Wiley & Sons, 1987).

22. D. Porter, "Foreword," *Understanding Growth Management* (Washington, D.C.: Urban Land Institute, 1989).

23. Porter, "Foreword," vi.

24. For an explanation of Von Thünen, see Randall, *Resource Economics*.

25. A. Randall, *Resource Economics*, 334.

26. Garreau, *Edge Cities*.

27. J.C. Hite, *Room and Situation: The Political Economy of Land-Use Policy* (Chicago: Nelson-Hall, 1979).

28. M. Gaffney, "Non-point Pollution: Tractable Solutions to Intractable Problems," paper presented at Conference on Political, Institutional, and Fiscal Alternatives to Accelerate Nonpoint Pollution Programs, Milwaukee, December 9, 1987.

29. See Frank, *The Costs of Alternative Development Patterns*; T. Snyder and M. Stegman, *Paying for Growth: Using Development Fees to Finance Infrastructure* (Washington, D.C.: Urban Land Institute, 1989).

30. P. Niebanck, "Growth Controls and the Production of Inequality," in D. Brower, D. Godschalk, and D. Porter, eds., *Understanding Growth Management* (Washington, D.C.: Urban Land Institute, 1989):105-122.

31. Fischel, *The Economics of Zoning Laws*, 336.

32. Hite, *Room and Situation*, 299.

33. R.L. Meyers and J.L. Ewell, eds., *Ecosystems of Florida* (Orlando: University of Central Florida Press, 1990):627.

34. Vesterby and Heimlich, "Land Use and Demographic Change."

35. Heimlich and Brooks, *Metropolitan Growth and Agriculture*.

36. G. C. Bjork, *Life, Liberty, and Property: The Economics and Politics of Land Use Planning and Environmental Controls* (Lexington, Mass.: D.C. Heath, 1980):18.

37. Fischel, *The Economics of Zoning Laws*.

38. Hite, *Room and Situation*, viii.

39. G. Meeks, Jr., *A Legislator's Guide to Land Conservation and Growth Management Policy* (Denver: National Conference of State Legislatures, 1990):42.

13

Not All Dreams Come True: Progressivism and the New Political Economy

James Hite

The Progressive paradigm in land-use policy analysis is no longer tenable. Although the Progressive ideology has dominated thinking about land-use policy for almost a century, the work of James Buchanan and Gordon Tullock, George Stigler, and Ronald Coase (and their followers) can no longer be ignored by land economists and public policy professionals.[1] A substantial portion of almost every issue of leading journals, like the *American Economic Review*, now carries scholarly work of the highest quality dealing with such important concepts of the new political economy as transaction costs, rational ignorance, and the efficient-market hypothesis. If the essence of Progressivism is to bring science into the public policy process, public choice theory, as an important part of the modern science of economics, must be given its due. Ironically perhaps, to be true to Progressivism, we must now finally kill it off.

Progressivism was an idealistic, optimistic ideology born of beautiful dreams of crusaders and reformers. But not all dreams come true. In this paper I reassess Progressivism in light of new insights developed by public choice theorists. My discussion is in four parts. In the first part, I examine the Progressive ideal and its influence on land-use policy. In the second, I focus on the fundamental concepts of public choice theory and the challenge they raise to the Progressive paradigm. I then review land-market theory and examine the incentives that the land market provides for land speculators to attempt to influence land-use policy. I conclude by raising the question whether land-use policy is worth worrying about and, assuming that it is, noting some ways that public choice theory might suggest to improve policy outcomes.

Land Economics and the Progressive Ideology

It is inevitable that the policies and activities of government will have significant effects on land use. At the most fundamental level, the laws of property recognized and enforced by government implicitly favor some types of land use over others. Environmental laws, taxation policy, defense spending, and a host of other governmental activities that are not directly focused on the shaping of land use inevitably influence, even if only subtly, the evolution of land-use patterns.

Since the time of the ancients, governments have also explicitly attempted to control land use. Mighty rulers from the time of Ramses I have built or rebuilt cities in accordance with some grand design. Some few of those ancient cities, even in ruins today, and more modern efforts, like Haussmann's Paris, excite wonder and admiration. But the idea that government should attempt to bring rationality to land use by resorting to science is of relatively recent vintage, a product of the Progressive Movement at the turn of the twentieth century.

Although less than precise about what it might be, Progressives believed that there was such a thing as "the public interest." That interest could be served by simply making public policy processes and public administration rational and by applying the principles of science to achieve efficiency. Pursuing what some scholars have called the "gospel of efficiency," the Progressives sought to purge policymaking of metaphysics by substituting verified scientific theories and empirical data.[2]

Land economics as a specialized field of study has deep roots in the Progressive Movement. Richard Ely, one of the founders of land economics in the United States, was also an intellectual leader in the Progressive Movement. His view that "governmental intervention [is] in order to secure 'all the conditions of a sound industrial system'" was seldom questioned by land economists.[3] With the development of modern welfare economics in the second quarter of the century, land economists fashioned a "scientific" justification for governmental intervention to correct externalities in land markets that lead to inefficiencies in land use and erode social welfare.

This justification was built on the undisputed observation that laissez-faire markets have imperfections, particularly when property rights cannot be (or have not been) fully defined.[4] Governments, therefore, as trustees for the public at large, must step in and either more fully specify property rights or use regulations to direct the allocation of resources in the "public interest." An important task of land economists was seen as developing the scientific information needed for government to know what would be the likely outcomes of various land-use policy options—to tell government policymakers how to fix market failures.

The Progressive ideology framed the way in which land-use policy has been approached in the United States during most of this century. It gave rise to the city planning movement and local land-use planning and zoning.[5] To be sure, there have been critics. But the only ones afforded much intellectual respectability were those who worried about how land-use planning could be reconciled with the "taking" clause of the Fifth Amendment to the Constitution.[6] Only a few, most notably Hayek,[7] challenged the fundamental reasoning that rational, scientific land-use policy was required in order to achieve efficiency in resource allocation.

The Public Choice Challenge

Even so, experience has shown that so-called rational planning does not always deliver the promises that the Progressive ideology held out. City planning did not prevent American cities from becoming congested, dirty, and largely ungovernable. Governmental intervention to protect natural resources and environmental amenities did not halt a rapid deterioration in environmental quality.[8] Something was wrong. But the failures were laid to deficiencies in scientific understanding and administrative structure, or to corruption.[9] They could, it was thought, be remedied by more studies, better science, and political reform. Only after Buchanan and his colleagues launched a new field of economic analysis, called public choice, did the fundamental problems inherent in the Progressive paradigm begin to become evident.

Buchanan's basic premise is both powerful and straightforward:

> The study of man must be based on a consistent set of assumptions; man does not become a different species in the voting booth or political assembly from what he is in the market.[10]

Conventional economic theory is based on the assumption that human activities in the marketplace are the results of rational utility maximization. That theory has proven to have considerable predictive power, and Buchanan suggests that human activities in the public policy arena are the results of the same attempts by rational individuals to maximize their utilities. The public choice paradigm is the result of logical reasoning based on such an assumption.

Public choice theorists do not deny that market failure can occur if there are goods that are nonexcludable and nonrival. If there are such goods, their allocation must be determined by political actions. Those actions will be nothing more nor less than individuals seeking to obtain through the policy process what they are unable to obtain in the marketplace, and they will be guided by rational calculations by each individual of the benefits and costs of alternative courses of action. Thus, if the expected benefits of seeking to influence land-use policy offset the costs, individuals will be active in trying to shape policy to serve their private objectives. That being the case, "there is no a priori reason to expect government action to improve the efficiency of the market allocation of resources."[11]

Public choice theory, therefore, is a direct challenge to the Progressive idea that public land-use policy can produce an allocation of land that is more efficient than that which would have been obtained in the absence of such policy. Indeed, the development of public choice theory has produced good reasons to expect that public land-use policy will not be guided, even by an invisible hand, toward some allocation of land use that maximizes social welfare. Instead, public choice models suggest that land-use policy will largely be the result of competition between those special interests that seek to use policy to obtain unearned economic rents. Understanding what this rent-seeking behavior means in regard to land-use policy requires an understanding of some fundamental aspects of land markets, which is the focus of the next section.

The Land Market

Randall and Castle have provided a concise, thorough, and rather rigorous theoretical analysis of the land market that readers might find useful if they wish to understand that market in all its subtle richness.[12] It is not necessary to review here all aspects of land-market theory. Yet it is worthwhile to recall the most fundamental thing about land prices, namely, the price of a parcel of land is derivative and depends on the current and anticipated future rents accruing to that parcel. If all future rents are fully and correctly anticipated and if the discount rate is constant, land neither appreciates nor depreciates in market value. Under such circumstances, the only return to holding land is a rate of return on the investment equal to the going rate of interest. But nothing in economics is ever quite that simple. Future rents are not fully and correctly anticipated by all parties operating in the land market. Different parties form different anticipations regarding future rents and from those differences come different judgments about what a particular tract of land might be worth in the market at any given time. Those different judgments account for the presence simultaneously of buyers and sellers and keep the land market fluid.

Yet as a general rule, it is accepted that capital gains from landowner-ship are possible only from events that increase rents in ways that the land market failed to anticipate.[13] So what is the point in owning land? One might own land because it is needed either as an input into produc-tion or as a site for a dwelling, but one could (if the land market fully and correctly anticipated all future rents) as easily and cheaply lease the required land. Alternatively, one might wish to own land to obtain a return on investment in the form of rents, but an equal return could be obtained from holding any other type of financial asset, some of which offer greater liquidity. One cannot rule out the holding of land as an asset for the same reasons certain conservative investors are attracted to the "widows and orphans" corporate securities: If the market fully and correctly anticipates all future rents, landownership is a safe investment for ensuring a steady flow of income equal to the going rate of interest. But none of these reasons is the sort of thing that would induce specula-tors to get into the land market.

Yet it is generally known that there is considerable speculation in the land market. Indeed, real estate speculation has been one of the roads to great riches in the United States. Those great riches were obtained be-cause the market did not fully and correctly anticipate all the events that affect land rents. Day-to-day and month-to-month changes in market psychology can open up opportunities to sell land at a profit. Yet if one subscribes to the efficient-market hypothesis, it must follow that spec-ulating in land is (for the most part) betting on being able to influence events so as to increase the rents flowing to ownership of a particular parcel, or at the very least, being able to convince participants in pro-spective land markets that a particular tract has been undervalued. In short, speculation in land is financially rewarding to those who can cause unanticipated things to happen that will increase, or appear to increase, the stream of future rents accruing to land generally or to spe-cific tracts of land of which those speculators are seized and possessed.

In the nineteenth century, such motivation caused land speculators to influence decisions about routes for railroads so as to favor their hold-ings. In the twentieth century, it has caused landholders to be concerned about interchanges for interstate highways, sitings of airports, and con-struction of water and sewer lines and other facilities that affect the rents that particular parcels of land can command. Such motivation has caused land speculators, operating under the guise of "developers," to lobby for highway bypasses to relieve traffic congestion in downtowns, thus opening up opportunities for development of suburban shopping centers, which drain the downtowns and lead to a collapse in down-town real estate values. Now it is causing speculators, or developers, to become leaders in downtown redevelopment in the hope of bringing the traffic back to Main Street.

I do not mean to imply that speculation is evil and that those engaged in it are immoral. Economists understand that speculation is a necessary thing to keep markets fluid and that speculators can perform useful economic functions by assuming the risk of holding assets. While land (as distinguished from real estate, which is land mixed with capital) will exist whether anyone invests in it or not, the U.S. system of land law requires that someone hold title to land. Land speculation, therefore, is inevitable in our system of land law. Human beings, being the acquisitive creatures they are, will therefore seek to use every opportunity available to realize the maximum gains from their holdings. Becoming involved in the making of public policy so as to maximize land rents on particular parcels is their right as citizens, and it is no surprise that many exercise that right with vigor.

In attempting to shape land policy, land speculators have two key objectives. The first is to obtain policies that promote economic growth. While it may be possible for speculators to achieve capital gains on land-holdings in an economy that is stagnant or contracting, the odds of achieving such gains are increased if the general economic environment is one of expansion. To the extent that economic expansion benefits the general public at large, the activities of land speculators in supporting economic growth policies are socially valuable.

The second objective, however, is to influence the distribution of economic growth so that it is not geographically neutral. Land-use policy is essentially about geography. Hence, it is the pursuit of the second objective that causes land speculators to be active participants in land-use policy decisions. Because land-use policy decisions have the potential for greater benefits and greater costs to land speculators than to ordinary citizens, land speculators have much stronger incentives than ordinary citizens to bear the transaction and information costs required to influence land-use policy.

Therein lies a problem. Given that the growth was going to occur some place, the struggle of land speculators to influence its geography is a zero-sum game. The investments in transaction and information costs made by speculators as part of their struggle to obtain a disproportion-ate share of the resulting rents are deadweight losses to society such as occur with any type of rent-seeking behavior.[14]

Is there any possible institutional arrangement that could prevent these societal losses? In the abstract, there are such arrangements, and it may be that there are practical adjustments in institutions that would minimize the losses. But so long as there are private property rights in land that allow the owner to capture unanticipated increases in rents, it is reasonable to expect that there will be agents who will speculate in land in hopes of capital gains.

It is possible to conceive of minimal governments that deliberately reduce activities having effects on geography. The "new resource economists" go beyond Buchanan and argue that one need only specify property rights fully and then government can (and should) step back and let the market operate.[15] Yet even if the very difficult technical and political problems in specifying property rights were overcome (a process that inevitably would be influenced by rent-seeking behavior), it is not realistic to expect that governments that perform minimum essential functions can avoid all activities that might favor one place over another. If governments do anything that affects the spatial distribution of economic activities, they will have an impact on land use, thus on land rents, and thus on land values. Much of what shapes land-use patterns inevitably is going to occur not in the marketplace but in the political arena.

That being the case, there is still another alternative: Adopt the reforms proposed by Henry George and tax away all increases in land rents. Such an approach would eliminate the incentive for land speculation, and consequently, it would eliminate the incentives for rent-seeking behavior. In the abstract, the Georgian approach has a great deal of appeal to land economists, but its revolutionary implications for private property rights in land cannot be denied. It is difficult to see any practical way to move from the existing system of property rights in land to a Georgian system without causing significant windfalls and wipeouts for those holding land at the time of the changeover. The likelihood of those windfalls and wipeouts is probably such as to make a Georgian-based reform politically unacceptable.

Conclusion: What Now?

If the logic of the public choice theorists makes the Progressive paradigm untenable, is it any longer legitimate to expect that governmental intervention can make the land market better serve the cause of efficiency? Probably not. Governmental policies and programs will continue to influence land-use patterns, and it seems highly unlikely that those policies and programs can be anything more than compromises among the special interests with sufficient stakes in political outcomes to justify bearing the information and transaction costs inherent in becoming involved in public choices.

This conclusion does not necessarily lead to despair, however. Information and transaction costs can be affected by technology. Anything that reduces the cost of accessing information will make it more likely that rational ordinary citizens, acting in their own self-interest, will become involved in shaping and implementing land-use policy. Anything that makes it less costly for ordinary citizens to communicate with other ordinary citizens will enable them to organize themselves into interest groups that challenge the power over land-use policy of other interest groups. Just as the printing press helped set the stage for modern democracy, recent advances in information and communications technology have the potential to lower information and transaction costs and bring more and more citizens into the public choice arena. As computer technology spreads and more people become comfortable using computerized data bases, as fax machines spread and new fiber-optic communications make it easier to be in touch with others located at a distance, the special interest groups that have historically influenced policy choices will face increased competition.

The challenge for land economists is to assist this process. New tools, like geographic information systems, offer opportunities not only for assembling and organizing more information but also for making it available in ways that are accessible to ordinary citizens. The technology supporting geographic information systems is not yet sufficiently advanced to make it feasible to offer access through personal computers in millions of private homes, but the rapid advances in the technology suggest that such a possibility may not be beyond reach for long. Land economists can play a useful role by helping collect data relevant to land-use policy that are compatible with the requirements of geographic information systems and by developing user friendly analytic tools that might be accessible to lay citizens interested in asking "what if" questions of geographic information systems.

In the end, none of these things may make a great deal of difference. Yet just as increased competition improves the efficiency of market outcomes, increased competition in the public choice arena can be expected to improve (at least, at the margin) land-use policy outcomes. Even such modest improvements, however, are unlikely if land economists and others interested in land policy continue to be beguiled by the idealism of Progressivism. The public choice theorists teach us that the real problems in land-use policy are barriers to entry in the form of information and transaction costs. Those costs can be lowered, and while one should not expect utopia even if the costs are zero, finding ways to reduce those costs is the only rational hope for improving land-use policy.

Notes

James Hite is professor, Department of Agricultural Economics, Clemson University.

1. See B.L. Benson, "Why Are Congressional Committees Dominated by 'High Demand' Legislators? — A Comment on Niskanen's 'View of Bureaucrats

and Politicians,'" *Southern Economic Journal* 48(1981):68-77; A. Breton, *The Economic Theory of Representative Government* (Chicago: Aldine, 1974); J.M. Buchanan and G. Tullock, *The Calculus of Consent* (Ann Arbor: University of Michigan Press, 1968); R. Coase, "The Problem of Social Cost," *Journal of Law and Economics* 3(1960):1-44; M.T. Maloney and R.E. McCormick, "A Positive Theory of Environmental Quality Regulation," *Journal of Law and Economics* 25(1987):99-123; D.C. Mueller, *Public Choice* (New York: Cambridge University Press, 1979); W.A. Niskanen, *Bureaucracy and Representative Government* (Chicago: Aldine, 1971); G.J. Stigler, "The Theory of Economic Regulation," *Bell Journal of Economics and Management* 2(1971):3-21.

2. R. Nelson, "The Economics Profession and Public Policy," *Journal of Economic Literature* 25(1987):52.

3. Quoted in Nelson, ibid., 53.

4. See A. Schmid, *Property, Power and Public Choice* (New York: Praeger, 1987).

5. See G. Meeks, Jr., *State Conservation and Growth Management Policy* (Washington, D.C.: National Conference of State Legislatures, 1990):7-11.

6. B.H. Siegan, *Land Use Without Zoning* (Lexington, Mass.: Lexington Books, 1972); *Other People's Property* (Lexington, Mass.: Lexington Books, 1976); *Planning Without Prices* (Lexington, Mass.: Lexington Books, 1977).

7. F.A. v. Hayek, *The Road to Serfdom* (Chicago: University of Chicago Press, 1944).

8. See R.L. Stroup and J.A. Baden, *Natural Resources: Bureaucratic Myths and Environmental Management* (San Francisco: Pacific Institute for Public Policy Research, 1983):39-51.

9. See J.C. Hite, *Room and Situation: The Political Economy of Land-Use Policy* (Chicago: Nelson-Hall, 1979).

10. A. Sandmo, "Buchanan on Political Economy," *Journal of Economic Literature* 27(1990):51.

11. Ibid., 52.

12. A. Randall and E.N. Castle, "Land Resources and Land Markets," in A.V. Kneese and J.L. Sweeney, eds., *Handbook of Natural Resource and Energy Economics*, Vol. II (Amsterdam: North-Holland, 1985).

13. Ibid., 604.

14. See A.O. Krueger, "The Political Economy of the Rent-Seeking Society," *American Economic Review* 64(1974):291-303.

15. See Stroup and Baden, *Natural Resources.*

14

Public and Private Interests in Land in the United Kingdom

Alan Harrison

To understand how the British do things and how best they might attempt to change them, it is important to be aware of the historical basis of current arrangements. Only in that way can land's privileged tax status and the lack of statistical information about land be explained. History also helps one understand why access to the countryside in Britain is so often forbidden.

The Influence of the Past on Current Land Policies

At the beginning of the twentieth century, farming in Britain had long been exposed to the pressure of foreign competition. Its farms were large by West European standards, and 90 percent of them were held on a cash rental basis. The landlord was responsible for the provision and upkeep of fixed capital, and the tenant provided the working capital.

So much and more is well known. What is much less well understood is the extent to which landownership was rooted in politics. To possess land was to have access to political power, and the pattern of ownership that developed in its pursuit became highly concentrated in the hands of the aristocracy and squirearchy. The landowners were unwilling to believe this was the case, but when a count was made in 1875, based on the valuation rolls that existed at that time, it revealed a degree of concentration even greater than their critics had claimed. In total there were some million owners, but about 75 percent of the land was owned by about 7,000 of them, and 25 percent by a mere 710 (less than 1 percent of all owners). The large owners were politically powerful. They exercised enormous influence in both houses of Parliament. On their estates (the totality of farms each one possessed) they were able to negotiate tenancy contracts that severely restricted the tenant's freedom to manage the land in ways that were likely to hinder the owner's right to hunt, shoot, and fish. More generally, the public was denied the right of entry to properties, as well as access to public rights-of-way that had been in use since times beyond memory. The problem still awaits resolution today, and it is an issue to which this paper will return.

Despite its apparent financial stability, the landlord-tenant system has declined over this century from about 90 percent of land to a little over 30 percent. This has come about through massive sales to sitting tenants, especially during the severe farming depression in the 1920s and 1930s and because of legislation favoring tenants that resulted in the sale or taking in hand of high-priced, vacant-possession (unlet) land in more recent years of farming prosperity. Nevertheless, the concentration of private ownership has persisted to an astonishing degree given the efforts by society to bring about greater equality of ownership of wealth. Studies by individual researchers (Harbury and Rubinstein are noteworthy examples[1]) and a glimmer afforded by official statistics bear out this claim: In 1976, 1 percent of owners owned 52 percent of privately owned land, 5 percent owned 74 percent.

Three reasons explain the remarkable survival of concentrated landownership. First, government statisticians have never made any sustained effort to document landownership. Consequently, critics have never had a clearly identified target at which to aim. The origins of this statistical secrecy, if not entirely its survival, are found in the position of authority held by the large landowners and by those depending on and supporting them.[2] There still are no official statistics of landownership. Second, the preservation of estates in land has been a priority of the owners, who have created means to facilitate their ownership. In particular, estate-owning families have regularly restricted ownership to lifetime tenancies (strict settlements) in order to protect their wealth against the actions of profligate heirs. Third, and most important from a national standpoint, the legislature, with the approval and influence of landowners, has created a fiscal and legal environment that, given a modicum of business sense and good fortune, goes a long way to ensuring survival. In particular, landowners have enjoyed modest levels of taxation.

Landownership's historical and political genesis, then, combined with long periods of modest levels of taxation of wealth generally and land in particular, makes it easier to understand the survival and continuing influence of massive fortunes in land. Nevertheless, the system has had and still has its active, influential, and talented critics. Not only were they very nearly victorious in their own day, but many of their arguments are still employed by critics today.

Protests against large-scale landownership on the grounds that it deprived the poor of the means to produce food abound in British history, and even in the seventeenth century caused "rebels" to question the right to private property at all. But the model for later anti-landlordism is based mainly on Henry George's arguments. They received perhaps their most intellectually telling presentation in the campaigning of Joseph Chamberlain in the late nineteenth century for a tax on land values, but their most dynamic and rousing one in the oratory of David Lloyd George at the beginning of the twentieth century. As chancellor of the exchequer in the 1908 Liberal government, Lloyd George proposed, first, that a tax of a penny per pound (less than .05 percent) be levied on the capital value of all undeveloped urban and suburban land and, second and more threatening, that a tax of 20 percent be levied on any increase in the value of land resulting from public decision making and spending on development. The narrow issue of taxation became obscured, however, by the larger issue of the Lords' right to block finance legislation. The political alliances being formed weakened the cause of taxing land, and, although the government set up a Land Inquiry Committee, which recommended a number of what were considered radically left-wing measures, including the taxation of land and the funding of local authorities, the onset of World War I brought all to naught. Worse still, the Labour government of 1929 did not exist long enough to make law the land valuation act it introduced in 1931. "The cup was dashed from the lips of the landless.... The cause of land taxation had been won and lost again, this time within four months. It was never to be embodied in a statute again."[3]

It had been a remarkably close-run thing, but having lost the battle, that was that. The results were far reaching and require examination. On the one hand, local authorities were deprived of income from the taxation of land, what the British call *the rates*. On the other hand, land was to enjoy—and continues to enjoy—fiscal concessions over other forms of property. Yet another political watershed was to come with the end of World War II in 1945.

Labour Wins the Election After World War II

Central Planning Takes Over

Although farming depression and governmental neglect had quickly resumed at the end of World War I despite the nearly disastrous effects of the wartime blockade, the lessons of World War II were better learned. Laissez-faire was not to be trusted. The Socialist government that came into power immediately after the war ushered in an era of multisectoral central planning. Two measures are of particular interest: the 1947 Agriculture Act and the 1947 Town and Country Planning Act.

The two measures remain the major acts in force in their respective spheres, but they are by no means the only areas of interest here that the government at that time examined with a view to legislation. Indeed, even during the war the authorities had studied how, when the war was over, the countryside might be protected from urban development and how the public might have greater access to it. One of the more important of those early studies was the Dower report on *National Parks in England and Wales*,[4] and the Attlee (Socialist) government took steps immediately after being elected to legislate on the basis of it.

Earlier attempts to control development had been concerned particularly with the demolition of dangerous and unsanitary houses and, later, with the restriction of ribbon development. As Dawson points out, however,

> The control over land-use change afforded by [this] legislation was weak. Participation in planning by the local councils was optional; the mechanisms for the approval and amendment of plans were cumbersome; and the threat of having to pay compensation to landowners and developers who were prevented from carrying out their proposals discouraged local authorities from taking decisive action to deflect development away from the sites preferred by the market. By 1942 only about 5 percent of England and Wales was covered by approved schemes, although plans were being prepared for about two-thirds of the country.[5]

The 1947 Town and Country Planning Act was an altogether more powerful and comprehensive piece of legislation than anything that had existed before. Local authorities had to draw up development plans for their areas of jurisdiction; developers had to obtain planning permission from the appropriate local authority and their plans had to fit in with the authority's overall plan; and any increase in land value due to planning permission being granted (betterment) had to be paid over to the authorities in the form of a development charge.

The central government had a particularly powerful role in this planning system. It set out the broad terms of development policies, ratified and amended the local authority's development plans, and decided appeals against refusals to grant planning permission. The hierarchical nature of this system and the control its upper tiers exercise contrast with the U.S. system. The British system also contrasts in that, whereas Americans frequently appeal to the judiciary to settle planning disputes, the British seldom do.

It is evident that, had the philosophies and faith in central planning shared by British Socialists in the 1940s and 1950s continued to ensure their reelection, the pattern and thrust of legislation in later decades would have been very different from what they were. Nevertheless, it is because of what the Socialists left out of the planners' control that the land-use planning debate today is so contentious. In addition to development by central government and the so-called statutory undertakers of development (e.g., the nationalized industries), what was left out of the 1947 act was farming, improvements for agricultural purposes, and afforestation. Their omission was to prove crucial.

The 1947 Agriculture Act and the Development of Agricultural Fundamentalism

Not only was farming left free by the Town and Country Planning Act to develop, it was given massive technical and financial assistance to do so. Product prices were supplemented and guaranteed, and input prices were subsidized. New technology in the form of machines, superior breeds of crops and animals, and a whole range of chemical inputs that greatly enhanced disease and pest control became available. As scales of production were increased, there was massive replacement of labor by capital. As a result, output has increased to the point that it cannot be sold at world prices; upland and hill farming, dairying, and forestry have expanded far beyond what they would have been without massive financial support (all are currently under severe financial pressure nevertheless); and large areas of marsh- and moorland have been "improved," to the increasingly severe chagrin of the rest of society.

If it borders on the incredible that farming and forestry activities were not regarded as "development" while virtually the rest of society's land-using activities were, bear in mind, first, that farming's technological revolution was not foreseen by pre- and postwar conservationists, let alone politicians, and second, that urban sprawl was both foreseen and feared. As Shoard so aptly put it, "It was the speculative builder who was seen as the main threat to the countryside; the farmer was the willing but ailing guardian of the landscape who should be given whatever support he needed."[6] So great was this confidence that automatic planning consent was deemed to exist for all roads and buildings for forestry and farming, provided the said structures did not exceed 5,000 square feet in area.

Another, less publicized but no less far-reaching component must be added to this postwar saga of farming priority in British land-use planning: the totality of fiscal arrangements relating to property and local authority finance that were gradually put in place. Foremost among these measures was the continued exemption of farmland from rates (local authority taxes on all forms of property and the main source of locally generated income). When the enumeration of private landowner-ship took place in 1875, local valuation rolls already existed for levying rates on farmland. In 1929, however, in response to persistent pressures from the National Farmers' Unions, the government did away with them and they have not been levied since. Farmland was completely exempted and farmhouses partly exempted.

The consequences of the above have been far reaching. Domestic and business properties have been subjected to a direct and selective tax, although businesses do not have the right to vote in local elections. The funding of local authorities has been rendered less viable than it other-wise would have been. Local authorities have been particularly exposed to macrofunding effects as the economy's fortunes have waxed and waned with the magnitude of the public sector borrowing requirement and the consequent rising and falling of interest rates. The need for sup-plementation from central funds has been correspondingly increased, and the control of local authorities by central government has become harder to resist. Poundage rates on property values have varied more among local authorities than they would otherwise, and investment and employ-ment patterns have been correspondingly distorted. The danger that irre-sponsible voting patterns would emerge in some areas has increased.

In addition, rents on domestic properties have been controlled, but tax concessions have been granted to mortgagee purchasers of houses and of farms for occupation and letting. The supply of domestic proper-ties to rent has been depressed, and the demand for houses and farms has been exaggerated. Additionally, owner-occupied houses have been exempted from the capital gains tax. The result is that the British hous-ing market has become not only buoyant but highly speculative and volatile. Between 1971 and 1973 house prices in the United Kingdom increased by 60 percent in real terms, only to fall again by over one-half (real) over the following four years. Between 1982 and 1989 house prices rose by over 90 percent. This irregularity reflects, in particular, the value of building sites for which planning permission has been granted and is, in turn, reflected in market prices of farmland. Corresponding markets in Germany, for example, are much less unpredictable.[7]

Agricultural Landlords and Tenants

At the same time as the various fiscal measures were being put in place, the security of tenure granted to farm tenants was being extended to the point that a landlord found it virtually impossible to repossess his farm during his tenant's lifetime. (And beyond the tenant's lifetime, al-though only for a few years, with the help of legislation in the later

1970s—later rescinded, but even this fell short of the anti-landlord measures enacted by other member states of the European Community, EC.) Rents, which remained freely negotiable, although subject to arbitration within the tenancy legislation, came to represent a relatively modest return on the price of farms subject to tenancy, but, being open to review every three years, a rate of return that might, hopefully, offset the wealth-depleting impacts of the inflation that was besetting the British economy, particularly in the 1970s. There was also the possibility of enhancing rents by improving a farm's layout and its associated stock of buildings and other fixed equipment, and better still, at some stage, the chance to sell with vacant possession (unlet) and maybe, even, for development.

By the 1960s it was evident that the market in farmland was no longer a narrow, technologically constrained one.[8] Quite quickly the financial institutions (property companies, insurance companies, and pension fund holders) entered the market for let farmland. There was great interest in this development, as well as naive extrapolation of trends based on the amounts being bought at that time. Those dramatic, short-term movements were not sustained, however, as inflation subsided and farming fortunes deteriorated. The data in Table 14.1 show how quickly the change in interest came about.

While their involvement lasted, the financial institutions played a vital role in the greatly diminished market for new farm lettings. They did not restrict their interests exclusively to the let market, however, and the estimate that 19 percent of their land was farmed in hand is probably too low.[9]

TABLE 14.1 Net Sales(–) and Purchases of Vacant Possession and Tenanted Agricultural Land by Property Companies and Other Financial Institutions in England, Selected Years, 1978-1988 (hectares; 1 hectare = 2.47 acres)

| | Sales(–) and Purchases | | |
	Vacant Possession	Tenanted	Total
1978	9,319	8,476	17,795
1980	8,988	4,972	13,969
1982	6,399	5,326	11,725
1984	1,744	302	2,046
1986	–1,755	–695	–2,470
1988	–8,922	–3,542	–12,464

Sources: Ministry of Agriculture, Fisheries and Food; Agriculture Department (Welsh Office).

The longer term tendency for landlords to reduce the amount of farmland they rent to others, either by selling it to sitting tenants or outsiders or by taking it in hand to farm themselves, continues, although only slowly. During the 1980s the rate of loss of land from the rental sector was about 1.5 to 2 percent a year; most of that land was taken in hand or sold to sitting tenants, and only a small amount was sold as vacant possession. Legislation to increase the security of tenure of one generation of tenants has evidently been at the cost of reduced availability of tenancies for later would-be tenants.

In contrast, the amount of land held under partnership agreements outside the law relating to landlord and tenant has grown significantly in recent years, and attempts have also been made to legislate for medium (five-year) letting periods. Over the past two decades, land agents have directed more and more attention to designing ways of letting land without creating secure tenancies. The struggle by landlord and tenant to come to mutually acceptable agreements that are not unacceptably constrained by the law has not yet run its full course. The situation within the EC is even more complex and generally more unfavorable to landlords than it is in the United Kingdom. The final balance, however, is complicated by the advantages, broadly considered, enjoyed by farming over the postwar decades with regard to capital taxation, both on wealth and on its increments.

Wealth (inheritance) taxes in Britain, unlike those in other EC member states where the wealth-spreading effects of the Napoleonic Code have been greater, are levied on the total amount of wealth in the possession of the deceased at the time of death. Because they are progressive, moreover, they are designed to hit large fortunes hard, and no incentive is afforded the wealthy to avoid them by spreading their fortunes widely at death.

Despite the progressive rate of death duties, the survival of large family-owned estates in land has been remarkable. The explanation is twofold. First, legislation has regularly, although to varying degrees, left open the chance to give away wealth before death (with progressive savings up to complete avoidance if seven years elapse between gift and death). Second, trust ownership has been developed to enable landholdings to be spread widely among members of families.

The Attempts to Tax Development Gains

Further explanations are required of capital gains taxes and issues of so-called betterment. The severe control over and restriction of grants of planning permission by British planning authorities make the value of those grants that are issued all the greater. The expectation that such grants will eventually be made inevitably has its impact on farmland prices, and enormous, and widely resented, capital gains occur whenever planning permission is granted. The 1974 White Paper *Land*, which led to the Community Land Act of 1975, expressed the view of the government of the day as follows:

> The growth in value, more especially of urban sites, is due to no expenditure of capital or thought on the part of the ground owner, but entirely owing to the energy and enterprise of the community ... it is undoubtedly one of the worst evils of our present system of land tenure that instead of reaping the benefit of the common endeavor of its citizens a community has always to pay a heavy penalty to its ground landlords for putting up the value of their land.[10]

Henry George might easily have drafted the above paragraph a century earlier. Yet the Community Land Act of 1975 was the third attempt by postwar Labour governments to capture betterment values. And it fared no better than its predecessors. Like them, it aimed ultimately at the ownership of all development land by local authorities.

The program envisaged was as follows. First, local authorities were empowered to acquire, by negotiation or compulsorily, land needed for development over a 10-year period and to link that stock to a rolling 5-year program of actual development. At the end of that 10 years, they would be required to embark on a program of purchase of development land. In the meantime, betterment gains were to be collected through a development land tax (at a basic rate of 80 percent). Because all purchases of land for development by local authorities would be at current-use value, all development values would, it was envisaged, be effectively nationalized. No betterment values would be generated, and therefore, no device was needed to tax them away. The development land tax would no longer be required.

In the end, this scheme to municipalize land scarcely got off the ground—less than 2,500 acres were acquired in two years. In part this was because local authorities were particularly disadvantaged financially at that time, so that although property prices were relatively depressed few purchases fell within their scope. The scheme was abolished by a Conservative government in 1979, although the development land tax lasted until 1985; the capital gains tax of 30 percent is still in effect.

Apart from the costliness of collecting the development land tax, the unrealistically high level at which it was levied and the lack of success in identifying betterment values as such emphasize the need for the two major political parties, under the first-past-the-post method of election which the British employ, to develop an agreed philosophical approach to the subject. There is little, if any, sign that this will happen, however.

The precise rate of taxation levied on capital gains is not the only issue about which society in Britain should be concerned when seeking to evaluate the net cost of controlling social and other capital formation in the way it does. Also relevant are local authority-developer relationships and how they bear on the possible misappropriation of public funds by public servants and on the types of public good that developers are regularly induced to provide in return for permission to develop private housing and other projects. Among other things, do current arrangements achieve economies of scale? What are the transaction costs and problems when major schemes are involved? The subject seems to generate much less public debate than it merits.

Given the low proportion (25 percent) of local finances that are now raised locally, is it not time, as Muellbauer argues,[11] not only to take up the Layfield Committee's rejected recommendation (made in 1976) to introduce a local income tax within the framework of national income taxation, but also, this time, to supplement it with the taxation of imputed rents from land? By this means, not only would local finances be placed on a broader and healthier footing, but major fiscal distortions affecting the property market would be removed. Strangely, Muellbauer makes no reference to farming in a paper that pleads for a more comprehensive approach to fiscal issues.

Agricultural Fundamentalism at Bay: The Current Debate

The current agricultural debate embraces three issues that although overlapping, nevertheless provide helpful separate points of departure from which the subject can be examined. The issues are access, pollution, and planning and betterment.

Access

In Britain there is no automatic right of entry to a piece of land unless right of access is indicated. To enter a field, park, or garden is, therefore, in most cases to trespass. Trespass, however, is not a crime but a tort, that is, something against which only a civil action can be brought. Moreover, if such an action was brought, there would be no possibility of securing compensation unless damage to the property or person could be proved. The widely displayed sign that "trespassers will be prosecuted" is a completely hollow threat. Nevertheless, it is a source of great annoyance to all who wish to enjoy the countryside at first hand. Support is growing for the argument that right of access should always apply unless legally and expressly forbidden.

It is by no means certain, however, that such all-embracing right of access will be given to the public. Only as recently as 1985 an attempt was made to make trespassing a crime because of the problems arising from the number of caravan dwellers and their vehicles entering private property. And even more recently, press and radio comment called attention to corresponding problems because of the entry of people, their dogs, and their four-wheel-drive vehicles onto privately owned chalk downlands in order to hunt hares.

Despite this rather curious legal situation, the country is cross-crossed by a complex network of public footpaths, or rights-of-way. In England and Wales, they cover an estimated 120,000 miles, although that is much less than in the past. Such rights-of-way are much less common in Northern Ireland and in Scotland, and they seldom exist overseas. The protection and addition to public rights-of-way was yet another issue to which the postwar Attlee government addressed itself, in particular through the 1949 National Parks and Access to the Countryside Act (England and Wales only).

The Highways Act of 1835 had already made obstructing a public right-of-way (a footpath or bridleway) an offense. However, proving that a right-of-way existed (either from public record or from evidence of long-uninterrupted use—in practice usually 20 years) was quite another matter until the 1949 act required county councils to map all rights-of-way in their area. This marked an important departure, and although straying from the right-of-way constituted trespass, such rights-of-way could not be removed without obtaining public approval. Over a thousand formal applications to alter such paths are made every year, most of which are granted, so the public must be vigilant if its rights are not to be lost. It is a task at which the Ramblers' Association has worked hard and to good purpose for a number of decades now.

As Shoard points out,[12] however, a particular problem arises for the Ramblers' Association as unofficial watchdog over rights-of-way on woodland sold by the Forestry Commission to private persons. The commission has regularly allowed the public to visit its forests and has permitted the existence of footpaths for this purpose, although only as a "permissive" not a "public" right. The commission, however, does not reveal the names of persons who buy its woodlands because of what it calls "commercial confidentiality." The commission's attitude is yet another example of an arrangement that frustrates the public interest, and it takes the enthusiasm, competence, and stamina of a good detective to unravel and bring ownership to light.

Commons are also areas where ancient and by no means well-understood or well-publicized rights often apply. Commons are areas where the rights of persons other than the owner apply. The rights of the other persons, in effect, determine the type of common in question. First, there might be commons on which certain individuals are legally entitled to carry out some carefully specified activity (e.g., to take turf or graze animals). Second, the common might be wasteland. Third, the common might be land that is publicly owned and managed for the good of the community.

There are no commons, as such, in Scotland or Northern Ireland, although land of corresponding status exists. However, in England and Wales they extend to an estimated 1.5 million acres. Curiously, the public has complete freedom to wander at will on only one acre of commons in five. Elsewhere, apart from on footpaths, the charge of trespass might easily arise.

Should an owner seek to enclose common land, the consent of the commoners (i.e., those holding rights on the common) must be obtained. In an attempt to clarify who those persons were, a royal commission was set up in 1955, and a Commons Registration Act was passed in 1965 requiring county councils to register all commons in their areas. The act resulted in commoners' rights being recorded, but it did not grant the right of access by the public that the royal commission had recommended. Further legal protection of commons stems from the duty to provide a compensating area (usually more) if a common is acquired by compulsory purchase for development purposes. In addition, the 1925 Law of Property Act granted the legal right of access for "air and exercise" to commons within urban areas and prohibited building and fencing on commons that "impede public access."

Following the 1925 Law of Property Act, deeds of access to commons were granted up to the mid-1930s. However, the war and early postwar years revealed the possibilities of farming and forestry on such lands, and the practice was not continued. In his report *National Parks in England and Wales*, cited above, Dower had deplored the block planting of conifers by the Forestry Commission, but he had not expected the practice to be continued after the war. He was quite wrong in this respect and in failing to anticipate the heavy subsidizing by government of private plantings as time went on.

The Forestry Commission is obligated to consult with conservation bodies with regard to the expansion of forestry, but at the end of what can be very time-consuming examination and appeals procedures, the Forestry Commission and its regional advisory committees have the final say, even after the view of the appropriate minister of state has been obtained. So far as the commission's own planting is concerned, it is up to the local authorities to approach the commission (and not the other way around), but in the event of disputes, the minister who is invited to arbitrate rules and not merely advises. There are good grounds for arguing that the procedures for consultation are not democratic. An insufficiently wide range of persons and bodies participates, and the deliberations are not made public.

Agricultural Pollution

The debate on agricultural pollution has become more polarized as it has developed. One part has become increasingly focused on site-specific toxic emissions and, therefore, increasingly subjected to expert scientific analysis. The other part has remained focused on more general "environmental deterioration," which makes it hard, if not impossible, to identify who benefits and who is harmed, let alone to quantify cost and benefits. Below, the more important of the specific types of pollution are described briefly in turn. The environmental deterioration question is then examined mainly in terms of the measures being taken to reduce it, namely, legislation on environmentally sensitive areas (ESAs) and sites of special scientific interest (SSSIs).

Specific Pollution Problems

Noise. Although the noise nuisance resulting from farming has never been quantified, even in terms of the crude number of complaints, the noise generated is modest by industrial, transport, and general urban standards. On the other hand, the noise of milking machines and grain driers, the two worst offenders, can come at particularly early and particularly late hours and be all the more resented on that account.

Smells. Information provided by the Institution of Environmental Health Officers reveals that there were 556 complaints about smells arising from slurry in 1987-88 and 696 in 1989-90. Complaints about smells emanating from farm buildings numbered 310 in 1987-88 and 379 in 1989-90. The Ministry of Agriculture is currently drafting a code of good agricultural practice to avoid smells from spreading slurry and from housed livestock.

Smoke. As of 1993 the burning of straw and stubble will be illegal. The National Society for Clean Air, which monitors smoke pollution, reported that, in some areas in 1990, there was a nuisance of dark smoke coming from burning waste material, especially tires, on farms.

Food Safety. The 1990 Food Safety Act requires that environmental health officers ensure that food premises are properly constructed and run. Farm shops and other farm premises more directly concerned with products at the consumer end of the food chain are required to register under the act. Operators are required to be properly trained.

Water. Water use and water pollution are probably the most serious site-specific pollution problems. Not only does water taken from rivers for irrigation reduce river flows, it is likely, on its return, to be contaminated to varying degrees with pollutants (nitrates in particular), as is rain falling onto cropland. The threat is by no means confined to inorganic as distinct from organic fertilizers, nor is it one related in a simple way to local topography. Rather, it appears to be closely related to the nature of the intervening vegetation, certain types of which are much better suited to intercepting pollutants.

It is becoming increasingly common for water companies to offer farmers reduced rentals in return for adhering to certain constraints in order to cut down pollution of aquifers. The use of constrained tenancy agreements is also a feature of farming in areas designated as nitrogen sensitive.

General Environmental Deterioration

Currently, the public and legislators are focusing a great deal of attention on environmentally sensitive areas and sites of special scientific interest. The latter are widely regarded as novel features, yet they have existed for four decades. Under the National Parks and Access to the Countryside Act of 1949, the Nature Conservancy (later to become the Nature Conservancy Council) is required to notify local authorities of what areas within their jurisdiction are of special scientific interest. These are sites that, regardless of area, include the best remaining examples of particular wildlife habitats, provide a good environment for rare plants and animals, or contain other interesting geological or physiographical features. Such sites now cover some 7 percent of Britain.

The ESA scheme, which dates only from the mid-1980s, is designed to reduce the damage to the landscape from intensive forms of farming by paying farmers to follow approved management systems. The scheme has received considerable publicity and Minister of Agriculture Gummer takes pride in it: "We have led the way in Europe in developing the schemes for Environmentally Sensitive Areas. Other Member States are now following our lead and it is clear that the EC Commission wants to encourage further the wider adoption of environmentally sensitive farming practices."[13] Nevertheless, ESAs extend to only a little over 250,000 acres, less than 1 percent of the area of England and Wales. Payments to farmers in ESAs are based on standard packages; farmers in SSSIs are compensated for the loss of profits.

Some idea of the size of the task of environmental protection facing these and other schemes can be gained from the finding of a Department of the Environment Countryside Commission survey[14] that, between 1947 and 1980, England and Wales experienced a 22 percent reduction in hedgerows and a 25 percent reduction in "semi-natural" habitats. Additionally, a Nature Conservancy Council study[15] concluded that, between 1949 and 1984, 80 percent of limestone grasslands, 50 percent of lowland mires, 30 to 50 percent of lowland woodlands, 40 percent of lowland heath, and 30 percent of upland moors had been lost or seriously damaged. More recent studies also document the continuing loss of moors and heathland to cropland in the national parks and also serve to emphasize that so-called national parks in Britain are privately owned, occupied, and exploited, albeit subject to special rules.

Planning and Betterment Issues

The starting point from which legislation to reform agricultural and environmental policy must begin is well recognized. There is widespread regret that so little of the postwar transformation of agriculture was foreseen by politicians and their professional advisers and that farming and forestry operations were, by definition, excluded from the sorts of control to which other sectors of the economy were subjected.

The transformation of rural communities that has taken place, however, is not a shallow technical one but rather a root-and-branch matter. Because rural land use was regarded in such an exclusive sense, displaced farm workers found it hard to find alternative employment in rural areas. A two-way migration began, but it was of unemployed rural workers into the towns and of commuting and retired urban classes into the villages, where not surprisingly, they were able to bid up the price of the few properties that came on the market beyond what the locals could afford. The newcomers, moreover, had enough funds left over to restore and expand the cottages and old farm buildings they had bought to create micropockets of luxury and convenience—*urbs in rure* indeed. The story does not end there, however, for once in place the new and new-style countryfolk do all within their power to prevent others from coming in to share (destroy) the positional goods they themselves have sought. Just what Hirsch, in his book *Social Limits to Growth*, warned years ago must happen.[16]

All the antifarming forces are still at work. Moreover, they are ranged against a greatly weakened farming industry. Farming is under great financial pressure because it cannot generate the profits required to service its debt, yet its low-geared balance sheet—because of high land prices—is still one that the typical industrialist envies.[17] The evidence of overproduction grows clearer and clearer, and its costs are more and more resented. Animal welfare and health scares are almost a regular feature of the all-too-indignant and alarmist tabloid press. The Ministry of Agriculture is less frequently appointed as final and sole arbiter in land-use appeals cases than in the past. Moreover, the claim that some farming act charged with constituting a nuisance is "good agricultural practice" is no longer the cast-iron defense it used to be.

The forward-looking philosophy required to inspire policymakers from now on is widely agreed and nowhere, probably, more elegantly and helpfully expressed than by Newby:

Rural Britain, which was once agricultural Britain, has become, and remains, middle-class urban Britain.... The public at large still tends to see the countryside in terms of landscapes and wildlife habitats, and rarely as a set of working communities ... The future growth of rural communities will not be provided by agriculture, nor even by forestry, but by manufacturing and service industries, especially those in the high technology sector which do not need to be based in the towns ... As far as town and country planning is concerned, there is a need to recognise that "appropriate" development in rural areas no longer constitutes blacksmiths and basket weaving. Hi-tech industrial development is not environmentally intrusive, nor is it locationally specific. For the first time since the Industrial Revolution, rural areas are in a position to compete on an equal basis with towns and cities for the benefits of technological innovation.[18]

The broad-based nature of the message is clearly set out and implies the need for planners to implement it. It is not envisaged as a process that will come about of its own accord as a result, say, of bringing the price of farming products and factors more nearly in line with world levels. It is something that can be "engineered," but is it a matter that can be handed over to the current engineers (of whom there is no small number)?

The Roles of Different Planning Bodies

Thus far, in this paper reference has been made only to government departments and to quasi-governmental bodies, but there is one very important nongovernmental body that fulfills a truly national role. It is the National Trust, formed in 1895 with the aim of "holding land in the public interest." It exists by public subscription and is accountable through its various management committees to its members. Its actions have inspired the setting up of government and quasi-governmental bodies. The first was the Council for the Preservation of Rural England.

Currently, the National Trust is the country's second largest public landowner. It has over 600,000 acres in its possession, much of it extensive areas of upland. It is a model owner in terms of the ways in which it marks out and maintains public footpaths on its properties. It regularly offers tenancies that constrain farming practices in order to protect the natural environment, and it assists its tenants to farm profitably under them.

But the National Trust and other landowners whose aim is conservation in one form or another (e.g., the Royal Society for the Protection of Birds) are, by the very nature of their purpose and the area in which they operate, bound to be subjected to a large measure of influence from central government. This arises because large tracts of land they hold are located in 10 areas designated as national parks subject to detailed control of land use as specified by the national park authorities. These authorities are composed of the nominees of central government and of members from the county councils where the parks are. The plans they are obliged to draw up must be approved by central government.

Central government has also been given powers (under the New Town Act of 1946) to designate new towns and to set population targets for them. In addition, central government also funds several regional organizations that have powers to acquire, develop, and reclaim land. The Highlands and Islands Development Board and the Scottish and Welsh development agencies are the most noteworthy examples.

Whereas the accountability of government departments is directly, through the minister, to Parliament (which has the additional advantage of Treasury examination and criticism), quasi-governmental bodies in Britain of the sort just referred to have been formed to achieve particular purposes with a minimum amount of accountability. This is certainly the case with the national parks and countryside commissions. In practice these rural authorities tend to provide services that have major spillover effects that, being essentially social in nature, are difficult if not impossible to quantify on the benefit side.

But as has already been argued, following Shoard,[19] there is evidence that the membership of committees responsible for administering these various bodies not only does not reflect the full range of public interests, it is heavily slanted toward landowners' interests. Moreover, the committees do not make public all the information in their possession, which is required if they are to be held accountable for their action (e.g., with regard to certain exemptions from transfer and inheritance taxes in return for granting public access to the lands involved).

As yet, the ESA and SSSI schemes have not been subjected to a full cost-benefit appraisal, but the cost of ESA schemes, which are based on standard management programs, appear to have settled at about £100 per hectare (1990 prices). The situation is radically different for SSSIs, which as noted are based on estimated profits foregone. Shoard provides the following example of alarming financial implications:

> Under a management agreement secured in 1948, the Nature Conservancy Council is committed to compensating Boulsbury Wood's owners ... to the tune of £21,150 every year. The agreement runs for sixty-five years and payments are index linked. At 1983 prices this means that the benefits to the owners will be £1.3 million. The nation will benefit from the conservation of the essential features of Boulsbury Wood. However, the agreement confers no extra public access to the Wood, so apart from what can be glimpsed from the public path and road the bulk of what is conserved must be left to the imagination of those citizens who will be contributing their money.[20]

In similar manner, the Scottish National Heritage, the corresponding body for Scotland, is engaged in negotiating conservation terms with the titled owner of the Altnaharra estate, described as "one of western Europe's last great wildernesses." The sum required to compensate the owner runs into millions of pounds and has prompted one member of the trust to comment, "It is a law that has been turned into a racket for people who have the time and money to take the National Conservancy Council for Scotland to the cleaners. It offers money to people who threaten to damage precious sites."[21]

Given the runaway costs on the above scale, the hit-and-miss nature of linking some conservation programs to inheritance tax concessions for individual owners, and the failure to guarantee full representation of the public's interests on the management boards of quasi-governmental bodies, it is not surprising to find increasing demands for more central control of conservation and access issues and for bringing out into the public domain all the information relating to the deals struck. To this end, it is sometimes argued that only if a tax is levied regularly on all rural land can "the principle that land is different from other capital assets" be established. Thereafter, not only would conservation contracts and associated payments disappear, but so would subsidies paid directly to farmers and foresters. "In place of the counterproductive mishmash that exists at present there would be a means of implementing a genuine national policy on the countryside which would not only be effective but also capable of responding quickly to change in society's demands from rural land."[22] The proposal appeals in that it would provide, point by point and acre by acre, a levy on which attention could be focused in the central evaluation of the symmetry of interests involved. That said, the implication that what society demands from rural land can not only be quickly identified but also traded for the relevant proprietary interests wherever they lie is hard to accept. Nevertheless, simplistic and overly optimistic though the proposal may be, it does aim at a comprehensive bargaining framework in which the goal of accountability is paramount, even if the full range of transaction costs is seldom taken into account.

Britain's Membership in the European Community

The issue of accountability is further complicated and probably not at all well understood by the British public because it is affected by Britain's membership in the EC. Under the terms of membership, Britain (like other member states) is required to take into account the environmental effects of development schemes (European Commission Directive, July 1988). But there is no machinery designed specifically to bring such matters to the attention of the relevant commissioner in Brussels. Certainly, Britain's Inspectorate of Pollution does not have the duty to report to Brussels. Rather, matters about which members of the public believe there are grounds for complaint must be brought directly to the attention of the EC's commissioner for the environment. And this members of the public do. (Recently, for example, the public has expressed concern in that way about the extension of the M3 motorway through Twyford Down in Hampshire and about other matters.) The disposition of complaints of this sort is that, in the event of their meriting it, the EC commissioner sends a letter to the appropriate minister of state—in the case of the M3 and Britain, the minister of transport.

The EC commissioner, however, has no power to compel Britain to conform. Indeed, only if an unsatisfactory reply is obtained from the British minister will a formal case be made by the commissioner that Britain is in breach of the relevant environmental directive. The matter might, and probably will, be settled amicably and to the commissioner's satisfaction at that point. But if it is not, the matter is placed before the European Court of Justice, which does have the authority to take steps to compel Britain (or any other member state) to toe the line.

All these operations, from the writing of initial letters of complaint to the final settlement in Luxembourg and every resultant action taken by everyone else affected, represent transaction costs. Whether they represent in the end better value for the money than any other possible set of arrangements will depend on facts—how they work in practice. But it is not in their favor in this respect if they are misunderstood, or resisted, by the persons affected.

Before concluding that relying on locally generated letters of complaint must inevitably be a costly way to alert a supranational body to the need for action, it is worth reflecting on just one example of how difficult it is to translate a local complaint into institutional reaction. On just one day (October 23, 1991) letters published in the London *Times* made the following points: (1) the European Commission had received over 5,000 letters about threatened damage to just one beauty spot; (2) local authorities bypass national authorities (like the Department of Transport) and raise matters with Brussels in the expectation of better treatment; and (3) where no single local authority exists (for example, for an area like the South Downs, which spans a number of counties, that the public might believe threatened), it might well prove impossible to set up a joint committee of local authorities capable of acting effectively.

A lead article in the London *Times* of October 19, 1991, expressed the view that the EC's environmental directive recognized that Europe has a "common heritage" with regard to such matters. However, whether it might ever go beyond achieving administrative conformity to the stage of embracing innovative policymaking is quite another matter. Moreover, the doubt is given even more substance when the interactions among the different formal EC institutions are taken into account.

The issue of policy initiation and institutional accountability within the EC is clouded with macropolitical problems. Additionally, questions of monetary policy on their own, without reference to issues of federalism and the surrender of national sovereignty, might easily—some would argue would inevitably—bring about a greater concentration of power in Europe. The contrast with the United States is striking and ironic in that it has been argued by one British authority that the American system of land-use planning has left local authorities free to encourage high-revenue-generating properties to come into their areas and to neglect the needs of the poorer members of society. The solution he advocates is to add a further tier of control to the existing planning machinery that can "override state, regional and township plans."[23]

In Britain, like it or not, a supranational tier of control exists. The fact that many do not know it is there and even fewer understand exactly how it works does not prevent the more articulate aggrieved from making use of it in order to put right things that their national institutions appear to fail to correct.

Conclusion

In the final instance, examination of British land-use planning arrangements reveals not only how many executive authorities have been set up, but that an even larger number of bodies have been created to harry, monitor, and challenge them. The situation is not reassuring, however. What is now in place in Britain is far from general and more impressive in terms of the machinery, as such, than in terms of what, in its totality, it is required to do. It is bureaucratic and only modestly tinged with the guiding hand of democracy. It has, as yet, made little effort at self-evaluation. Although much is made, by some administrators, of what is being done to monitor and evaluate the modest number of ESAs and SSSIs that have been set up, by no stretch of the imagination can it be represented as a basis for appraising the cost-effectiveness of what is currently being done.

Given the strength of the environmental lobby, it is surely time for a much more thoroughgoing debate. Given the wide-ranging fiscal distortions stemming from the plethora of central and local planning, taxation, pricing, and control measures bearing directly on land, its owners, and tenants and on its associated capital resources and their owners and tenants, it must be a more economically aware and forward-looking discussion than hitherto. Many are simply confused by the complexity of it all.

Even more serious in the longer run than bureaucratic complexity is likely to be the fact that Britain is earning the reputation for being rigidly biased toward the use of direct controls and prejudiced against using the many cost-effective economic instruments increasingly being employed in other countries. The latter include charges on effluents, users, and products, as well as administrative charges, like control and authorization fees. Moreover, the charges can be linked to differential taxes either to achieve more nearly neutral budget effects or to alleviate resulting social hardships.

Britain and also the United States have much to do in these respects. And Britian has much to undo in preparation.

Notes

Alan Harrison is professor, Department of Agricultural Economics and Management, University of Reading, U.K.

1. C.D. Harbury, "Inheritance in the Distribution of Personal Wealth, "*Economic Journal* 72, 228 (1962):845; and W.D. Rubinstein, *Men of Property* (London: Croom Helm, 1981).

2. Although the registration of title to land became law in England and Wales in 1862, an effective beginning was not made until the Land Registration Act of 1925. Progress has been slow, however, and although registration is obligatory in areas that collectively house the greater part of the country's population, many farming counties are scarcely touched by it. In addition to the direct disadvantages associated with the absence of registration of title at times of transfer, statistics of aggregate patterns of ownership have to be built up from small-scale, ad hoc studies and are, therefore, seriously deficient.

3. M. Shoard, *This Land Is Our Land* (London: Paladin Grafton Books, 1987):96.

4. Ministry of Town and Country Planning, *National Parks in England and Wales*, report by J. Dower, Cmnd 6628 (London: Her Majesty's Stationery Office, 1945).

5. A.H. Dawson, *The Land Problem in the Developed Economy* (London: Croom Helm, 1984):67.

6. Shoard, *This Land Is Our Land*, 429.

7. J. Muellbauer, *The Great British Housing Disaster and Economic Policy,* Economic Study No. 5 (London: Institute for Public Policy Research, 1990).

8. One result of this is that, despite continuing expert examination of the latest data on farmland prices and the multiplicity of factors influencing them, there is little agreement that a general model has yet been specified that is capable of finely tuned statistical explanation of past performance of the market, let alone one that possesses any significant predictive power.

9. A. Harrison, with R.B. Tranter, *The Changing Financial Structure of Farming*, Centre for Agricultural Strategy, Report 13 (University of Reading, 1989); The Rt. Hon. Lord Northfield, *Report of the Committee of Inquiry into the Acquisition and Occupancy of Agricultural Land*, Cmnd 7599 (London: Her Majesty's Stationery Office, 1979).

10. HMSO White Paper, *Land*, Cmnd 5730 (London: Her Majesty's Stationery Office, 1974).

11. Muellbauer, *The Great British Housing Disaster*.

12. Shoard, *This Land Is Our Land*, 263-264.

13. The Rt. Hon. John Gummer, M.P., "Opening Address," in Centre for Agricultural Strategy, *Agricultural Policy and the Environment*, Paper 24 (University of Reading, 1991):14.

14. Countryside Commission, *Monitoring Landscape Change* (Cheltenham, 1986).

15. Nature Conservancy Council, *Nature Conservancy in Great Britain* (Petersborough, 1984).

16. F. Hirsch, *Social Limits to Growth* (London: Routledge & Kegan Paul, 1977).

17. Harrison, *The Changing Financial Structure of Farming*.

18. H. Newby, "The Economic and Social Context of Farming and the Countryside Environment," in Centre for Agricultural Strategy, *Agricultural Policy and the Environment*.

19. Shoard, *This Land Is Our Land*.

20. Ibid., 452.

21. K. Gill, London *Times*, November 25, 1991.

22. Shoard, *This Land Is Our Land*, 530.

23. *Dawson, The Land Problem in the Developed Economy*, 183.

15

Britain, America, and the Rural Land-Use Bargain

Ronald J. Oakerson

A Key Difference in Land-Use Institutions

The institutional arrangements for rural land-use control in the United Kingdom and the United States differ in one key respect:

- In the United Kingdom, the base rule governing the conversion of farmland to nonagricultural use is a blanket restriction—conversion is prohibited (as a matter of national policy) unless special permission is granted for nonagricultural development by means of case-by-case administrative review.
- In the United States, the base rule is nearly the reverse—conversion is in general permitted (in the absence of national and, in most cases, state policy) unless local authorities choose to enact restrictions (still subject to constitutional standards that apply to any use of the police power).

Both arrangements are maintained with the support of farm constituencies, explained in part by associated tax policies. In the United Kingdom, agricultural land is exempt from property taxation, but strong efforts are made to tax away gains to landowners from the designation and sale of land for development purposes. In the United States, agricultural land is subjected to property taxation (although often according to special rules), but there is no discriminatory tax treatment of capital gains realized from the sale of agricultural land for nonagricultural purposes.

Conceivably, both institutional arrangements could reach the same result, that is, a comparable degree of farmland conversion. It is the difference in the assignment of transaction costs that distinguishes the

British and American systems of land-use control and that will account for different results. If the transaction costs of creating exceptions to the base rule are high, as might be expected in both cases, the likelihood is that both arrangements generate results that are considerably less than socially efficient. In Britain, there are the nearly inevitable distortions in the rural land market with respect to housing that follow from a blanket restriction on development, plus Harrison's suggestion that the *quid pro quo* for protecting farmland has not been adequate—that "society" might seek something more from the bargain than the mere preservation of farmland as open space. At stake are issues of public access and use, as well as the preservation of "natural" areas from conversion to agriculture or forestry. The American arrangement, while arguably underproviding for farmland preservation (even as open space), does offer a variety of institutional possibilities for generating local solutions to land-use problems that the market may not solve.

Institutional Alternatives Within the U.S. System

The basic institutional choice for controlling land use within the U.S. system is between (1) some use of local police power and (2) the collective purchase of development or use rights either by securing an easement or by contracting for certain restrictions on use. The second alternative operates through normal market transactions (or less likely, through an eminent-domain proceeding). Is there a principle for guiding the choice between these two institutional alternatives? Some guidance may be available from the *symmetry or asymmetry of interest* among the affected parties. Consider the following argument.

Where interests are fairly symmetrical, the parties can choose to give up a *liberty* (such as the liberty to develop farmland for nonagricultural use) in exchange for the *security* derived from a prohibition (such as zoning for agricultural use). The collective good obtained from the trade-off is the security that one's community will continue to be a farming community. It is a subjective trade-off, one that depends on farmers' preferences and the calculation of various risks. It is not unreasonable to suppose that a preference for farming as a way of life (not simply as an economic activity) would extend to preservation of the immediate farming community. However, farmers clearly differ—and there is some reason to believe that often farm communities differ—in their degree of attachment to farming. If there is substantial agreement among a community of farmers on the trade-off between liberty and security, the police power would appear to be a reasonable instrument of collective action—reasonable on market-equity principles. Each person gives up roughly equivalent liberties in exchange for a greater common good.

Where interests are asymmetrical, that is, where some parties are asked to incur a cost for the benefit of others, the police power is less justifiable and a purchase-of-easement or contractual approach would seem more appropriate in market-equity terms. If, for example, a local community is asked to forego development opportunities in order to provide amenities for others, the larger community should perhaps be required to pay for the acquisition of limited proprietary claims on the local community. Relatively "unspoiled" natural areas that provide recreation to nonresidents (such as the Adirondacks of New York State) represent this sort of problem.

To take a more complex example, if farmland preservation goes beyond preservation of open space to include restrictions on farming practice (e.g., preserving buildings), the risk to farmers potentially increases. Building preservation or, even more so, technology restriction potentially impairs the ability of local farmers to compete in commodity markets that extend far beyond the local community. Should the interest in preservation be strictly local, the risk of a less competitive farming community is simply part of the price of preservation; it affects the trade-off between liberty and security discussed above. If there is a larger interest in preservation, however, the purchase of rights-in-use has the advantage of compensating farmers for a loss of income. A one-time purchase of easement secures for the collectivity a permanent entitlement, but it exposes farmers to greater uncertainty and risk over time. A long-term contract subject to renegotiation leaves full property rights in the hands of the farmer, but it exposes the farmer to less risk of future loss.[1]

At the same time, the police power has greater flexibility than easements that "run with the land," to the extent that they do so. If preferences change, a community can modify zoning regulations, and variances from a zoning restriction on grounds of economic hardship are possible. Future generations are less bound by the decisions of their predecessors. Long-term contracts are also a more flexible instrument than easements. The choice of a particular legal instrument requires trade-offs that depend on judgments about an uncertain future. Both police-power and purchase-of-easement/contractual approaches may be appropriate and feasible in different circumstances. The freedom of state and local communities to choose among these institutional alternatives increases their capacity to craft solutions that satisfy the diverse time-and-place characteristics of specific problems.

Under the current line of constitutional interpretation by the U.S. Supreme Court, the reserved powers clause of the Tenth Amendment appears to pose no bar to the creation of a national system of land-use regulation. Two lines of decisions have combined to produce this result:

(1) a very permissive construction of the federal commerce power enumerated in Article I and (2) a construction of powers reserved to the state that become no more than a residual power after the enumerated powers have been defined.[2] The combined effect is to open wide the door to national land-use legislation in terms of constitutional authority, although not necessarily in terms of political feasibility or policy desirability.

The information needed to practice effective land-use regulation may often be highly localized—sometimes farm specific, but the collective interest in land-use control is frequently broader in scope. There is no perfect solution to this dilemma given significant information costs. Direct federal regulation (e.g., U.S. wetlands policy) sacrifices local adaptability to obtaining policy uniformity—or at least its appearance. Both federal and state policy may be better directed toward the creation and facilitation of diverse problem-solving capabilities at various levels of collective action. Such arrangements are more apt to generate local information about problems than to suppress information. The police-power approach sketched above is consistent with an institutional arrangement that allows the formation of special farmland-protection districts through local referendums. States that use general enabling legislation to authorize local communities to create a variety of special districts for various purposes increase the capacity for local problem solving and collective action. Especially important is the ability to create local jurisdictions with boundaries that match the boundaries of a problem or that define an appropriate community of interest. Existing general-purpose governments may or may not be adequate to address any given land-use problem. The basic unit of local government in rural America varies significantly among the states—in some states, it is a relatively small unit, the township, but in others it is a relatively large unit, the county.[3]

Comparing American and British Institutions

The American and British arrangements rest on different assumptions about the nature of the problem being addressed, require different modes of analysis and different types of policy information, imply much different approaches to problem solving and policy formulation, and lead in widely different future directions.

The American arrangement is based on the assumption that land externalities are local (or regional) phenomena to be addressed locally. The British arrangement might be understood as associating agricultural land-use regulation with the extent of the commodity market, or at least the basic unit of "international trade" (until recently assumed to be the nation-state). There is something to be said for both points of view. As noted above, the efforts of local communities to regulate land use according to local preferences can be frustrated by the need to remain competitive in commodity markets. The extent of the market is not irrelevant to land-use control.

Both approaches also require information, and they place great demands on analysts. For too long, American localities depended on the services of a planning profession that assumed it could arrange land uses as so many pieces in a puzzle. The problem is quite different. In particular, it is important that local communities understand the potential impact of forces outside the community and respond in timely fashion. Many local responses are too little, too late. The information needs of central planners, however, are, if anything, even greater. To be able to make appropriate exceptions to a general policy requires information that is time and place specific, which cannot be gleaned from aggregate data series.

The American system is one in which the aggregate result emerges from a large number of local political bargains—bargains struck under rules that vary somewhat (although not sharply) from state to state. The local bargains are exogenously constrained, and some observers would suggest that formal local authority is far greater than real local discretion. While this view is no doubt correct to some extent, if exogenous constraints were fully controlling, local bargains would not differ significantly at all. The American system is designed to be market responsive while vesting in states and localities the authority to correct market imperfections through collective action. The British arrangement, by contrast, is one that depends on a national political bargain and is designed to coordinate rural land-use regulation on a national basis. The logic of the British solution, however, pushes now toward a European bargain rather than simply a British bargain, and, as Harrison points out, the British are out of step with the other members of the European Community on many points related to land and agriculture. What would happen if the European states were to attempt to integrate their rural land-use policies is an open question. The logic of the British solution may have reached its practical limit at the national borders. But if the British solution was to be succeeded by a European solution, from an American perspective one may ask, "What becomes of problem solving?"

Notes

Ronald J. Oakerson is senior scientist, Workshop in Political Theory and Policy Analysis, Indiana University.

1. This appears to be the basic approach being applied in the United Kingdom to the farming of environmentally sensitive areas (ESAs) and sites of special scientific interest (SSSIs). See Harrison, in this volume. Another institutional possibility is to combine regulation with subsidies—an approach being pursued by the U.S. government in relation to soil conservation (see the Food Security Act of 1985).

2. See *Garcia v. San Antonio Metropolitan Transit Authority* (105 S. Ct. 1005, 1985). For a discussion of the issues, see L.A. Hunter and R.J. Oakerson, "An Intellectual Crisis in American Federalism: The Meaning of *Garcia*," *Publius: The Journal of Federalism* 16(1986):33-50.

3. See Advisory Commission on Intergovernmental Relations, *The Organization of Local Public Economies* (Washington, D.C., 1987).

PART FOUR

Land Information

Scientific investigators must stand ready to make use of all types of data and to judge their accuracy not merely in terms of metrical precision but on the basis of how well they reveal patterns of actual human experience.

—L. Salter, Jr., *A Critical Review of Research in Land Economics*, 1946

16

Land Information: Taxing as a Data Source

John O. Behrens

Information, simply stated, is knowledge that is communicated. This applies to information about land as well as information about anything else. The "knowledge" here can pertain to any one of several aspects, attributes, or capabilities associated with the particular land involved. In this paper I consider three aspects of land from the standpoint of information needs and sources. Then, I look at three recent developments that may satisfy land information needs, and briefly examine the issue of access to public information.

Types of Information Needed

Ownership and Tenure

Information needs concerning ownership and tenure can relate to the price associated with land transfer, the value of the land, the rental it might earn, improvements (if any) to the land, the identity of owners and occupiers, and the nature of the land's actual or highest and best use. In *Land Law and Registration*, Simpson defines *tenure* as the holding of land, whether allodially or otherwise. That is its meaning here.[1]

The sources of information about ownership and tenure are diverse and reflect the variety of purposes that condition the preparation and presentation of the information conveyed. Legal documents, such as certificates of title, deeds, mortgages, leases, and easements, reveal the basic facts about who owns what. Such information, in the hands of the public officials responsible for recording any changes in ownership evidenced by the documents, buttresses the public notice function accomplished by recording a transaction.

In the United States recording a land title is usually a county duty, except in Connecticut, Rhode Island, and Vermont, where city and town governments have the responsibility. A few of the remaining states have more than one recording office in a single county. In the entire country, there are about 3,500 recording officials, some of whom are elected, some appointed. Their job has evolved from English conveyancing, transplanted to the United States.

Originally an element in promoting alienation of land within the framework of the Land Ordinance of 1785, recording achieves the public notice necessary for giving the instrument of conveyance priority over adverse claims. Recorded documents are also admissible in court as evidence without further proof. Also, if an original document is lost or destroyed, a certified copy of the record entry can be admitted as secondary evidence. If delivery of deed is disputed, recordation sustains a presumption of delivery and may satisfy the delivery requirement.

Land Development

The recording officials, in a sense, typify the public and private officials who satisfy the need for land information. The multifaceted exercise known as land development could not occur without a substantial group of people supplying information about soil characteristics, topography, size, mineral and other resource deposits, as well as the value of the property, as it is and as it will be if improved according to the plan for its development. Building inspectors, engineers, planners, and zoning officials, together with architects, construction supervisors, and investors combine, fortuitously if not deliberately, to inform owners about property detail so as to make possible, if not certain, the reality of optimum development. Multiplying a single project by many, in numerous places and amid varied circumstances, always with accurately reported individual results (successful or not), yields the aggregate information necessary for land-related analysis, evaluation, and policymaking.

Property Taxation

Taxation is an aspect of civic life that carries with it the need for copious land information. The latter aggregate is associated, in one way or another, with considerable portions of the $1,160 billion in total tax revenue collected (for the year ending September 30, 1991), by the 83,237 governments (1 federal, 50 state, 83,186 local) in the United States. Of that revenue total, 40.3 percent, or $467.6 billion, came from federal taxes on individual income, down slightly from the 41.2 percent of five years earlier.[2] Federal individual income tax revenues include a portion of unknown magnitude representing gains from the sale of real property, information about which is now obtained from Form 1099-S (discussed below).

The country's total tax revenue above also includes $167.6 billion in state and (primarily) local property taxes, which now provide 14.4 percent of total tax revenue, up from 13.4 percent five years ago. Among tax types, only the federal individual income tax contributes more revenue than property taxes, despite the caps placed on real property taxes since 1978 by Proposition 13-type policies.

The administration of property taxation depends on assessed values, the work products of the 13,500 tax assessors in the United States. The assessment records involved, many of them in digital form, constitute the most comprehensive cadastral data base in the country. In 1986 the assessors arrived at a gross total assessed value of $4.8 trillion for all taxable real and personal property. That amount included $4.1 trillion for 108 million parcels of locally assessed taxable real property, which represents a 1986 market value of approximately $10.25 trillion. Corresponding figures for 1991, assuming a somewhat lesser percentage of growth, are $5.7 trillion in assessed value of 118 million parcels of locally assessed taxable real property, with a market value of approximately $14 trillion.[3]

The assessor is the public official who discovers, officially lists or otherwise exhibits, and values each taxable property in the jurisdiction, as of the legally prescribed date each year. Each assessed value has to be consistent with the assessed value of each of the other taxable properties in each of the use categories or other classifications that are valid in the jurisdiction. In the United States all realty parcels are in a single class in 29 states and the District of Columbia, to be assessed at the market level in the District of Columbia and 17 states, and at specified single percentages of market value in 12 states (see Table 16.1). Each realty parcel in another group of 17 states is subject to two or more specified assessed value percentages.

The four remaining states follow other assessment schemes. California adopted an acquisition-value system on June 8, 1978, when voters there approved Proposition 13. This radical departure from a uniform standard calls for assessment as of base year 1975, with subsequent annual increases of no more than 2 percent annually until an applicable change in ownership occurs. Whenever that happens, the property must be reappraised at market value. The maximum tax at all times is 1 percent of assessed value. Indiana requires that assessors value each property at one-third of its "true tax value," a depreciated cost estimate.

TABLE 16.1 De Jure Classified Assessment Levels, Real Property, State by State, United States, 1991

State	Percentage(s) of Market Value
Alabama	10,* 20, 30
Alaska	MV
Arizona	5, 10,** 14, 16, 25, 30
Arkansas	20
California	Base year 1975, or MV (at change of ownership)
Colorado	14.34,** 29
Connecticut	70
Delaware	MV
District of Columbia	MV (5 rates)
Florida	MV
Georgia	40
Hawaii	MV
Idaho	MV
Illinois	One-third (Cook County, 9 value levels)
Indiana	One-third of true tax value
Iowa	Usually 4 roll-back classes
Kansas	12,** 30
Kentucky	MV
Louisiana	10,** 15, 25
Maine	MV
Maryland	40% growth factor
Massachusetts	MV (4 rates)
Michigan	50 (6 equalization levels)
Minnesota	24 "tax capacity" rates, each multiplied by market value
Mississippi	10,* 15, 30
Missouri	19,** 12, 32
Montana	3.86,** 3, 8, 12, 3.84, 3.088, 2
Nebraska	MV
Nevada	35
New Hampshire	MV
New Jersey	Between 20 and 100%, selected by each county
New Mexico	One-third
New York	2 value levels for each assessing unit, except 4 each for New York City & Nassau County
North Carolina	MV
North Dakota	9,** 10 (4 classes, but only 2 value levels)
Ohio	Not exceeding 35%
Oklahoma	Not exceeding 35% for "highest and best use" actually used
Oregon	MV

—Continues

TABLE 16.1 (Continued)

State	Percentage(s) of Market Value
Pennsylvania	Not to exceed 75% in 4th- to 8th-class counties; MV otherwise
Rhode Island	Not to exceed 100%
South Carolina	4,** 1.6, 2.4, 6, 9.5, 10.5
South Dakota	MV
Tennessee	25,** 40, 55
Texas	MV
Utah	66.9,** 95
Vermont	1
Virginia	MV
Washington	MV
West Virginia	60 (3 rates)
Wisconsin	MV
Wyoming	9.5,** 11.5, 100

Notes: MV = market value; * = single-family only; and ** = single-family and multi-family. In some instances, more than one class may have the same specified assessment level. Unlabeled percentages are other than residential for classifying states.

Sources: In each instance, the state department with local assessment, tax, or administrative responsibilities (or equivalent title), and U.S. Department of Commerce Clearinghouse, *State Tax Guide* (Washington, D.C., 1991).

Minnesota now has further refined its "tax capacity" system, which directs that the total or applicable portion of the market-level assessed value be multiplied by the applicable rate among several specified tax rates. New York State prescribes two realty classifications for each assessing jurisdiction, except New York City and Nassau County, each of which has four.

In the precomputer era, assessors needed a quick and convincing way of arriving at assessed values if they were to assess and give individual attention each year to the scheduled fraction of the many thousands of properties in their charge. The result was a de facto preference for the cost approach, which was based on a manual of in-place cost units, plus or minus lump sum or unit-oriented adjustments for departures from or enhancements to "standard" structures. Sales and rental data, if readily available, were sometimes used to check the reasonableness of the depreciated cost calculations. The process stressed uniformity of method more than correlation of the classic three approaches (depreciated replacement cost, capitalized income, and comparison of sales prices).

In today's land information environment, computer-assisted mass appraisal (CAMA) is frequently the dominant assessment method. It usually features sales-oriented valuation that reflects use of statistical techniques like multiple regression analysis, often although no longer exclusively for residential property. Computers have also transformed how assessment records are maintained and have given rise to frequent requests by entrepreneurs for entire assessment rolls in digital form, sometimes including sales prices. Since much if not all of such information is public, assessors supply it in accordance with the applicable open records or freedom of information statute. Fees, if any, may be limited to the cost of reproduction, especially if "free access" in open-records laws holds sway over "cost recovery" (see below). One commercial source offers on-line access to any assessed value and associated data, often including sales prices, for any property in 30 states and the District of Columbia, with the remaining states eventually to follow. Similarly, commercial sources in Colorado, Florida, Georgia, and elsewhere will lease, and in some instances sell, machine-readable copies of entire assessment rolls, including sales prices as well as assessed values, for hundreds of counties.

Obtaining sufficient information on representative sales prices can, however, still be difficult. This underscores the potentially substantial benefits that can result from mutually agreeable arrangements between state and local tax officials, and between them and the Internal Revenue Service (IRS), to share potential new sources of land information data on sales price now collected by the IRS through Form 1099-S.

New Sources of Land Information

Form 1099-S

Form 1099-S (Form for Proceeds from Real Estate Transactions) is a potential new source of nationwide land information. In accordance with Treasury Decision 8323, the person responsible for the closing of every real estate transaction (usually sale) occurring on January 1, 1991, or thereafter, must report, on Form 1099-S (see Figure 16.1), the gross proceeds (usually sales price) and certain other information to the IRS.[4] Exempt from this requirement are corporations (corporations are temporarily exempt because a computer program for matching records is not yet available), government units, and parties to a sale with gross proceeds of less than $600. Where reporting is necessary, the person with that responsibility is required to use magnetic media if 250 or more transfers are involved annually.

The Final Regulations (26 CFR 1.6045-4) issued for Treasury Decision 8323 implement the reporting requirement in Section 6045(e), which was added to the Internal Revenue Code by Section 1521 of the Tax Reform Act of 1986. Prior to Treasury Decision 8323, temporary regulations

7 5 7 5   ☐ VOID   ☐ CORRECTED

FILER'S name, street address, city, state, and ZIP code			OMB No. 1545-0997	**19 92**	**Proceeds From Real Estate Transactions**

FILER'S Federal identification number	TRANSFEROR'S identification number	1 Date of closing (MMDDYY)	2 Gross proceeds $	**Copy A**

TRANSFEROR'S name | 3 Address or legal description (including city, state, and ZIP code)

For Internal Revenue Service Center

Street address (including apt. no.)

City, state, and ZIP code

File with Form 1096. For Paperwork Reduction Act Notice and instructions for completing this form, see **Instructions for Forms 1099, 1098, 5498, and W-2G.**

Account number (optional) | 4 Check here if the transferor received or will receive property or services as part of the consideration ▶ ☐

Form **1099-S**   Cat. No. 64292E   Department of the Treasury - Internal Revenue Service

---

☐ CORRECTED (if checked)

FILER'S name, street address, city, state, and ZIP code			OMB No. 1545-0997	**19 92**	**Proceeds From Real Estate Transactions**

FILER'S Federal identification number	TRANSFEROR'S identification number	1 Date of closing	2 Gross proceeds $	**Copy B For Transferor**

TRANSFEROR'S name | 3 Address or legal description

Street address (including apt. no.)

City, state, and ZIP code

This is important tax information and is being furnished to the Internal Revenue Service. If you are required to file a return, a negligence penalty or other sanction may be imposed on you if this item is required to be reported and the IRS determines that it has not been reported.

Account number (optional) | 4 Transferor received or will receive property or services as part of the consideration (if checked) · · · ▶ ☐

Form **1099-S**   (keep for your records)   Department of the Treasury - Internal Revenue Service

---

☐ VOID   ☐ CORRECTED

FILER'S name, street address, city, state, and ZIP code			OMB No. 1545-0997	**19 92**	**Proceeds From Real Estate Transactions**

FILER'S Federal identification number	TRANSFEROR'S identification number	1 Date of closing	2 Gross proceeds $	**Copy C For Filer**

TRANSFEROR'S name | 3 Address or legal description (including city, state, and ZIP code)

Street address (including apt. no.)

City, state, and ZIP code

For Paperwork Reduction Act Notice and instructions for completing this form, see **Instructions for Forms 1099, 1098, 5498, and W-2G.**

Account number (optional) | 4 Check here if the transferor received or will receive property or services as part of the consideration ▶ ☐

Form **1099-S**   Department of the Treasury - Internal Revenue Service

FIGURE 16.1 Internal Revenue Service Form 1099-S; for reporting proceeds from real estate transactions.

(1.6045-3T), effective January 1, 1987-December 3, 1990, implemented Section 6045(e) on a limited basis, that is, they required the reporting of sales of one to four family residences, including co-ops, condominiums, and vacant land. Prior to the Tax Reform Act of 1986, the IRS relied on voluntary reporting, usually by the seller, for information on realty sales. The forms used were 2119 (Sale or Exchange of Principal Residence), 4797 (Gains or Losses from Sales or Exchanges of Assets Used in Trade or Business), and 6252 (Computation of Installment Sale Income).

A 1986 study on capital gains noncompliance had revealed that in tax year 1979, only three-fourths of an estimated $36.4 billion in capital gains had been reported.[5] That meant $8.8 billion less in taxable capital gains income that year. Thus did Section 1521 emerge. The reporting it mandates applies to all use categories of realty and all kinds of ownership, current or future. Its coverage extends to fee-simple interests, life estates, reversions, remainders, perpetual easements, and previously created rights to use or possession for all or a portion of a year (such as leaseholds and timeshares), provided such rights have at least 30 years to run.

Possible sharing of data collected through Form 1099-S (preferably amended to provide more space for location description, property-use type, assessor's parcel number, and county name) arguably has potential for enhancing IRS enforcement of compliance tasks, even as it assists state and local tax officials. Agreements between the latter and the IRS are possible, in accordance with Section 6103(d)(1) of the code and any applicable freedom of information and privacy laws. A similar agreement, in accordance with Section 6103(j)(1)(a) of the code, is possible with the Census Bureau in connection with the latter's quinquennial surveys of taxable property values.

Model Law on Real Property Transfer Information

A second potential source of land information is the Model Law on Real Property Transfer Information, approved by the American Bar Association in 1988 and already a matter of interest to several state legislatures. The purpose of the model law is to "provide simple, timely, and cost-effective collection of essential data that will be made available to government officials and taxpayers alike, concerning real property transfers...." The model law provides for a declaration that would be a public record and would contain the following information about each transferred property:

- assessor's parcel number
- property address
- conveyance document execution date or actual date of transfer

- ownership interests transferred
- existence of personal property, if any
- names and addresses of transacting parties
- property tax billing address
- property use (residential, commercial, industrial, agricultural, vacant land, other)[6]
- "full" price paid (excluding payments for legal and other services and taxes)
- seller-provided financing
- family or business relationship between the parties

The model law, together with the technology available today, can help bring closer the attainment of uniformity in assessed values as a practical goal. Assessing jurisdictions in several states now conduct annual reassessments. The best way to monitor the extent to which uniformity is achieved is to conduct an assessment ratio study. About 45 states do so, usually annually. A ratio study is a systematic attempt, carried out in accordance with statistical principles, to compare the assessed values of individual properties with their actual worth, the latter usually indicated by "arm's length" sales prices. The study uses enough sales to support calculation of measures of central tendency and dispersion and to indicate de facto assessment levels and the uniformity achieved at those levels. One frequently helpful source of sales prices is documentation for realty transfer taxes now maintained by the District of Columbia and 36 states. (Each such tax is a levy on the transfer of realty; the rates range from 0.01 percent to 2.2 percent. Local transfer taxes may add 1 percent or more.) About three-fourths of the states require affidavits or declarations containing price and other details, including the signature of transacting parties (see example shown as Figure 16.2). Use of the model law format would promote standardization and designation of such documentation as public records. Currently, at least 10 states deem transfer tax affidavits to be confidential.

The only nationwide study of assessment-sales price ratios is the one begun in 1957 and conducted in every fifth year since, except 1987, by the Census Bureau as part of its quinquennial Census of Governments. This study, now in progress for 1992, produces de facto assessment levels and coefficients of intra-area dispersion for jurisdictions throughout the country.

TIGER Abroad in the Land

A third new information source is the Topologically Integrated Geographic Encoding and Referencing (TIGER) geographic support system created for the 1990 census by the Census Bureau, in cooperation with

WISCONSIN REAL ESTATE TRANSFER RETURN — CONFIDENTIAL Submit all parts to Register of Deeds with document(s) to be recorded.

I. GRANTOR:

1. Name _____

2. Address - New address if property transferred was residence

3. Grantor is ☐ Individual ☐ Partnership ☐ Corporation ☐ Other

II. GRANTEE:

4. Name _____

5. Property Address

6. Grantor /grantee relationship: ☐ Financial ☐ Family ☐ Other ☐ None ☐ Corp/Shareholder/Subsidiary ☐ Partnership

7. **Send tax bill to: Name and address**

III. ENERGY 8. Is this property subject to the Rental Weatherization Standards, ILHR67?
☐ Yes ☐ No Exclusion code ____ If W-11, explain _____

IV. PROPERTY TRANSFERRED

9. ☐ City ☐ Village ☐ Town _____
County _____

10. Street address _____

11. Tax parcel number _____

12. Lot no.(s) _____ Blk. no.(s) _____
Plat name _____

13. Section _____ Township _____ Range _____

14. **Legal Description** metes and bounds: (attach 4 copies if necessary)

V. PHYSICAL DESCRIPTION AND PRIMARY USE

15. Kind of property
☐ Land only
☐ Land and buildings
☐ Other (explain) _____

16. Primary use
a. ☐ Residential
☐ Single family/condominium
☐ Multi-family - # units _____
☐ Time share unit

17. Estimated land area and type
a. Lot size _____ x _____
b. Total acres _____
c. MFL / FC / WTL acres _____
d. Ft. of water frontage _____

b. ☐ Commercial _____ business use
c. ☐ Manufacturing
d. ☐ Agricultural
Adjoining land? ☐ Yes ☐ No
e. ☐ Other (explain) _____

VI. TRANSFER

18. Type of transfer: ☐ Sale ☐ Gift ☐ Exchange ☐ Other (explain)

19. Ownership interest transferred: ☐ Full ☐ Partial (explain) _____

20. Does the grantor retain any of the following rights? ☐ Life estate ☐ Easement

21. ☐ Deed in satisfaction of original land contract? Dated? _____

22. Points (prepaid interest) paid by seller $ _____

23. Value of personal property transferred but **excluded** from (25) $ _____

24. Value of property exempt from local property tax **included** on (25) $ _____

VII. COMPUTATION OF FEE OR STATEMENT OF EXEMPTION

25. Total value of REAL ESTATE transferred $ _____

26. Transfer fee due (line 25 times .003) $ _____

27. TRANSFER EXEMPTION NUMBER, sec. 77.25 _____ or Orig. L.C. ☐

28. Grantee's financing obtained from
a. ☐ Seller
If box a or b is checked, complete Part VIII - Financing Terms
b. ☐ Assumed existing financing
c. ☐ Financial institution / Other 3rd party
d. ☐ No financing involved

VIII. FINANCING TERMS (FOR SELLER/ASSUMED FINANCED TRANSACTIONS ONLY)

29. Total down payment $ _____ (Line 29 = Line 25 minus Lines 30a, b and c excluding payments for personal property)

	30. Amount of mortgage/land contract at purchase	31. Interest rate (stated)	32. Principal and interest paid per payment	33. Frequency of pymts	34. Length of contract	35. Date of any lump sum (balloon) payments	36. Amount of lump sum
a.	$ _____	_____ %	$ _____	_____	_____	__ _/_ _/_ __	$ _____
b.	$ _____	_____ %	$ _____	_____	_____	__ _/_ _/_ __	$ _____
c.	$ _____	_____ %	$ _____	_____	_____	__ _/_ _/_ __	$ _____

37. If the dollar amount paid per payment (32) is scheduled to change (not as a result of a change in the interest rate), fill in the line letter from above _____.
Enter the date of change __ _/_ _/_ __ and the amount it will change to $ _____ .

IX. CERTIFICATION We declare under penalty of law, that this return has been examined by us and to the best of our knowledge and belief it is true, correct and complete.

	Grantor or agent	Grantor's social security number or FEIN	Date	Grantor's telephone number ( )
SIGN HERE	Grantee or agent	Grantee's social security number or FEIN	Date	Grantee's telephone number ( )
	Print name and address of grantor's agent			Agent's telephone number ( )

	Document number	Vol./Im.	Page/Jac.	Date recorded	Date and kind of conveyance		Conv. code 1 2 3 4
LEAVE THIS AREA BLANK	Parcel number	Assmt. year 19 ___		☐ Field	Sales number		
	Parcel classification RES COM MFG AGR S/W FOR 1 2 3 4 5 6	L _____ I _____ T _____	County _ _ Tax dist _ _ Assmt. dist. _ _	☐ Use ☐ Reject			

Wisconsin Department of Revenue

PE-500 (R. 10-91)

DEPT. OF REVENUE COPY

FIGURE 16.2 Sample state (Wisconsin) form for reporting real estate transfers.

the U.S. Geological Survey. The TIGER system has a unique new file structure, and its data base incorporates theories of topology, graph theory, and other mathematics. Its geometry consists of single lines (1-cells) representing roads, hydrography, boundaries, railroads, and miscellaneous features; intersections of the lines (0-cells); and areas enclosed by the lines (2-cells), which are the polygons. The latter would be parcels if TIGER were a cadastral system, which it is not (although it can be used in association with cadastral systems). Its 2-cells link the areal cover to the geometry.

The TIGER system is a disciplined, mathematical description of the geographic structure of the United States in one computer file (a "virtual map"). It contains every street and road, name of each, range of addresses located along each section of every street, in the 354 largest urban areas of the country, all railroads and names of operating companies, all bodies of water and their names, together with boundaries, names, and numeric codes for 1990 geographic tabulations. A key aspect is its "integrated" character. This makes it possible for internal computer linkages to "tell the computer" precisely which records in one part of the data base belong to, and with, specific records in another part of the data base. This provides the capability to tabulate data in hierarchical fashion with speed and accuracy. Ramifications from prospective applications abound, and expectations are buoyed by the Census Bureau's decision to maintain TIGER integrity throughout the 1990s, through means like the following:

- A base program that calls for updating boundaries annually for all counties and for all other governmental entities with a population of 5,000 or more, and quinquennially for each such entity with a population of 2,500 or more.
- Extended coverage of address control files so that displayed address ranges will include 85 percent of all addresses, instead of the current proportion of 60 percent.
- Completion of initiatives currently under way, including a pilot project with the Geographic Information Council of Washington State, for improved state map coverage.
- Completion, in cooperation with the U.S. Postal Service, of a pilot project to incorporate new roads within the TIGER system on a regular basis.

The Accessibility Spectrum

Many a local tax assessor now has at least two jobs: (1) valuer as always, the "old pro" (regardless of age) on how much property is worth, and (2) information officer, custodian of data bases that contain

the most comprehensive and current inventory of property in the jurisdiction, together with much information about people. Much of all such
data is in the public domain because it arises out of performance of a
public function.

Inexorably, then, access to such data involves public policy rooted in
open-records or freedom of information laws at one end of the spectrum
and in privacy laws at the other. Underlying all is a basic proposition:
Whether completely open or tightly controlled, or somewhere in between, accessibility has perhaps the highest priority among elements
bearing on public information decisions. The pervasive thrust of freedom of information legislation, at any echelon, is promoting openness in
government. That promotion goes forward along a spectrum that extends from unfettered accessibility to the decidedly controlled accessibility that safeguards privacy.

The laws involved include the federal Freedom of Information Act,
originally passed in 1966 and amended several times since (substantially
so in 1986, including revised fee and fee waiver provisions, summarized
below), which is applicable to records of agencies in the executive
branch of the federal government; the Federal Privacy Act, enacted in
1974 and amended in 1989; and state open-records or freedom of information laws (each state has one) and privacy laws (about 40 states have
them).

Perhaps the major issue in this regard currently is the nature of the
response to requesters, including the charging of fees. A suggested general rule is that, in the absence of any published fee schedule rooted in
statute or regulation, public agencies are obliged to provide copies of
public records promptly, regardless of form, at a fee no greater than the
cost of reproduction.

The U.S. Freedom of Information Act now has more specific provisions regarding fees, with the passage of the 1986 amendments, which
became effective on April 27, 1987.[7] In general, agencies should charge
fees that recover for them the "full allocable direct costs they incur." An
example of a "direct cost" is the salary of an employee conducting a
search, defined as basic rate of pay plus 16 percent of that rate to cover
benefits.

For a computer search, the agency should charge the cost of operating
the central processing unit (CPU) for operating time directly attributable
to searching for the records, plus operator/programmer salary appor-
tionable to the search.

Specific provisions are made for each of the following categories of
requesters:

- commercial users
- educational and noncommercial scientific institutions

- requesters who are representatives of the news media
- all others

Generally, all except commercial use requests provide for 100 pages of reproduction without charge, plus free search time. The latter is two hours for "all other" requesters, after which search charges are activated.

The overall fee waiver provision states that documents shall be furnished "without any charge" or at a reduced charge if disclosure is "in the public interest because it is likely to contribute significantly to public understanding ... and is not primarily in the commercial interest of the requester."

Conclusion

Public information at all levels of government will remain in the forefront of public interest and attention in the days and years ahead. Public information about land, and property in general, constitutes a vitally important segment of such data. At the local level this means frequent involvement, with crucial responsibility, for assessors, no matter what part of the accessibility spectrum is affected by a specific request. Assessors naturally accumulate the most comprehensive data base of cadastral information available locally, and the restive, increasingly sophisticated public knows this. The twin policy objectives of freedom of information and respect for privacy should condition individual requests and official public responses, especially in a democracy. Stated or unstated, explicit or implicit, they naturally influence land information needs and sources, in particular, the source that may be more ubiquitous than any other, namely, taxation.

Notes

John O. Behrens is an attorney; fellow, Advisory Commission on Intergovernmental Relations; and president, Institute for Land Information. This paper is an original effort, the sole responsibility of its author. Opinions expressed are those of the author and not necessarily those of any organization.

1. See S.R. Simpson, *Land Law and Registration* (New York: Cambridge University Press, 1976):27.

2. For all revenue figures, see Bureau of the Census, *Quarterly Summary of Federal, State, and Local Tax Revenue, July-September 1991*, GT/91-Q3 (Washington, D.C., 1992):Tables 1-3.

3. For 1986 assessed values and numbers of parcels, see Bureau of the Census, *1987 Census of Governments*, Vol. 2, *Taxable Property Values*, GC87(2)-1 (Washington, D.C., 1989):6, 11, also ix-x. Corresponding figures for 1991 are based on subjective inferences from text Tables C and D and aggregate and size-weighted

ratios in Tables 11 and 13 of Bureau of the Census, *1982 Census of Governments,* Vol. 2, *Taxable Property Values and Assessment-Sales Price Ratios* (Washington, D.C., 1984):20 and 47. See also "Nationwide Real Estate Sales Database Has Numerous Uses," in *GIS World* 5, no. 2(1992):68.

4. See *Federal Register,* December 13, 1990:51282-51290.

5. Assistant Commissioner for Planning, Finance, and Research, *Capital Gains Income Reporting Noncompliance: 1979 Estimates by Type of Assets and Type of Error,* Research Division (Washington, D.C.: Internal Revenue Service, 1986).

6. Unfortunately, the text is so worded that single-family residence is distinguishable only if a broker is involved.

7. See Office of Management and Budget, FR Document 87-6951, Filed March 26, 1987, published in *Federal Register* 52, no. 59 (March 27, 1987). Reprinted as Appendix E in *Guidebook to the Freedom of Information and Privacy Acts,* 2d ed., compiled and edited by J.D. Franklin and R.F. Bouchard (Cranbury, N.J.: Clark, Boardman, Callaghan, 1992).

17

The Survey of
Taxable Property Values

Gerard T. Keffer

For analytic and policy reasons, many people need to know the size, composition, and value of inventories of property. They also are interested in the relationship of assessed values to each other and to market values and in the tax burdens borne fully, partly, or not at all by individual properties. Further, people seek information about the organizational structures within which the (mostly) local function of tax assessing is carried out in the United States.

In this paper I examine land information needs and sources, in particular the Bureau of the Census's Survey of Taxable Property Values (TPV). I discuss three principal topics: (1) issues affecting TPV surveys, (2) understanding the assessing environment, and (3) results of the 1987 TPV survey. To meet land information needs more fully, the dialogue regarding existing land information sources must be raised and broadened. This paper is one attempt to do that.

Background

The TPV survey has been conducted in its current form every five years since 1957. Unlike any other Census Bureau data collection effort, the survey is parcel oriented. It is a source of fiscal as well as some spatial data on the nation's real property base, especially the taxable portion, which is currently estimated to include 120 million parcels, with a market value in excess of $15 trillion. Survey results include estimates of numbers of parcels and assessed values in each of seven major property-use categories, assessment-sales price ratios, coefficients of dispersion, and property tax rates. These data are provided for a sample of approximately 2,000 primary assessing jurisdictions (mostly counties) throughout the nation.

The survey involves four major activities. First is a canvass by mail of state officials with responsibility for assessment administration. This "census of governments" results in benchmark aggregates, as of applicable valuation dates, of assessed values in each of the approximately 9,200 county (or equivalent) primary assessing jurisdictions in the country.

The second activity is the enumeration of a sample of realty sales occurring within each of the approximately 2,000 sample primary assessing jurisdictions within a specified six-month period. For each sale selected, the Census Bureau obtains the applicable presale assessed value from the assessment roll (a public record) and the actual use and sale price of the property. To date, all TPV surveys have obtained the property-use and selling prices by sending a confidential questionnaire to one of the transacting parties. The availability of assessed value and sales price information permits calculation of ratios and dispersion coefficients. For the 1982 census, the bureau sampled about 180,000 sales from a depressed 1981 real estate market that produced only 2 million sales for the six-months covered (generally July-December 1981). For the 1992 census, the bureau increased the sample to about 250,000 property sales. (For budget reasons, the bureau did not conduct a ratio study in 1987.)

The third activity is enumeration of a sample of the assessed values of real property parcels in each of the approximately 2,000 sample jurisdictions. The parcel sample for the 1987 census exceeded 1.5 million, of the nationwide total of 108 million taxable parcels. In 586 of the sample areas for 1987, enumeration of over 750,000 parcels was handled by computer-assisted means.

The Census Bureau's Field Division enumerators manually collected the assessed value data for the past three censuses. For each TPV survey a field staff of over 300 is employed through the Census Bureau's 12 regional offices for six to eight months. Processing the field-enumerated data requires the assistance of a staff of several dozen at the bureau's Data Preparation Division (Jeffersonville, Indiana). To complete computer-assisted or central source enumeration, the bureau obtains data through state and local governments and private vendors.

Finally, in the fourth activity, the Census Bureau obtains tax billing information for each sampled property sold, when located in selected large cities and their surrounding county(ies). For 1982 the cutoff level was cities with a population of 200,000 or more. This activity is designed to obtain data for calculating effective and nominal tax rates. An *effective tax rate* is the amount of the tax bill expressed as a percentage of the sales price. A *nominal tax rate* is the amount of the tax bill expressed as a percentage of net assessed value, after deducting partial exemptions for homesteads, senior citizens, veterans, and so on.

Data Users and Uses

The major users of TPV survey data fall into three categories. First, some data users base their own statistics (and conclusions) on the estimates derived from the census of governments portion of the survey. This requires a thorough understanding of concepts and definitions underlying the estimates. At least for these users, any change in the survey's scope or content would be resisted. They have a vested interest in the status quo. Second, other data users rely on the data for analysis. For these users, reliability of data and consistency of time series are more of a concern. Finally, still other data users act as intermediaries, providing data directly from Census Bureau reports to their clients. Here, there is a danger that data will be misused due to a lack of appreciation by the intermediary and/or final recipient of the meaning and reliability of the original data.

Below is a partial list of data users in one or more of the above categories:

- federal agencies
- state and local governments
- professional associations
- universities and colleges
- financial institutions
- research institutes
- taxpayer advocacy groups
- private citizens

Issues Affecting TPV Surveys

As part of the planning for the 1992 TPV survey, the Census Bureau had to address several issues, including property-use coding and parcel identification systems, state involvement in local assessment administration, the universe of unclassified realty sales, and the changing role of market value.

Use Coding and Parcel Identification Heterogeneity

Assessors use many coding systems. This applies to property-use categories as well as parcel identification numbers. This variability complicates efforts to collect and process data, especially when exact computer matching is required. Coding the actual use of properties is frequently difficult because all such state or local codes must be converted to a limited set used for Census Bureau statistics.

State Involvement in Local Assessment Administration

Some states mandate, and others strongly encourage, standardization and computerization of local assessment rolls. Some states have also achieved agreement on standards for assessment ratio studies. In Arizona, Florida, and New York, for example, the state routinely produces or acquires a copy of each local assessment roll on computer tape for use in its ratio studies and appraisal work. Such activity (assuming access to state tapes) facilities the bureau's survey work. With the ever-increasing use of automation, Census Bureau survey design, data collection and processing, and release of statistics are expected to be more efficient, timely, and cost effective in the future.

Universe of Unclassified Realty Sales

The Census Bureau obtains realty sales data from local public records. The grantor-grantee indexes and deed books used for initial sample selection generally contain no indication as to property-use type. That information is obtained either from secondary public records at state or local offices or through a questionnaire sent to property buyers and sellers. Since the basic unclassified sample must be large enough to yield sufficient coverage for each property use being surveyed, the kind of property use least subject to market activity has a disproportionate influence on initial sample size required. A classified (by use) sales universe would greatly facilitate future sample design and enumeration activities.

Changing Role of Market Value

Estimated market value remains the assessor's basic work product. Nowadays, however, that value is more of a starting point than the ultimate basis for tax burden apportionment. Property tax bills now are influenced not only by tax rate and assessed value, but also by taxpayer age or income, nature of property use, and in recent times, even by the date of acquisition or type of financing involved. Thus, while assessed values and sales prices (basic ingredients of the TPV survey) remain very important, they often tell substantially less than the full story about property tax productivity, equity, and uniformity.

Understanding the Assessing Environment

At the heart of understanding and effectively using information from the TPV surveys is understanding the assessing process as it is prescribed in the states and implemented by local governments. Quite simply, an understanding of national data on real property taxation requires an understanding of assessing.

Assessment Organization and Administration

The fundamental assessing entity is the primary assessing jurisdiction. This is simply one of the contiguous territories (counties, municipalities, or townships) that together occupy the entire geographic area of a state. The assessing official in each of the primary assessing jurisdictions has initial responsibility for determining the base for local general property taxes levied by local governments and, where applicable, by the state government.

In 1986 there were 13,588 primary assessing jurisdictions. Except for Hawaii's change from one state jurisdiction to four county jurisdictions, there has been little alteration in the organizational pattern within the past three decades. State involvement in local assessing, however, has increased, as exemplified by developments in South Carolina and Wisconsin, where all assessing of manufacturing property now takes place at the state level.

Assessed Values and Taxable Values

For the TPV survey to ensure nationwide comparability, the Bureau of the Census regards an *assessed value* as the one officially determined for tax purposes. Specifically, it is the value determined for county or county-equivalent government tax purposes, as of the specified valuation date.

Despite its conceptual simplicity, *assessed value* covers a variety of circumstances and is not always known as "assessed value." There are, in fact, three types: (1) conventional, that is, each parcel in a primary assessing jurisdiction is assigned a single assessed value, which becomes final subject only to specified appeal procedures; (2) the assessed value in counties, or equivalent areas, with more than one assessor to produce either one value or more than one value per property; and (3) the assessed value or values resulting from application of prescribed procedures that inflate, deflate, or otherwise adjust the assessor's original work product.

Legal Standards for Assessed Values

Assessing is the responsibility of appointed or elected county or other officials. Their job includes discovering, listing, and valuing property subject to local general property taxation as of specified valuation dates. Two characteristics affect and reflect assessment performance: conformance with value levels, at market or other specified value level(s) prescribed in the particular state's constitution and statutes; and uniformity with the assessed value of other taxable properties subject to the same prescribed legal level(s).

Each state, in its constitution or statutes or both, prescribes one legal standard for all assessed values, or a group of standards covering specified types of property. The legal standard may be the same for realty and personalty, or there may be specified differences. Regardless, the standards almost always are related to market value.

In 1986, 21 states and the District of Columbia called for assessments at market value or some equivalent—"full and true value" in Alaska, "true value in money" in Delaware, "actual value" in Nebraska, and "fair market value" in Virginia. Another group of 15 states specified a single percentage of market value or a way of calculating a single percentage annually. Fourteen states have no single realty assessment level. For these states, "classified property taxation" was in effect in 1986, as summarized below:

State and Number of Classes

Alabama	3	Mississippi	2
Arizona	10	Missouri	3
Colorado	3	Montana	12
Iowa	4	North Dakota	4
Louisiana	5	South Carolina	5
Michigan*	6	Tennessee	3
Minnesota	23	Utah	2

*Classification by equalization categories.

One type of legal standard affecting realty is the assemblage of benefitted-use (sometimes called current-use) laws. This kind of legislation exists in all states except Wisconsin, which uses an income tax credit. The main characteristic of such laws is the instruction to assessors to estimate the value for the realty affected on the basis of the current use of the site, rather than the "highest and best use" for the site.

The purpose of benefitted-use laws is to benefit the particular use or uses specified, frequently agricultural, open space, or historical. There are three types of such legislation: preferential use, deferred taxation, and contracts and agreements. In some instances, a single state may employ two or even all three of the possible types.

Preferential-use laws direct assessment on the basis of the use or uses specified, without providing any tax consequence in the event such uses change. Twenty-two states had such laws in 1986. Often eligibility for such assessment depends on preexisting benefitted use for a specified number of years. There also may be minimum requirements for property size and for income attributable to what the property produces (crops, for example).

Deferred taxation prescribes "benefits use assessing" as long as the qualifying use continues. With any change, however (for example, the sale of property), a deferred tax is activated, its rate applicable to the difference in value between what the property is worth at the benefitted use and what it would command at highest and best use. In 1986, 31 states had such provisions. In the states affected, the assessment rolls may show both values for each affected parcel (the benefitted-use assessment and the conventionally estimated assessment).

Contracts and agreements are simply that, contractual arrangements available under the law by means of which taxpayers agree to use the subject property for purposes and under conditions specified, for a stated period of time, in exchange for assessment of the property on a benefitted-use basis as long as the contract is in effect. Fourteen states, by 1986, had enacted legislation of this type.

An in-depth understanding of benefitted-use laws in each of the states is imperative to the successful conduct of each TPV survey. Concomitantly, the assessed values and related ratios for the "benefitted" property categories produced as part of the surveys constitute the only uniform data set on their de facto assessments. For this reason, these data are used extensively by state and local assessing and taxation officials and others who have an interest in this subject.

A total (worth) of all property values includes the value of totally exempt realty, such as governmental, religious, educational, and charitable property, plus tangible and intangible personalty not subject to taxation. Quantifying totally or partially taxable assessed values versus totally exempt amounts on a common basis continues to be a difficult task.

In recent times both assessed and market values have varied considerably. The real estate market has been subject to inflation, recession, high interest rates, and a multitude of "creative" financing arrangements. Each of these factors influences how assessed values relate to market values.

Some Results of the 1987 TPV Survey

The Real Property Tax Base

The realty tax base (net assessed value) in 1986 was $3.91 trillion (see Table 17.1). Between 1981 and 1986, the net assessed value of locally

TABLE 17.1 Summary of Gross and Net Assessed Values and Changes Therein, 1956, 1966, 1976, 1981, and 1986 (dollar amounts in billions)

Assessed Value Type	1956	1966	1976	1981	1986
Total gross assessed value	280.3	499.0	1,229.1	2,958.2	4,817.8
Total net assessed value	272.2	484.1	1,189.4	2,837.5	4,619.7
State-assessed property	22.5	41.6	84.7	159.0	242.9
Locally assessed property	249.7	442.5	1,104.7	2,678.4	4,376.9
Real property	202.8	378.9	959.1	2,406.7	3,910.7
Personal property	46.9	63.6	145.6	271.6	466.3

| | Percent Change | | | | |
	1956-1966	1966-1976	1976-1981	1981-1986	1956-1986
Total gross assessed value	78.0	146.7	140.7	62.9	1,618.8
Total net assessed value	77.8	145.7	138.6	62.8	1,597.2
State-assessed property	84.9	103.6	87.7	52.8	979.6
Locally assessed property	77.2	149.6	142.5	63.4	1,652.9
Real property	86.8	153.1	150.9	62.5	1,828.4
Personal property	35.6	128.9	86.6	71.6	894.2

Note: Because of rounding, detail may not add to totals.

Source: Bureau of the Census, *Census of Governments, Taxable Property Values* (Washington, D.C., 1957, Vol. 5; 1967, Vol. 2; 1977, Vol. 2; 1982, Vol. 2; 1987, Vol. 2).

assessed realty increased by 63 percent. Over the 30 years of the survey, the corresponding increase stands at over 1,800 percent.

Between 1956 and 1986, the gross assessed value of locally assessed realty increased nearly 1,900 percent, from $210 billion to $4.1 trillion (see Table 17.2). The rate of increase has grown dramatically, especially since 1966. Total gross assessed value of locally assessed realty that year reached $393 billion, after an increase of 87 percent since 1956. Values then moved up much more rapidly, climbing by 152 percent by 1976 and then more than quadrupling by 1986.

One profound influence on assessment methods was the introduction of the computer, as noted earlier. With machine assistance, assessors can accomplish mass appraisal every year, which was not feasible in the past. Local assessments, therefore, are now more likely to be reflective of current market trends, especially for residential property.

A noticeable proportionate decline in the realty value base is evident for the acreage category (including farms and nonresidential rural land). As shown in Table 17.2, in 1986 acreage realty contributed only 7.5 percent of the taxable base, continuing a decline (interrupted only in 1976) from 13.9 percent in 1956. This change may be linked to the profusion of benefitted-use legislation now common in all states in one form or another.

Realty Tax Base—Numbers of Parcels by Use Categories

In 1986, acreage and farm parcels accounted for over 16 million parcels, or 14.8 percent of the total (see Table 17.3). This nationwide proportion continued its steady decline from a high of 23.3 percent in 1956.

Throughout the TPV survey, parcel counts follow the definitions of the local assessors. On occasion this means that they reflect statutory limits on size or other aspects that may require separate identification in local assessment rolls.

One of the shortcomings of the TPV survey is the lack of parcel size data and the ability to calculate the property tax burden per unit of area. The Census Bureau is trying to remedy this data gap in future surveys. However, because about one-third of all assessing jurisdictions do not record the size of parcels on their assessment rolls, this will be a formidable and costly endeavor. The best chance for remedying this situation appears to be through further standardization of local property records. The Census Bureau will allocate additional resources to achieving this goal in the future.

Decline, Growth, and Durability

State and, primarily, local revenues from property taxes were approximately $162 billion for the year ending June 30, 1991. This is over 12

TABLE 17.2 Gross Assessed Values, Locally Assessed Realty, and Use Categories, 1956, 1966, 1976, 1981, and 1986 (dollar amounts in billions)

Use Category	1956	1966	1976	1981	1986
U.S. total, all use categories	209.8	393.2	992.5	2,514.9	4,104.5
Acreage and farms	29.1	43.4	117.6	247.8	309.3
Vacant platted lots	4.8	10.2	38.0	109.4	189.2
Residential (nonfarm)	113.5	236.3	587.3	1,520.0	2,511.6
Single-family houses only	95.1	196.7	495.3	1,328.7	2,180.3
Commercial and industrial	58.0	97.2	239.8	549.3	997.5
Commercial	34.8	60.0	166.0	353.5	710.5
Industrial	22.6	37.1	73.7	195.8	286.9
Other and unallocable	4.4	6.0	9.8	88.3	97.0
			Percent Distribution		
U.S. total, all use categories	100.0	100.0	100.0	100.0	100.0
Acreage and farms	13.9	11.0	11.9	9.9	7.5
Vacant platted lots	2.3	2.6	3.8	4.4	4.6
Residential (nonfarm)	54.1	60.1	59.2	60.4	61.2
Single-family houses only	45.4	50.0	49.9	52.8	53.1
Commercial and industrial	27.7	24.7	24.2	21.8	24.3
Commercial	16.6	15.3	16.7	14.1	17.3
Industrial	10.8	9.4	7.4	7.8	7.0
Other and unallocable	2.1	1.5	1.0	3.5	2.4

Note: Because of rounding, detail may not add to totals.

Source: Bureau of the Census, Census of Governments, Taxable Property Values (Washington, D.C., 1957, Vol. 5; 1967, Vol. 2; 1977, Vol. 2; 1982, Vol. 2; 1987, Vol. 2).

TABLE 17.3 Numbers of Parcels, Locally Assessed Realty, and Use Categories, 1956, 1966, 1976, 1981, and 1986 (number of parcels in thousands)

Use Category	1956	1966	1976	1981	1986
U.S. total, all use categories	61,158	74,832	88,194	98,394	107,890
Acreage and farms	14,185	14,085	13,893	14,778	16,004
Vacant platted lots	12,694	14,250	17,492	19,483	19,484
Residential (nonfarm)	30,924	42,329	51,971	58,162	64,754
Single-family houses only	29,973	40,436	48,750	54,983	61,114
Commercial and industrial	2,291	2,487	3,663	4,113	4,479
Commercial	1,942	2,112	3,179	3,562	3,946
Industrial	298	376	485	551	533
Other and unallocable	1,067	1,679	1,175	1,861	3,169
			Percent Distribution		
U.S. total, all use categories	100.0	100.0	100.0	100.0	100.0
Acreage and farms	23.3	18.8	15.8	15.0	14.8
Vacant platted lots	20.8	19.0	19.8	19.8	18.1
Residential (nonfarm)	50.6	56.6	58.9	59.1	60.0
Single-family houses only	49.0	54.0	55.3	55.9	56.6
Commercial and industrial	3.7	3.3	4.2	4.2	4.2
Commercial	3.2	2.8	3.6	3.6	3.7
Industrial	0.5	0.5	0.5	0.6	0.5
Other and unallocable	1.7	2.2	1.3	1.9	2.9

Note: Because of rounding, detail may not add to totals.

Source: Bureau of the Census, *Census of Governments, Government Finances* (Washington, D.C., 1957, Vol. 5; 1967, Vol. 2; 1977, Vol. 2; 1982, Vol. 2; 1987, Vol. 2).

times the $13 billion collected 34 years ago, in 1957, when the Census
Bureau first conducted the TPV survey.

The history of property taxes since 1957 has been one of steady
growth, as seen in Table 17.4. They remain the source of three of every
four local tax dollars. Moreover, collections in recent years have arrested
the rate of decline that had reduced what property taxes contribute to
total local revenue, from more than two of every five dollars in 1957 to
one out of four in 1990.

Despite caps, limits, exemptions, and assorted relief measures en-
dorsed or spawned by the 1978 vote in California for Proposition 13,
property taxes remain the most prolific single revenue source within
local control. In absolute terms they yield more every year, the lone
exception in contemporary times being the reduction between fiscal
years 1978 and 1979 following adoption of Proposition 13 in California.

State and Local Structural Changes

Between fiscal years 1957 and 1990, the property tax yield decreased
from 43.4 to 25.5 percent of total local revenue, as seen in Tables 17.4
and 17.5. Local governments still depend on the property tax, but within
limits imposed not by tax capacity but by public pressure for alternative
revenue sources. Service fees and charges have become common, along
with local government efforts to maximize earnings on investments.

Conclusion

All states and individual assessing areas closely monitor the assessed
value and estimated market value of their real and personal property.
Given the vast differences in legal standards, exemptions, property-use
categories, definitions of "arm's length sales," statistical measures derived, and so on, the nationally consistent approach of the Census Bureau's TPV survey has gained broad acceptance as the standard by
which other systems should be judged. As more programs are shifted
from the federal level to state and local levels, and the burden to support them also shifts, the main source of local revenue—the property
tax—will come under increasing scrutiny. Questions regarding assessment uniformity and property tax equity will be raised with greater fre-
quency. The Census Bureau's Survey of Taxable Property Values is
expected to play a significant role in addressing these and other related
administrative and policy issues.

Gerard T. Keffer is chief, Taxation Branch, Census of Governments, Bureau
of the Census. The views expressed are the author's and do not necessarily represent policies or views of the U.S. Department of Commerce.

TABLE 17.4 Revenue from Property Taxes, 1956-57 to 1989-90 (dollar amounts in millions)

Fiscal Year	State and Local Governments			State Governments			Local Governments		
	Property Tax Revenue	Percentage of		Property Tax Revenue	Percentage of		Property Tax Revenue	Percentage of	
		Revenue From All Sources	Total Tax Revenue		Revenue From All Sources	Total Tax Revenue		Revenue From all Sources	Total Tax Revenue
1989-90	155,674	15.1	31.0	5,848	0.9	1.9	149,825	25.5	74.5
1985-86	111,711	14.3	29.9	4,355	0.9	1.9	107,356	24.7	74.0
1981-82	81,918	15.0	30.8	3,113	1.0	1.9	78,805	25.2	76.0
1976-77	62,527	18.5	35.5	2,260	1.1	2.2	60,267	30.7	80.5
1971-72	42,133	22.2	38.7	1,257	1.1	2.1	40,876	36.1	83.5
1966-67	26,047	24.4	42.7	862	1.4	2.7	25,186	39.0	86.6
1961-62	19,056	27.4	45.9	640	1.7	3.1	18,416	42.6	87.9
1956-57	13,097	28.5	45.1	479	1.9	3.3	12,618	43.4	87.0

Source: Bureau of the Census, *Census of Governments, Government Finances* (Washington, D.C., 1956-1957 through 1989-1990, series GF no. 5).

TABLE 17.5 Percentage Distribution, State and Local Government Revenue Structures, 1957, 1965-66, 1975-76, and 1985-86 (dollar amounts in millions)

	State Governments				Local Governments				Exhibit: Total Revenue
	1957	1966-67	1976-76	1985-85	1957	1966-67	1976-77	1985-86	1985-86
Revenue from all sources	100.0	100.0	100.0	100.0	100.0	100.0	100.0	100.0	434,751
Intergovernmental revenue	15.9	23.4	23.8	20.5	26.2	31.2	39.2	33.9	147,256
From federal government	14.2	22.3	22.5	19.3	1.2	2.9	8.5	4.7	20,433
From state governments	—	—	—	—	25.0	28.3	30.7	29.2	126,824
From local governments	1.7	1.1	1.3	1.2	—	—	—	—	—
Taxes, all types	58.9	52.3	49.4	47.4	49.9	44.8	38.1	33.4	144,997
Property taxes	1.9	1.4	1.1	0.9	43.4	39.0	30.7	24.7	107,356
Income, individual	6.3	8.0	12.5	14.0	.07*	1.4*	1.9*	1.6	6,948
Income, corporate	4.0	3.7	4.5	3.8	—	—	—	0.4	1,588
Sales and gross receipts	34.2	30.4	25.6	23.3	3.5	3.0	4.2	5.2	22,628
Other	12.4	8.8	5.8	5.3	2.3	1.5	1.3	1.5	6,477
Current charges	5.0	6.9	6.2	6.2	8.6	9.7	9.7	11.6	50,413
Miscellaneous general revenue	2.8	2.7	3.6	7.7	3.5	4.1	4.2	8.7	37,996
Other	17.3	14.7	16.9	18.2	11.8	10.1	8.8	12.4	54,088

*Corporate income taxes combined with individual income taxes for local governments in 1976-77 and earlier *Government Finances* reports.

Source: Bureau of the Census, *Census of Governments, Government Finances* (Washington, D.C., 1957, vol. 5; 1967, vol. 5; 1977, vol. 5; 1987, vol. 5).

18

Integrating Land-Related Program, Survey, and Inventory Data

Ralph E. Heimlich

A common conclusion in much writing about difficult policy issues is that more information is needed. Issues related to land use, ownership, and taxation are not immune from the cry for "more data." At the same time, there are constant reminders that this is an "information age"— knowledge is power and a myriad of inputs cascade from every direction on a real-time basis. With this paper, I want to start a countertrend: I think we have enough data, possibly even a superfluity. Ours is more aptly described as a "data age." Although we are constantly inundated by a flow of data, our ability to extract much information that goes directly to the pressing issues is limited. I believe that the fundamental problem is the failure to integrate data collected by members of various disciplines, for a variety of purposes, under the auspices of various institutions. The cause is an attachment to two-dimensional thinking in a multidimensional world. That is, analysts anticipate relatively few connections between aspects of an issue and, hence, perceive different data elements as unrelated. I believe the problem is greatest between "things" (physical data) and "people" (socioeconomic data) and constantly plagues those concerned with natural resource issues. Lack of integration is also apparent, however, between different aspects of socioeconomic data, such as data on the economics of production and data on land ownership, tenure, and taxation.

An example from the area of farmland-retention policy will help to illustrate the situation.[1] Several key questions surround the subject of farmland retention: How much land is being converted to urban uses? What is the quality of the farmland being lost? What are the factors contributing to loss of farmland? How effective are farmland-retention programs? What do they cost?

A wealth of data exists on many aspects of this issue. For example, the Census of Agriculture tracks the net changes in agricultural land uses, at least for land that remains within the farm sector. Soil survey and national resource inventory (NRI) data measure the quality of land in agricultural production. The Agricultural Economics and Land Ownership Survey (AELOS) provides information about the ownership of farmland. Data are also available on changes in population, employment, and income in counties and towns where farmland is located. And data are available on at least some of the farmland-retention programs administered by state agencies. With all of these data, why is it that so little can be said about what works and doesn't work regarding farmland retention and other land-related issues?

Two-Dimensional Data in a Multidimensional World

The answer to the question above is that almost all of these data are organized in a one- or two-dimensional fashion. By that, I mean that I can get county listings of, say, changes in cropland and farmland enrolled in use-value assessment programs, but I can't get a county listing of cropland changes by enrollment in use-value assessment programs. Further combinations of data elements—such as cropland changes, by program enrollment, by land quality, by ownership—are completely impossible. At best, I know how much change in each of these attributes occurred in a particular county. But there is no way to link data elements directly to get at the more meaningful relationships that would help illuminate many of these issues.

Constraints of money, time, and respondent burden are common to all data collection. Beyond these, however, are three reasons why data integration is so difficult. First, different disciplines or professions have different ideas about the kinds of data to collect. Soil scientists are comfortable inventorying soil types or erosion rates, but they don't see the need for information about who owns the land. Production economists collect detailed data on production costs, but they don't see the need for information on either land quality or tenure. Every group is constrained by its own professional myopia.

Second, the purpose for which the data are collected determines the kind and scope of data obtained. Local assessors or purchase-of-development-rights (PDR) managers acquire data needed to run their programs, but they won't (or can't) record details that might help explain participation in the program. Researchers are careful to collect data on variables that theory indicates might explain behavior, but they may not record details specific to participation in particular programs. This is where limited time, money, and respondent willingness cause data gatherers to compromise larger information needs, even if they do recognize those larger needs.

Finally, institutional affiliations limit one's ability to think more globally about data needs. An analyst in a state agency is oblivious to the need for commonality of data beyond state borders. A federal researcher cannot be expected to take full account of peculiarities in local assessment practices, even if those can be determined, in favor of trying to generalize to some degree.

Institutional and Technical Solutions

It should be clear that all disciplines, purposes, and institutions would be better served if all of the data elements and public records collected that pertain to the same land could be linked. How could this be achieved? The dichotomy between people-based and equipment-based solutions may be appropriate.

Institutional Solutions

An institutional answer is the obvious one: Institutions could simply agree to cooperate in data collection efforts and in the design of public record documents. However, as in many other instances of cooperative behavior, it is likely that the large transaction costs involved in even discussing cooperation outweigh the marginal gain that might accrue from cooperation. Transaction costs, as well as increased direct collection costs and respondent burden, would be maximized if each institution tried to collect all the data that everyone needs.

One area of cooperation that could avoid much of the transaction costs and yet could increase the ability to link data would be an agreement to collect a common identifying element. This could be people based, such as Social Security number, or it could be land based, such as county code or geographic coordinates. The now ubiquitous Federal Information Processing Standard (FIPS) coding of geographic units is a time-proven example. However, it is rare to see anything more than a geographic identification code (usually not FIPS coded) on most socioeconomic data. This is particularly true for public record information collected by state and local government agencies.

A most promising system, called the Topologically Integrated Geographic Encoding and Referencing (TIGER) system, has evolved from the U.S. Geological Survey's (USGS) National Digital Cartography (NDC) and the Census Bureau's Geographic Base File/Digital

Information Map Encoding (GBF/DIME) systems.[2] Jointly developed by the Census Bureau and USGS, TIGER is a national geographic information system (GIS) that is being used to organize information collection, processing, and publication for the 1990 Census of Population and Housing. The TIGER system deserves serious consideration as a useful framework on which to organize future land analyses. It integrates information on boundary, hydrological, and transportation features from the USGS Digital Line Graph data system and Census Bureau information on population, housing, income, agricultural land use, and local governments. It can include land-use/land-cover and soils data, but they are not part of the initial data set.

The TIGER system is the first that will provide a nationally consistent structure for land information with sufficient detail and precision to serve local land information needs.[3] Both TIGER and the earlier GBF/DIME system are more suited for research on urbanization than on rural lands because the information in the systems is proportional to Census Bureau collection blocks, which are in turn primarily based on the U.S. road, street, and drainage system and are not linked to agricultural parcels. Neither system includes agricultural land use. The 1990 census data are being made available in the TIGER format, which is compatible with digital cartographic systems.

Technical Solutions

For those who have little faith in institutional solutions to our woes, dependent as they are on the ability of people to agree with each other, there are always the impersonal solutions offered by technology, which can enable people to work separately from each other. One of the technical solutions to data integration most widely put forth is the GIS. Such systems are used to store data collected from various sources into a common, geographically referenced computer environment. Data integration is thus accomplished by juxtaposing, or layering, unrelated data elements on the basis of geographical proximity. In effect, a GIS uses geographic coordinates, as the common identifying element, to link data elements.

Some difficulties remain, however, even assuming that everyone is willing to add his or her data collection/public record efforts to a common data pool linked by a GIS. Some of the difficulties are technical ones related to what coordinate system (latitude and longitude, Universal Transverse Mercator, and so on) and what GIS software or hardware to use. Most of these difficulties have technical solutions that bridge between the alternatives and are better left to more technical forums. Beyond these problems, however, remain more fundamental problems of definition, resolution, simultaneity, and disclosure.

The definitional problem concerns specifying the geographic location associated with the data element being collected. For example, a point source of water or air pollution can be represented by the geographic coordinates of the discharge pipe or stack. A farm field can be represented by the polygon describing its boundaries. But what location can be ascribed to a farm enterprise? Home address? The boundaries of all owned parcels? The parcels operated by the farmer? There is a reluctance on the part of social scientists and public officials to invest the time and effort needed to digitize parcel boundaries, particularly during a survey interview.

The problem of resolution has to do with how closely the location attributed to a data element should be defined. Resolution is intimately tied to the scope of analysis or the purpose of the data or public record, and it is also a factor of the storage and handling capacities of the particular GIS. At the watershed or county level, very precise geographic location may be necessary to associate socioeconomic characteristics and physical characteristics accurately. That same degree of precision is probably not needed at the national or regional level. From the national perspective, efforts to achieve such precision will be wasted because the degree of resolution in the GIS itself would not reflect the increased precision obtained in the data. Yet such precision may be essential for studies with a narrower scope.

The simultaneity problem is the temporal analog of the resolution problem. Does it matter that the cropping system information obtained for a parcel pertains to one year while the stream-quality monitoring data are for the previous year? How far apart in time can observations on various owner-operator and landscape characteristics be and still be usefully related to one another? Can observations be taken over a multi-year period and still be treated as representative of the whole period, as is done for NRI data, which are taken over a three-year period?

Finally, as in all realms of data collection, there is the increasing problem of disclosing confidential information. This applies to geographically referenced data as well as the more familiar cases for survey data. In the early 1980s the Economic Research Service (ERS) had plans for a program of work examining changes in land use and conservation behavior predicated on merging data from the 1977 NRI, the 1978 Landownership Survey, and the 1982 NRI. Because some landowners had complained that university classes and personnel of the U.S. Department of Agriculture (USDA) were repeatedly revisiting the NRI sample points, the Soil Conservation Service (SCS) deleted all point-identification fields from the 1982 data set. This effectively precluded any attempt to merge successive sample observations and mooted the entire research effort. Five years later, SCS responded to the opportunity to link successive samples by presenting the 1987 and 1982 data elements merged into a single record. However, there are still no geographic coordinates coded on the record that would allow it to be merged with other data sources.

Turning Data into Information

In principle, at least, technology is providing a nearly continuous flow of data that could be used in a GIS. In physical terms, Landsat and SPOT satellites provide remotely sensed, multispectral scanning data on land and water surface conditions. The USGS National Stream Quality Accounting Network (NASQAN) and Water Data Storage and Retrieval (WATSTORE) system automatically provide data on water quantity and quality from 8,000 stream-monitoring stations. On the socioeconomic side, state and local programs generate public records covering landownership, assessment, taxation, and participation in a host of voluntary programs. Federal programs generate similar public records for participants, such as USDA farm program participation.

This flood of data is difficult and expensive to access, however, and considerable processing would be required before such data could even conceivably make up an information layer in a functioning GIS. The tasks of acquiring, processing, summarizing, and storing such a flood of data are so daunting that they are seldom undertaken. When they are accomplished, it is usually in the context of relatively small demonstration projects for limited areas. What few large-scale, continuously updated, integrated GIS systems are in existence face ongoing technological obsolescence as newer and better computer systems are developed.

A fundamental clash between what I call engineering and research mentalities is involved here. The engineering mentality recognizes that it is technically possible to collect on a continuous basis a wide array of data covering the entire landscape in wall-to-wall fashion. Automated acquisition and processing of satellite-based, remotely sensed data for direct and repeated input to a GIS is an example of this kind of thinking. The fact that this is an enormous undertaking in terms of time, money, and institutional commitment over any but the smallest geographic scope is only seen as an obstacle to be overcome.

By contrast, the research mentality recognizes that a lot can be learned about any phenomena of interest by using a statistically based spatial sample. This approach is especially useful at broader geographic scales, where the reliability of statistical estimates can match the performance of inventory data. Statistical sampling is seldom viewed as a continuous or ongoing process, although periodic replication may occur as the usefulness of the data obtained becomes apparent. Examples include USDA's natural resource inventories and the repeated studies of land-use change conducted by ERS in fast-growth counties.

A kind of hybrid of the two approaches can be envisioned. The continuous stream of data generated by satellites or public recordkeeping could be periodically sampled to provide a usable data set. Examples are provided by the public-use sample of federal income tax returns, which are stripped of any possible disclosure information and made available for research and analysis. One hitch in this scheme is that much of the continuously acquired data is not organized to make sampling convenient. For example, Landsat is available as whole or half scenes, each occupying an entire magnetic tape, which form the minimum purchasable unit. There may be a technical solution to this problem that involves sampling directly from the satellite downlink, but building a sample from the archived tapes would require a huge amount of data processing.

Possible Futures: Confessions of a Pessimist

I have to admit to a continuing degree of pessimism concerning the eventual success of either institutional or technical solutions to the data integration problem. While some of this may reflect my own flawed personality, far more is due to the distance between what I see as necessary precursors to either solution and the current situation. Data integration probably will require a more fundamental integration among parts of agencies responsible for running day-to-day programs and analyzing or evaluating their performance.

Some progressive local governments have integrated public record systems cutting across all functions with the strategic or long-run planning function. At the state level, Wisconsin and Oregon are pursuing changes in land records that would facilitate data integration for analysis and strategic planning.[4] I see little evidence of such functional integration in the land-based resource areas of federal government, despite congressionally mandated requirements for program evaluation contained in the Soil and Water Resources Conservation Act of 1977 and the Forest and Rangeland Renewable Resources Planning Act of 1974. The research establishment seems even less likely to push for data integration. In part, this may be due to a tendency to view each emerging issue affecting land as somehow new, despite large similarities between integrated data needs for addressing land issues that have persisted over a number of years.

I see no reason to believe that the obstacles to data integration that prevent implementation of broadly applied GIS systems covering large geographic areas and incorporating a wide variety of data types and sources will be overcome soon. The pioneering work on the Census Bureau/USGS TIGER system may prove to be an exception if it can be broadened beyond the immediate needs of the Census Bureau. This could occur if other federal agencies can be persuaded to add geocoding to their systems and convert existing data sources to a TIGER-compatible format. Private vendors may find sufficient incentive to develop such compatible data sets, but none of the data sets particularly relevant to land issues seems a likely candidate for such commercial success.

Researchers should constantly be reexamining data collection and public record activities to make it easier to relate them to each other. Those who are, like myself, primarily a data user, should make every effort to devise ways of linking available data sets to make the best use of existing information before succumbing to the cry for "more data, please!"

Notes

Ralph E. Heimlich is an agricultural economist, Economic Research Service, U.S. Department of Agriculture. The views expressed are the author's and do not necessarily represent policies or views of the U.S. Department of Agriculture.

1. My colleagues in the Economic Research Service (ERS) and I tried to address the data integration problem to some extent in our data collection effort on fast-growth counties, and we examined the larger context of data problems associated with urbanizing areas. See R.E. Heimlich and R.C. Reining, "The Economic Research Service in Urbanization Research," in R.E. Heimlich, ed., *Land Use Transition in Urbanizing Areas: Research and Information Needs* (Washington, D.C.: Economic Research Service and Farm Foundation, 1987):73-89; M.C. Vesterby and R.E. Heimlich, "Land Use and Demographic Change: Results from Fast-Growth Counties," *Land Economics* 67, no. 3(1991):279-291.

2. G.T. Keffer, R. Marx, and K.E. Anderson, "A Prospective Case for a National Land Data System: Recent Developments at the Census Bureau and U.S. Geological Survey," in B. Niemann, Jr., ed., *Computers in Public Agencies, Sharing Solutions*, Vol. I, *Land Record Systems*, Proceedings of the Urban and Regional Information Systems Association (Ottawa, 1985):29-40; and W.B. Mitchell, S.C. Guptill, K.E. Anderson, R. Fegeas, and C.A. Hallam, *GIRAS: A Geographic Information Retrieval and Analysis System for Handling Land Use and Land Cover Data*, USDI Professional Paper 1059 (Reston, Va.: U.S. Geological Survey, 1987).

3. R.W. Marx, "The TIGER System: Automating the Geographic Structure of the United States Census," *Government Publications Review* 13(1986):181-201.

4. K.J. Dueker and P.B. DeLacy, "GIS in the Land Development Planning Process: Balancing the Needs of Land Use Planners and Real Estate Developers," *Journal of the American Planning Association* 56, no. 4(1990):483-491.

19

Land Information
Needs and Sources: A Comment

Paul E. Smith

In general, land ownership and taxation are essentially informational issues. Data and information to serve program operation and statistical purposes are at the heart of modern management, whether in government or the private sector. Behrens, Keffer, and Heimlich (in this volume) have successfully addressed problems regarding the sources of information, the interpretation of information, and the retrieval of data after they have been accumulated. I would add a fourth area of concern, namely, the correct interpretation of data that lack a high degree of uniformity in the definition of standards and terms that underlie their reporting by a multitude of sources.

A classic problem stemming from the lack of uniformity of standards is illustrated by the assessment of real property. There are thousands of assessors in the United States, each of whom functions in a separate, distinct way. Their functions and authorities are mandated by various laws of the 50 states. They are limited by options provided by their local jurisdictions. And they manage according to their own training and background.

No single agency or instrument ensures consistency of law or practice in the area of assessment. The International Association of Assessing Officers (IAAO) serves as a conduit through which data may flow from and to the membership and to various public and private agencies. The IAAO, however, is unable to force individual members to report any data at all, much less to do so by uniform standards.[1] Thus, there are major inconsistencies in the data, as well as the potential for deficiency or inaccuracy.

Certainly, IAAO would like to have up-to-date statistics that would aid assessors in estimating market values within and between jurisdictions. Assessors need such information to assist them in discovering, listing, and valuing real property uniformly, but obtaining it is often a futile endeavor because most property owners consider the assessor an adversary and withhold essential information for fear it may result in higher assessments.

The same reluctance is sometimes evident in contacts with information repositories that hold their information to be of a confidential nature. The result is the assessor's data may not be as reliable as they could be. While the assessor's files are generally public records and available to everyone, openness by property owners and other government repositories is needed as well. Sharing data should not be a one-way street.

Definition of terms and a high degree of uniformity in definitions are other essential attributes that seem to be elusive. Joan Youngman (in this volume) aptly stated that legislation is wonderfully vague when it comes to defining such terms as *market value*. Most definitions of market value include the requirement of an arm's length sale. Between the legislatures and the courts, however, there appear to be as many different definitions of market value as there are different lengths of arms.

To sort, analyze, and present data correctly, researchers must be able not only to determine what the data represent in direct comparison with other data but also to find, that is retrieve, the data accurately and quickly. This is becoming more and more of a task as increasing amounts of data are stored in computers. The ability to store vast amounts of data has created a nightmare for the researcher, who knows the data are there but also knows the time it takes to find the data before they can be analyzed. The knowledge that the data are somewhere in the black box is of no value unless one is able to pull specific items together quickly and easily.

Retrieving data is not easily accomplished without identifiers common to all sources. It is clear to anyone who has researched deeds or reviewed assessors' records and tax maps that there are many different property identifiers and map numbering systems. Data are stored and retrieved from various files by different identifiers. Even within the same jurisdiction there may be different identifiers for the same parcel of land. The increasing use of geographic information systems offers a possible solution to the problem. But there has been no great effort to correlate separate geographic information systems, even by adjoining jurisdictions.

The conclusion that I draw from all this is that if agencies and individuals really need access to land information as badly as they say they do, agreement, cooperation, and definition of terms and conditions must be forthcoming. Legislation is necessary across jurisdictional lines to achieve the use of common identifiers for property and taxpayers, and additional incentives must be found to encourage universal reporting of data to a central repository with the capability to furnish basic data for specific analysis in timely fashion.

Notes

Paul E. Smith is an assessor, Fairfax County, Virginia.

1. J. Eckert, ed., *Property Appraisal and Assessment Administration* (Chicago: The International Association of Assessing Officers, 1990).

20

The Literature of Land
Ownership and Taxation

John P. Michos

This bibliography is a guide to the literature on the economics of agricultural land ownership, tenure, and taxation published since 1980. It consists primarily of journal articles, but some books and monographs are cited. The citations are arranged in two sections: "Land Ownership and Tenure" and "Real Property Taxation." The land ownership and tenure section reflects new themes and models, as well as traditional themes. The section on real property taxation includes discussions of the burden and incidence of a real property tax, taxation of land rent, and land-use assessment and its implications.

In the past decade, microeconomists have developed many new models of property rights, transaction costs, moral hazard, adverse selection, and risk and uncertainty. Such models have many applications for research on land ownership and tenure. For example, models of transaction costs and property rights are being used to analyze how property rights develop from an evolutionary process that decreases uncertainty and increases efficiency in land markets. Because the opportunity costs of inputs are different for the landlord and the tenant, moral hazard and risk and uncertainty models provide new insights into the characteristics of cost-sharing arrangements. Models of risk and uncertainty and of adverse selection are being used to demonstrate the relationship between output-augmenting activities, such as investment, and the adoption of new technology. All of these issues are important to an understanding of land ownership and tenure. The entries in this bibliography should be of significant assistance to those investigating these areas.

In addition, traditional subjects in the literature of land ownership and tenure continue to be of importance, especially for policy analysis.

Landownership concentration and characteristics bear importantly on policies for cropland development and soil conservation. Leasing arrangements have important implications for resource allocation and soil conservation. An inspection of the literature on land tenure reveals that more research is needed on the effects of farm tenure on agricultural efficiency. These and other traditional topics are covered in this bibliography.

As for agricultural land taxation, the majority of the literature since 1980 has dealt with the taxation of agricultural land rent and the merits of a use-value assessment of agricultural land. Research on the incidence and burden of agricultural taxation has subsided because a consensus on the effects of these policies has been attained. Conversely, no consensus has been reached on the subject of the taxation of land rent. Increasing governmental land regulation and land taxation indicate that research on land rent is of increased importance. The rise in private and public interest in agricultural land rent, and how different assignments of rights affect the rent, has many implications for economic efficiency.

Use-value assessment has been enacted by taxing authorities to achieve two goals: (1) to make the real property tax fair and (2) as a consequence of an unprejudiced property tax, to preserve farmland. In theory, use-value assessment can delay the conversion of agricultural land to other uses, but many believe the program is ineffective and encourages speculation. Now that some form of use-value assessment has been in place in all states for over 10 years, empirical analysis is possible. Whether use-value assessment preserves agricultural land or encourages speculation and how the interaction of different interests appropriating land rent affects efficiency are important issues. This bibliography points to literature on these issues, as well as issues dealing with tax burden and incidence.

Land Ownership and Tenure

Abdel, R., "Optimality and Production Efficiency of Some Cropsharing Systems," *Journal of Economic Studies* 15, no. 1 (1988):53-70.

Alig, R.J., and R.G. Healy, "Urban and Built-Up Land Area Changes in the United States: An Empirical Investigation of Determinants," *Land Economics* 63, no. 3 (1987):215-226.

Allen, F., "On Share Contracts and Screening," *Bell Journal of Economics* 13, no. 2 (1982):541-547.

Alston, L., "Tenure Choice in Southern Agriculture, 1930-60," *Explorations in Economic History* 18, no. 3 (1981):211-232.

Apland, J., R.N. Barnes, and F. Justus, "The Farm Lease: An Analysis of Owner-Tenant and Landlord Preferences Under Risk," *American Journal of Agricultural Economics* 66, no. 3 (1984):376-384.

Babb, E.M., "Critical Choices Relating to the Economic Structure of the Farming Sector: Discussion," *American Journal of Agricultural Economics* 62, no. 5 (1980):954.

Baker, L., and P.J. Thomassin, "Farmland Ownership and Financial Stress," *Canadian Journal of Agricultural Economics* 36, no. 4 (1988):799-811.

Bardhan, P., and N. Singh, "On Moral Hazard and Cost Sharing Under Sharecropping," *American Journal of Agricultural Economics* 69, no. 2 (1987):382-383.

Baron, D., "Agricultural Leasing in the Cornbelt: Some Recent Trends in Land Tenure, Price Inflation," *Journal of the American Society of Farm Managers and Rural Appraisers* 45, no. 1 (1982):28-33.

―――――, "The Effects of Tenancy and Risk on Cropping Patterns: A Mathematical Programming Analysis," *Agricultural Economics Research* 34, no. 4 (1982):1-9.

Basu, K., "Technological Stagnation, Tenurial Laws, and Adverse Selection," *American Economic Review* 79, no. 1 (1989):251-255.

Bell, C., "Reforming Property Rights in Land and Tenancy," *World Bank Research Observer* 5, no. 2 (1990):143-166.

Berry, W., "A Defense of the Family Farm," in F. Comstock, ed., *Is There a Moral Obligation to Save the Family Farm?* (Ames: Iowa State University Press, 1987):325-333.

Bitney, L.L., "Leasing Practices: An Extension Viewpoint," in P. DeBraal and G. Wunderlich, eds., *Rents and Rental Practices in U.S. Agriculture* (Washington, D.C.: Farm Foundation, 1983):133-135.

Boxley, R.F., "Farmland Ownership and Distribution of Land Earnings," *Agricultural Economic Research* 37, no. 4 (1985) 40-44.

Braverman, A., and J.E. Stiglitz, "Cost-Sharing Arrangements under Sharecropping: Moral Hazard, Incentive Flexibility, and Risk," *American Journal of Agricultural Economics* 68, no. 3 (1986):642-652.

―――――, "Landlords, Tenants and Technological Innovations," *Journal of Development Economics* 23, no. 2 (1986):313-332.

Brenneman, R., and S.M. Bates, eds., *Land-Saving Action: A Written Symposium by 29 Experts on Private Land Conservation in the 1980's* (Covelo: Island Press, 1984).

Byrne, P.J., "Land Ownership and the Agricultural Land Market," in M. Pacione, ed., *Progress in Agricultural Geography* (London: Croom Helm, 1986):195-218.

Canto, V.A., "Property Rights, Land Reform, and Economic Well-Being," *Cato Journal* 5, no. 1 (1985):51-66.

Currie, J.M., *The Economic Theory of Land Tenure* (New York: Cambridge University Press, 1981).

Datta, S.K., D.J. O'Hara, and J.B. Nugent, "Choice of Agricultural Tenancy in the Presence of Transaction Costs," *Land Economics* 62, no. 2 (1986):145-158.

Dillman, D.A., and J.E. Carlson, "Influence of Absentee Landlords on Soil Erosion Control Practices," *Journal of Soil Conservation and Water* 37, no. 1 (1982):37-41.

Doran, H.E., "Small or Large Farm: Some Methodological Considerations," *American Journal of Agricultural Economics* 67, no. 1 (1985):130-132.

Feder, G., and D. Feeny, "Land Tenure and Property Rights: Theory and Implications for Development Policy," *World Bank Economic Review* 5, no. 1 (1991):135-153.

Geisler, C.C., and F.J. Popper (eds.), *Land Reform, American Style* (Totowa: Littlefield, Adams; Rowman and Allanheld Press, 1984).

Gupta, M.R., "Production Uncertainty, Lender's Risk and Landlord's Incentive to Innovate in an Interlinked Credit-Share Cropping Contract," *Journal of Quantitative Economics* 6, no. 1 (1990):11-18.

Harris, P.E., "Land Ownership Restrictions of the Midwestern States: Influence on Farm Structure," *American Journal of Agricultural Economics* 62, no. 5 (1980):940-945.

Jacobs, H.M., and D.D. Moyer, "Constructing a National, Rural Land Transfer Data Base," *Journal of Soil and Water Conservation* 41, no. 4 (1986):231-234.

Kaplan, H.M., "Farmland as a Portfolio Investment," *Journal of Portfolio Management* 11, no. 2 (1985):73-78.

Klemme, R.M., and R.A. Schoney, "Economic Analysis of Land Bid Prices Using Profitability and Cash Flow Considerations in Finite Planning Horizons," *North Central Journal of Agricultural Economics* 6, no. 2 (1984):115-127.

Koo, A.Y.C., "Toward a More General Model of Land Tenancy and Reform: Reply," *Quarterly Journal of Economics* 96, no. 4 (1981):731.

Laband, D.N., "Restriction of Farm Ownership as Rent-Seeking Behavior: Family Farmers Have It Their Way," *American Journal of Economics and Sociology* 43, no. 2 (1984):179-189.

Lee, L.K., "The Impact of Landownership Factors on Soil Conservation: Reply," *American Journal of Agricultural Economics* 62, no. 5 (1980):1070-1076.

————, "Land Tenure and Adoption of Conservation Tillage," *Journal of Soil and Water Conservation* 38, no. 3 (1983):166-169.

Ling, K., and C. Siung, "Impact of Farm Size on the Bidding Potential for Agricultural Land: Comment," *American Journal of Agricultural Economics* 62, no. 4 (1980):845-846.

Lockeretz, W., "Discussion: Land Markets and Landowners," in R. Heimlich, ed., *Land Use Transition in Urbanzing Areas: Research and*

Information Needs (Washington D.C.: Farm Foundation in Cooperation with Economic Research Service, 1989):71-72.

Mukesh, E., and A. Kotwal, "A Theory of Contractual Structure in Agriculture," *American Economic Review* 75, no. 3 (1985):352-367.

Murrell, P., "The Economics of Sharing: A Transactions Cost Analysis of Contractual Choice in Farming," *Bell Journal of Economics* 14, no. 1 (1983):283-293.

Otsuka, K., and Y. Hayami, "Theories of Share Tenancy: A Critical Survey," *Economic Development and Cultural Change* 37, no. 1 (1988):31-68.

Quan, N.J., "Concentration of Income and Land Holdings: Prediction by Latent Variables Model and Partial Least Squares," *Journal of Development Economics* 31, no. 1 (1989):55-76.

Quibria, M.G., and R. Salim, "Toward a More General Model of Land Tenancy and Reform: Comment," *Quarterly Journal of Economics* 96, no. 4 (1981):725-730.

Rao, V. and C. Tosporn, "The Inverse Relationship Between Size of Land Holdings and Agricultural Productivity," *American Journal of Agricultural Economics* 63, no. 3 (1981):571-574.

Reid J.D., "The Theory of Sharecropping: Occam's Razor and Economic Analysis," *History of Political Economy* 19, no. 4 (1987):551-569.

Roth, M., "Land Ownership Security and Farm Investment: Comment," *American Journal of Agricultural Economics* 71, no. 1 (1989):211-214.

Roumasset, J., and M. Uy, "Agency Costs and the Agricultural Firm," *Land Economics* 63, no. 3 (1987):290-302.

Runge, C.F., "Strategic Interdependence in Models of Property Rights," *American Journal of Agricultural Economics* 66, no. 5 (1984):802-806.

Sand, D., "Conservation Easements and the Conservation Movement," *Journal of Soil and Water Conservation* 40, no. 4 (1985):337-338.

Scott, A., "Property Rights and Property Wrongs," *Canadian Journal of Economics* 16, no. 4 (1983):555-573.

Shetty, S., "Limited Liability, Wealth Differences and Tenancy Contracts in Agrarian Economies," *Journal of Development Economics* 29, no. 1 (1988):1-22.

Taslim, M.A., "Short-Term Leasing, Resource Allocation, and Crop-Share Tenancy," *American Journal of Agricultural Economics* 71, no. 3 (1989):785-790.

Taver, L.W., "Use of Life Insurance to Fund the Farm Purchase from Heirs," *American Journal of Agricultural Economics* 67, no. 1 (1985):60-69.

Whatmore, S., R. Munton, and T. Marsden, "The Rural Restructuring Process: Emerging Divisions of Agricultural Property Rights," *Regional Studies* 24, no. 3 (1990):235-245.

Wunderlich, G., "The U.S.A.'s Land Data Legacy from the 19th Century: A Message from the Henry George, Francis A. Walker Controversy over Farmland Distribution," *American Journal of Economics and Sociology* 41, no. 3 (1982):269-280.

Zulauf, C.R., "Changes in Selected Characteristics of U.S. Farms During the 1970's and 1980's: An Investigation Based on Current and Constant Dollar Sales Categories," *Southern Journal of Agricultural Economics* 18, no. 1 (1986):113-122.

Real Property Taxation

Anderson, J.E., "Property Taxes and the Timing of Urban Land Development," *Regional Science and Urban Economics* 16, no. 4 (1986):483-492.

Anderson, J.E., and H.C. Bunch, "Agricultural Property Tax Relief: Tax Credits, Tax Rates, and Land Values," *Land Ecnonmics* 65, no. 1 (1989):13-22.

Aslanbeigu, N., and A. Wick, "Progress: Poverty or Prosperity? Joining the Debate Between George and Marshall on the Effects of Economic Growth on the Distribution of Income," *American Journal of Economics and Sociology* 49, no. 2 (1990):239-256.

Barrows, R., and K. Bondverd, "The Distribution of Tax Relief Under Farm Circuit-Breakers: Some Empirical Evidence," *Land Economics* 64, no. 1 (1988):15-27.

Bentick, B.L., "Capitalized Property Taxes and the Viability of Rural Enterprise Subject to Urban Pressure," *Land Economics* 56, no. 4 (1980):451-456.

————, "A Tax on Land Value May Not be Neutral," *National Tax Journal* 35, no. 1 (1982):113.

Bentick, B.L., and T.F. Pogue, "The Impact on Development Timing of Property and Profit Taxation," *Land Economics* 64, no. 4 (1988):317-324.

Bergstrom, J.C., and J.R. Stoll, "Southern Differential Assessment Programs: Issues, Status and Policy," *Journal of the American Society of Farm Managers and Rural Appraisers* 49, no. 2 (1985):34-39.

Bills, N.L., and R.N. Boisvert, "Impact of New Procedures for Estimating Agricultural Use Values in New York," *Journal of the Northeastern Agricultural Economics Council* 10, no. 2 (1981):63-69.

Blake, D.R., "Property Tax Incentives: An Alternative View," *Land Economics* 55, no. 1 (1979):521-531.

Blewett, R.A., and J. Lane, "Development Rights and Differential Assessment of Agricultural Land: Fractional Valuation of Farmland Is Ineffective for Preserving Open Space and Subsidizes Speculation," *American Journal of Economics and Sociology* 47, no. 2 (1988):195-205.

Bowman, J.H., and W.A. Butcher, "Institutional Remedies and the Uniform Assessment of Property: An Update and Extension," *National Tax Journal* 39, no. 2 (1986):157-169.

Braden, J.B., "Some Emerging Rights in Agricultural Land," *American Journal of Agricultural Economics* 64, no. 1 (1982):19-27.

Brueckner, J.K., "A Modern Analysis of the Effects of Site Value Taxation," *National Tax Journal* 39, no. 1 (1986):49-58.

Bryan, D., "Natural and Improved Land in Marx's Theory of Rent," *Land Economics* 66, no. 2 (1990):176-181.

Chamley, C., B.D. Wright, "Fiscal Incidence in an Overlapping Generations Model with a Fixed Asset," *Journal of Public Economics* 32, no. 1 (1987):3-24.

Chicoine, D.L., and A.D. Hendricks, "Evidence on Farm Use-Value Assessment, Tax Shifts, and State School Aid," *American Journal of Agricultural Economics* 32, no. 1 (1987):266-270.

Chicoine, D.L., and J.T. Scott, "Agricultural Use-Valuation Using Farm Level Data," *Property Tax Journal* 2, no. 1 (1983):1-12.

————, "Farmland Use-Value Assessment: Illinois Approach," *Journal of the American Society of Farm Managers and Rural Appraisers* 46, no. 2 (1982):16-22.

Chicoine, D.L., S.T. Sonka, and R.D. Doty, "The Effects of Farm Property Tax Relief Programs on Farm Financial Conditions," *Land Economics* 58, no. 4 (1982):516-523.

Douglas, R.W., "Capital Migration Land Rent Changes and Site Value Tax Adequacy," *Regional Science Perspectives* 10, no. 1 (1980):35-43.

Dunford, R.W., "A Survey of Property Tax Relief Programs for the Retention of Agricultural and Open Space Lands," *Gonzaga Law Review* 15 (1980):675-699.

Dunford, R.W., and D.C. Marousek, "Sub-County Property Tax Shifts Attributable to Use-Value Assessments of Farmland," *Land Economics* 57, no. 2 (1981):221-229.

Dunford, R.W., and D.E. O'Neil, "An Analysis of Alternative Approaches to Estimating Agricultural Use Values," *Agricultural Law Journal* 3, no. 2 (1981):285-307.

Eckart, W., "The Neutrality of Land Taxation in an Uncertain World," *National Tax Journal* 35, no. 2 (1983):221-229.

Ervine, D.E., D.L. Chicoine, and P.D. Nolte, "Use-Value Assessment of Farmland: Implications for Fiscal Stability," *North Central Journal of Agricultural Economics* 8, no. 1 (1984):17-28.

Ervine, D.E., R.M. Schoening, and R.W. Madsen, "Reassessment and Use-Value Appraisal of Farmland: Potential Property Tax Impacts," *Journal of the American Society of Farm Managers and Rural Appraisers* 46, no. 2 (1982):54-59.

Ferguson, J.T., "Evaluating the Effectiveness of Use-Value Programs," *Property Tax Journal* 7, no. 2 (1988):157-164.

Follain, J.R., and T.E. Miyake, "Land Versus Capital Taxation: A General Equilibrium Analysis," *National Tax Journal* 39, no. 4 (1986):451-470.

Forkenbrock, D.J., and P.S. Fisher, "Tax Incentives to Slow Farmland Conversion," *Policy Studies Journal* 11, no. 1 (1982):25-37.

Ghosh, J., "Differential and Absolute Land Rent," *Journal of Peasant Studies* 13, no. 1 (1985):67-82.

Giertz, J.F., and D.L. Chicoine, "Tax Evaluation of Farmland: Non-Neutrality with Respect to Inflation," *National Tax Journal* 37, no. 2 (1984):253-258.

Ginter, D.E., "A Wealth of Problems with the Land Tax," *Economic History Review*, 2d series, 35, no. 3 (1982):416-421.

Harl, N.E., "Special Use Valuation: An Exercise in Fence Building," *American Bar Association Journal* 68 (1982):50-53.

Harriss, C.L., "Transition to Land Value Taxation: Some Major Problems," in D.M. Holland, ed., *The Assessment of Land Value* (Madison: University of Wisconsin Press):213-251.

Hartwick, J.M., "On the Development of the Theory of Land Rent," *Land Economics* 65, no. 4 (1989):410-412.

Hite, J.C., and B.L. Dillman, "Protection of Agricultural Land: An Institutionalist Approach," *Southern Journal of Agricultural Economics* 13, no. 1 (1981):43-53.

Hoffman, S.A., "Farmland and Open Space Preservation in Michigan: An Empirical Analysis," *Journal of Law Reform* Summer, (1986):1107-1197.

Ihori, T., "Economic Effects of Land Taxes in an Inflationary Economy," *Journal of Public Economics* 42, no. 2 (1990):195-211.

Jones, P.T., and D.J. Epp, "Site-Value Taxation of Real Estate and Land Use at the Rural-Urban Fringe," *Journal of Northeast Agricultural Economics* 9, no. 1 (1980):101-110.

Little, C.E., "Farmland Preservation: Playing Political Hardball," *Journal of Soil and Water Conservation* 39, no. 4 (1984):229-231.

Mark, S.M. "A New Case for Differential Assessment of Prime Farmland," *Journal of Soil and Water Conservation* 37, no. 4 (1982):210-212.

Mills, D.E., "The Non-Neutrality of Land Value Taxation," *National Tax Journal* 34, no. 1 (1981):253-258.

Olson, E.G., "Use Value:Weakness and Remedies," *Journal of the American Society of Farm Managers and Rural Appraisers* 48, no. 1 (1984):31-36.

Ozuna, T., Jr., and L.L. Jones, "Farmland Conversion in the U.S. and Texas," *Journal of the American Society of Farm Managers and Rural Appraisers* 50, no. 1 (1986):17-22.

Persky, J., and W.D White, "A Rather Neoclassical Contribution to Marxian Rent Theory," *Land Economics* 64, no. 2 (1988):196-198.

Plaut, T.R., "Urban Expansion and the Loss of Farmland in the United States: Implications for the Future," *Journal of Agricultural Economics* 62, no. 3 (1980):537-542.

Pogue, T.F., "The Incidence of Property Tax Relief via State Aid to Local Governments," *Land Economics* 59, no. 4 (1983):420-431.

Pomp, R.D., "What is Happening to the Property Tax," *Assessors Journal* 15 (1980):107-126.

Quadrio-Curzio, A., "Rent, Income Distribution and Orders of Efficiency and Rentability," in L. Pasinetti, ed., *Essays on the Theory of Joint Production* (London: Macmillan, 1980).

Ring, R.J., Jr., and L. Jansen, "The Effects of Use-Value Assessment on County and School District Tax Revenues and on State Aid to Education," *Property Tax Journal* 2, no. 4 (1983):247-257.

Roberts, N.A., and H.J. Brown, eds., *Property Tax Preferences for Agricultural Land*, Landmark Studies (New York: Universe Books):1980.

Robison, L.J., D.A. Lins, and R. VenKataraman, "Cash Rents and Land Values in U.S. Agriculture," *American Journal of Agricultural Economics* 67, no. 4 (1985):794-805.

Rose, J.G., "Farmland Preservation Policies and Programs," *Natural Resources Journal* 24, no. 3 (1984):591-640.

Sexton, T.E., and R.J. Sexton, "Re-Evaluating the Income Elasticity of the Property Tax Base," *Land Economics* 62, no. 2 (1986):182-191.

Skinner, J., "If Agricultural Land Taxation Is So Efficient Why Is It So Rarely Used?" *World Bank Economic Review* 5, no. 1 (1991):113-133.

Tideman, T.N., "A Tax on Land Value Is Neutral," *National Tax Journal* 35, no. 1 (1982):109-111.

Turnbull, G., Jr., "Land Taxes and Land Use," *National Tax Journal* 35, no. 2 (1987):265-269.

Wildasin, D.E., "More on the Neutrality of Land Taxation," *National Tax Journal* 35, no. 1 (1982):105-108.

Wilson, G.J., "The Land Tax Problem," *Economic History Review* 2d, 35, no. 2 (1982):422-426.

Yamauch, H., "Use-Value Land Taxation and Conservation Economics: An Assessment of Tax-Zoning, with Implications for Conservation Easements," *Government and Policy Journal* 41, no. 1 (1984):199-210.

Ziemer, R.F., F.C. White, and I.D. Clifton, "An Analysis of Factors Affecting Differential Assessment Legislation," *Public Choice* 36, no. 1 (1981):43-52.

John P. Michos is an economist, Economic Research Service, U.S. Department of Agriculture. The views expressed are the author's and do not necessarily represent policies or views of the U.S. Department of Agriculture.

Appendix

Data on Agricultural Land Ownership, Tenure, Value, and Taxes

The Agricultural Economics and Land Ownership Survey (AELOS), conducted by the Bureau of the Census, and the annual surveys of land values and land taxation, conducted by the U.S. Department of Agriculture (USDA), illustrate two useful, but different, sources of data. AELOS, based on the Census Bureau's quinquennial survey of farm and ranch operators, is in many ways a unique survey. The UDSA's annual surveys of values and taxes concentrate on a few specific data items. Following a brief explanation of the surveys are five tables of selected data items that support the text of the chapters in this volume and illustrate the type of data available in the Bureau of the Census and USDA.

The mission and content of AELOS were described by Blackledge (Chapter 4). It remains only to emphasize that efficiencies of basing the survey on farmland owners, that is, adding nonoperating landlords, resulted in some shrinkage of the Census of Agriculture's universe of "land in farms" to the AELOS "privately owned farmland" (see Figure A.1). From the standpoint of interpretation, this difference is not serious, but users are cautioned to read carefully the explanatory material in published reports.

Data on taxation and valuation in the Census of Governments were discussed by Keffer (Chapter 17), and data on farmland taxes collected by USDA were described by DeBraal (Chapter 3). Lengthy series of annual estimates of agricultural land values, rents, and real property taxes are available from USDA. Value and tax data from USDA are tied to the quinquennial censuses of agriculture. These data are currently reported annually in a document entitled *Agricultural Resources: Agricultural Land Values and Markets Situation and Outlook Report*, published by the Economic Research Service, USDA (usually in June).

260

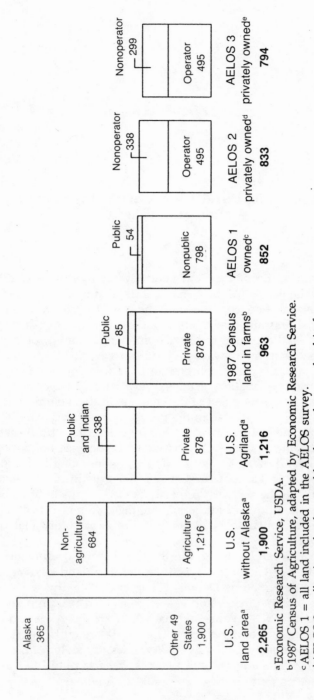

FIGURE A.1 The universes of agricultural land (millions of acres).

[a] Economic Research Service, USDA.
[b] 1987 Census of Agriculture, adapted by Economic Research Service.
[c] AELOS 1 = all land included in the AELOS survey.
[d] AELOS 2 = all private land owned by those who own land in farms.
[e] AELOS 3 = privately owned land in farms.

Listed below are the titles of the five tables that follow. Data for the tables were derived from AELOS and surveys of the Economic Research Service. John Jones, Economic Research Service, prepared the tables.

Table A.1:   Ownership of Agricultural Land, Operators and Non-operators, by State, 1988
Table A.2:   Owners, Leases, and Land, by Type of Lease and State, 1988
Table A.3:   Value per Acre of Farmland, by State, Selected Years, 1910-1992
Table A.4:   Taxes per Acre of Farm Real Estate, by State, Selected Years, 1910-1990
Table A.5:   Taxes per $100 of Market Value, by State, Selected Years, 1910-1990

TABLE A.1 Ownership of Agricultural Land, Operators and Nonoperators, by State, 1988

Region/State	All Owners			Owner-Operators (%)			Nonoperator-Owners (%)		
	Number	Acres (000)	Value ($mil.)	Number	Acres	Value	Number	Acres	Value
Northeast									
Maine	7,831	1,300	1,197	65	80	81	35	20	19
New Hampshire	4,127	428	1,482	58	75	51	42	25	49
Vermont	5,458	1,333	1,595	79	92	91	21	8	9
Massachusetts	7,675	642	3,350	69	82	86	31	18	14
Rhode Island	658	45	275	60	60	60	40	38	40
Connecticut	5,612	425	3,169	49	56	61	51	44	39
New York	60,374	8,186	9,904	56	75	75	44	25	25
New Jersey	10,389	846	6,308	55	63	63	45	37	37
Pennsylvania	77,398	7,062	13,303	47	65	57	53	35	43
Delaware	5,359	489	1,023	40	43	50	60	57	50
Maryland	21,391	2,194	6,630	51	57	61	49	43	39
Lake states									
Michigan	89,426	10,399	10,376	42	59	60	58	41	40
Wisconsin	111,091	17,752	14,496	56	66	67	44	34	33
Minnesota	124,471	28,110	20,864	53	58	59	47	42	41
Corn belt									
Ohio	116,216	14,248	17,219	54	57	56	46	43	44
Indiana	123,010	16,419	19,721	46	49	52	54	51	48
Illinois	173,191	28,622	40,252	35	35	33	65	65	67
Iowa	132,840	27,417	32,451	49	47	43	51	53	57
Missouri	134,824	30,290	19,564	66	68	69	34	32	31

Northern plains								
North Dakota	59,976	41,308	12,770	45	53	60	55	47	40
South Dakota	57,121	35,455	8,985	49	63	61	51	37	39
Nebraska	74,652	40,719	17,037	50	55	52	50	45	48
Kansas	124,941	51,981	21,201	53	54	57	47	46	43
Appalachia								
Virginia	59,651	8,449	10,925	59	70	74	41	30	26
West Virginia	18,395	3,051	2,062	75	78	77	25	22	23
North Carolina	105,256	9,085	12,877	42	46	52	58	54	48
Kentucky	110,520	13,810	12,924	72	77	75	28	23	25
Tennessee	83,298	10,377	10,973	74	73	75	26	27	25
Southeast								
South Carolina	34,796	4,893	4,800	52	59	64	48	41	36
Georgia	51,108	9,351	8,148	62	74	76	38	26	24
Florida	37,094	10,533	20,060	85	80	83	15	20	17
Alabama	57,920	8,576	7,291	69	66	71	31	34	29
Delta								
Mississippi	48,307	9,074	6,960	71	65	68	29	35	32
Arkansas	57,028	12,054	9,604	55	45	48	45	55	52
Louisiana	35,908	7,493	6,658	59	49	57	41	51	43
Southern plains								
Oklahoma	114,437	28,910	13,295	57	57	65	43	43	35
Texas	286,284	119,853	71,107	57	51	63	43	49	37
Mountain								
Montana	32,052	42,014	9,377	62	80	81	38	20	19
Idaho	35,868	12,107	7,790	53	63	62	47	37	38
Wyoming	11,459	22,840	3,361	60	70	71	40	30	29
Colorado	34,359	33,134	13,937	58	67	54	42	33	46
New Mexico	14,016	35,633	5,414	74	70	75	26	30	25
Arizona	6,368	8,246	5,195	70	63	64	30	37	36
Utah	18,393	6,803	3,410	69	70	74	31	30	26
Nevada	3,516	2,540	1,101	78	43	73	22	57	27

—Continues

TABLE A.1 (Continued)

Region/State	All Owners			Owner-Operators (%)			Nonoperator-Owners (%)		
	Number	Acres (000)	Value ($mil.)	Number	Acres	Value	Number	Acres	Value
Pacific									
Washington	38,023	12,866	10,061	66	43	66	34	57	34
Oregon	41,913	11,823	8,237	64	64	65	36	36	35
California	82,785	22,573	49,974	78	59	79	22	41	21
Alaska	588	354	132	69	26	67	31	74	32
Hawaii	4,909	1,044	2,624	59	59	53	41	41	47
United States	2,952,282	833,157	601,472	56	59	62	44	41	38

TABLE A.2 Owners, Leases, and Land, by Type of Lease and State, 1988

Region/State	All Leases				Cash Leases			
	Owners	Number of Leases	Acres (000)	Value of Land and Buildings ($ mil.)	Owners	Number of Leases	Acres (000)	Value of Land and Buildings ($ mil.)
Northeast								
Maine	2,942	3,626	184	165	2,586	2,852	146	134
New Hampshire	1,806	1,994	54	145	1,307	1,404	37	104
Vermont	1,636	2,043	217	326	1,309	1,534	113	125
Massachusetts	2,806	3,777	86	367	2,519	3,366	74	274
Rhode Island	291	314	8	50	273	290	8	46
Connecticut	3,084	3,550	144	981	2,649	3,101	131	882
New York	30,887	32,422	1,699	2,117	28,653	30,178	1,598	2,035
New Jersey	5,183	5,719	304	2,070	4,311	4,814	284	1,882
Pennsylvania	43,367	49,080	2,051	4,474	34,205	39,201	1,705	4,018
Delaware	3,522	3,909	245	359	2,847	3,147	203	295
Maryland	11,388	14,790	831	1,938	9,138	12,060	633	1,513
Lake states								
Michigan	53,954	64,241	3,408	3,234	46,723	55,288	2,738	2,619
Wisconsin	56,347	71,923	4,262	3,170	50,702	64,550	3,815	2,834
Minnesota	65,726	81,034	10,869	7,852	55,464	65,169	8,080	5,890
Corn belt								
Ohio	58,906	67,546	5,605	6,477	38,813	40,715	3,472	4,070
Indiana	73,720	93,779	7,346	8,364	37,694	39,721	3,461	3,932
Illinois	118,775	147,996	18,286	25,427	43,815	51,806	6,155	9,020
Iowa	74,555	92,869	14,441	16,271	44,997	53,907	7,327	8,275
Missouri	53,596	60,125	8,606	5,364	26,046	28,032	4,182	2,378

—Continues

TABLE A.2 (Continued)

Region State	All Leases				Cash Leases			
	Owners	Number of Leases	Acres (000)	Value of Land and Buildings ($mil.)	Owners	Number of Leases	Acres (000)	Value of Land and Buildings ($mil.)
Northern plains								
North Dakota	37,167	63,220	20,442	5,677	22,986	29,257	13,137	3,208
South Dakota	33,105	48,014	12,962	3,350	22,105	26,199	8,518	1,923
Nebraska	42,522	69,261	18,387	7,882	22,748	41,152	12,599	4,509
Kansas	73,322	113,195	24,678	8,896	33,501	41,707	10,560	3,434
Appalachia								
Virginia	27,707	30,455	2,147	2,301	23,558	25,408	1,674	1,684
West Virginia	5,119	6,011	573	379	3,761	4,334	434	282
North Carolina	66,959	80,632	3,782	3,929	51,856	59,304	2,888	2,914
Kentucky	42,470	46,536	3,112	2,987	32,575	35,359	2,251	2,235
Tennessee	26,724	32,857	2,718	2,273	16,648	19,665	1,645	1,453
Southeast								
South Carolina	17,501	20,391	1,468	1,168	16,403	19,074	1,391	1,102
Georgia	21,856	24,621	2,312	1,731	20,574	23,245	2,226	1,652
Florida	7,322	8,701	2,680	4,316	7,135	8,465	2,670	4,285
Alabama	22,081	24,323	2,484	1,712	17,888	19,624	2,042	1,313
Delta								
Mississippi	15,525	32,394	2,820	1,848	13,158	29,819	2,502	1,626
Arkansas	27,822	31,622	5,786	4,360	17,920	19,018	2,883	2,104
Louisiana	16,830	39,010	3,828	2,796	9,322	28,042	1,875	1,256
Southern plains								
Oklahoma	53,604	64,362	12,630	4,707	43,229	49,260	9,279	3,213
Texas	140,871	170,288	58,996	25,806	99,772	113,103	42,082	16,923

Mountain								
Montana	13,806	18,545	9,907	1,911	7,415	9,760	5,339	864
Idaho	19,033	22,033	4,314	2,822	11,152	11,635	2,578	1,603
Wyoming	5,356	6,826	7,496	989	3,994	5,111	6,583	802
Colorado	15,847	27,910	9,701	3,274	8,731	9,760	5,898	1,891
New Mexico	4,476	5,176	11,631	1,477	3,590	4,153	9,937	1,208
Arizona	2,162	2,631	3,073	1,655	1,888	2,339	3,022	1,581
Utah	6,720	30,535	2,015	807	5,618	29,327	1,847	686
Nevada	883	961	1,465	201	709	766	1,316	167
Pacific								
Washington	14,002	17,237	7,161	3,174	8,241	9,850	4,501	1,819
Oregon	17,532	21,177	4,102	2,469	11,992	13,891	2,303	1,528
California	23,311	32,126	9,908	12,644	16,243	23,617	7,833	9,910
Alaska	211	245	257	37	184	210	254	34
Hawaii	2,205	3,251	440	1,305	1,870	2,810	424	1,169
United States	1,466,542	1,895,283	331,923	208,035	990,817	1,216,399	216,655	128,707

TABLE A.3 Value per Acre of Farmland, by State, Selected Years, 1910-1992 ($)

Region/State	March 1							Feb. 1	Jan 1.	
	1910	1920	1930	1940	1950	1960	1970	1980	1990	1992
Northeast										
Maine	25	38	42	29	54	84	161	594	1,019	931
New Hampshire	26	35	39	34	73	104	239	1,004	2,237	2,045
Vermont	24	38	37	30	56	81	224	721	1,190	1,087
Massachusetts	68	99	130	109	190	314	565	1,608	3,763	3,439
Rhode Island	63	80	124	119	232	379	734	2,523	5,028	4,595
Connecticut	63	100	151	135	248	446	921	2,387	4,417	4,036
New York	54	69	73	55	92	145	273	720	974	1,051
New Jersey	84	110	170	122	293	528	1,092	2,947	4,634	4,774
Pennsylvania	56	75	79	59	107	188	373	1,464	1,807	1,820
Delaware	51	69	74	61	114	243	499	1,798	2,259	2,126
Maryland	48	81	81	65	125	290	640	2,238	2,420	2,255
Lake states										
Michigan	48	75	68	51	99	194	326	1,111	1,005	1,105
Wisconsin	57	99	79	52	89	133	232	1,004	803	870
Minnesota	46	109	69	44	84	155	226	1,086	805	873
Corn belt										
Ohio	69	113	79	66	136	248	399	1,730	1,204	1,249
Indiana	75	126	72	63	137	264	406	1,863	1,244	1,303
Illinois	108	188	109	82	174	316	490	2,041	1,389	1,500
Iowa	96	227	124	79	161	257	392	1,840	1,102	1,178
Missouri	50	88	53	32	64	115	224	902	679	689
Northern plains										
North Dakota	29	41	25	13	29	53	94	405	340	358
South Dakota	39	71	35	13	31	51	84	292	328	365
Nebraska	47	88	56	24	58	89	154	635	550	569
Kansas	40	62	49	30	66	101	159	587	462	484

Appalachia										
Virginia	27	55	51	41	82	140	286	1,028	1,516	1,363
West Virginia	26	43	39	30	59	75	136	669	613	719
North Carolina	20	54	47	39	99	186	333	1,219	1,263	1,264
Kentucky	29	60	44	38	81	137	253	976	981	993
Tennessee	24	53	41	36	77	132	268	976	996	985
Southeast										
South Carolina	25	65	36	30	69	137	261	900	909	931
Georgia	18	45	26	20	43	99	234	896	1,012	902
Florida	22	47	84	39	57	217	355	1,381	2,085	2,062
Alabama	14	28	29	21	49	91	200	780	839	832
Delta										
Mississippi	18	43	33	25	55	107	234	819	728	738
Arkansas	18	43	34	25	60	113	260	918	750	724
Louisiana	23	47	45	35	82	173	321	1,256	915	905
South plains										
Oklahoma	26	43	37	24	51	86	173	614	497	494
Texas	16	32	29	19	46	85	148	436	495	466
Mountain										
Montana	19	22	12	8	17	35	60	235	238	252
Idaho	46	69	45	33	70	112	177	698	661	687
Wyoming	11	20	9	6	13	22	41	161	149	138
Colorado	30	35	22	12	32	54	95	387	358	367
New Mexico	10	9	7	5	15	24	42	185	196	239
Arizona	38	30	18	6	15	48	70	267	263	302
Utah	35	48	39	21	43	60	92	530	389	425
Nevada	15	28	16	13	19	31	53	248	194	231
Pacific										
Washington	49	69	57	39	85	133	224	736	779	792
Oregon	39	50	38	27	60	88	150	587	571	603
California	52	105	112	71	154	360	479	1,424	1,704	1,765
48 states	40	69	49	32	65	117	196	737	668	685

TABLE A.4 Taxes per Acre of Farm Real Estate, by State, Selected Years, 1910-1990 ($)

Region/State	1910	1920	1930	1940	1950	1960	1970	1980	1990
Northeast									
Maine	0.27	0.55	0.81	0.84	1.29	1.94	3.44	6.16	9.52
New Hampshire	0.29	0.57	0.76	0.88	1.39	2.13	4.95	9.78	21.13
Vermont	0.20	0.45	0.58	0.54	0.86	1.42	4.04	7.83	14.43
Massachusetts	0.78	1.55	2.16	2.70	3.41	6.38	12.83	21.52	26.73
Rhode Island	0.44	0.81	1.35	1.70	2.46	6.10	14.87	30.84	48.22
Connecticut	0.46	1.08	1.63	1.86	3.20	5.91	13.99	19.51	26.08
New York	0.38	0.87	1.04	1.10	1.69	3.13	5.51	13.69	19.11
New Jersey	0.69	1.50	2.74	2.31	3.78	9.23	15.56	20.48	39.72
Pennsylvania	0.47	0.82	1.30	0.98	1.38	2.39	4.51	8.86	17.05
Delaware	0.24	0.68	0.50	0.33	0.58	1.07	2.23	2.01	1.70
Maryland	0.40	0.72	0.93	0.81	1.18	2.32	5.12	6.78	10.00
Lake states									
Michigan	0.37	1.23	1.34	0.46	0.80	2.36	4.67	17.75	33.18
Wisconsin	0.29	1.04	1.05	0.78	1.57	2.50	4.72	12.28	17.18
Minnesota	0.20	0.76	0.87	0.66	1.30	2.09	3.81	4.66	6.49
Corn belt									
Ohio	0.45	1.07	1.36	0.69	1.08	2.21	4.31	8.35	9.42
Indiana	0.48	1.26	1.47	0.76	1.36	2.42	5.43	7.11	8.11
Illinois	0.35	0.99	1.16	0.98	2.08	4.03	7.07	13.09	15.24
Iowa	0.33	1.10	1.24	1.00	1.92	3.06	5.87	9.83	10.94
Missouri	0.13	0.28	0.45	0.32	0.52	1.09	1.84	2.86	2.51
Northern plains									
North Dakota	0.13	0.44	0.38	0.22	0.43	0.65	1.18	1.99	2.27
South Dakota	0.12	0.45	0.44	0.28	0.46	0.69	1.27	2.54	2.86
Nebraska	0.15	0.42	0.44	0.30	0.64	1.11	2.04	4.90	7.43
Kansas	0.17	0.42	0.55	0.36	0.72	1.16	1.98	2.59	2.56

Appalachia									
Virginia	0.10	0.23	0.34	0.27	0.46	0.83	1.56	3.83	7.19
West Virginia	0.11	0.31	0.46	0.16	0.23	0.31	0.55	0.78	1.18
North Carolina	0.06	0.34	0.59	0.37	0.51	1.00	1.76	3.83	6.09
Kentucky	0.15	0.38	0.43	0.32	0.63	0.74	1.40	2.10	2.74
Tennessee	0.14	0.40	0.47	0.38	0.47	0.66	1.57	3.22	4.18
Southeast									
South Carolina	0.13	0.35	0.40	0.30	0.38	0.71	1.19	2.12	3.38
Georgia	0.10	0.28	0.30	0.14	0.32	0.43	1.36	3.46	5.54
Florida	0.09	0.46	0.70	0.32	0.54	1.42	2.98	6.34	11.97
Alabama	0.08	0.19	0.25	0.20	0.25	0.30	0.49	0.90	1.32
Delta									
Mississippi	0.13	0.50	0.63	0.34	0.37	0.42	1.03	1.60	2.12
Arkansas	0.13	0.33	0.32	0.28	0.32	0.73	1.35	2.14	2.92
Louisiana	0.14	0.55	0.57	0.31	0.40	0.67	1.25	1.79	2.54
Southern plains									
Oklahoma	0.14	0.38	0.47	0.24	0.36	0.51	0.94	1.56	1.86
Texas	0.05	0.16	0.23	0.14	0.26	0.47	0.89	1.47	2.60
Mountain									
Montana	0.06	0.14	0.14	0.11	0.21	0.31	0.64	1.20	1.47
Idaho	0.17	0.63	0.64	0.45	0.85	1.21	1.60	2.77	3.36
Wyoming	0.03	0.09	0.09	0.06	0.14	0.19	0.37	0.63	0.70
Colorado	0.10	0.27	0.28	0.20	0.35	0.59	0.95	1.40	2.38
New Mexico	0.02	0.05	0.07	0.04	0.09	0.15	0.25	0.23	0.40
Arizona	0.06	0.18	0.22	0.13	0.36	0.59	1.50	2.30	5.53
Utah	0.13	0.47	0.52	0.30	0.47	0.59	1.10	1.71	1.62
Nevada	0.06	0.21	0.15	0.15	0.17	0.26	0.52	0.63	0.53
Pacific									
Washington	0.25	0.67	0.71	0.32	0.62	1.15	2.26	3.55	5.02
Oregon	0.13	0.37	0.40	0.33	0.80	1.54	1.98	3.24	5.95
California	0.32	0.93	1.14	0.83	1.87	3.95	8.87	7.36	10.65
Hawaii	—	—	—	—	—	1.22	1.71	3.46	17.51
United States	0.19	0.51	0.57	0.39	0.69	1.21	2.27	3.83	5.27

TABLE A.5 Taxes per $100 of Market Value, by State, Selected Years, 1910-1990 ($)

Region/State	1910	1920	1930	1940	1950	1960	1970	1980	1990
Northeast									
Maine	1.06	1.54	1.97	2.87	2.38	2.30	2.14	1.08	0.55
New Hampshire	1.08	1.64	1.95	2.41	1.90	2.04	2.07	0.97	0.94
Vermont	0.82	1.17	1.58	1.76	1.55	1.76	1.81	1.12	1.21
Massachusetts	1.13	1.59	1.68	2.41	1.80	2.03	2.27	1.38	0.71
Rhode Island	0.70	0.99	1.10	1.38	1.06	1.61	2.03	1.24	0.96
Connecticut	0.71	1.08	1.08	1.30	1.29	1.33	1.52	0.82	0.59
New York	0.70	1.33	1.52	1.99	1.84	2.16	1.80	1.93	1.96
New Jersey	0.81	1.30	1.67	1.70	1.29	1.75	1.42	0.74	0.86
Pennsylvania	0.83	1.14	1.75	1.65	1.28	1.27	1.21	0.64	0.94
Delaware	0.45	1.04	0.68	0.51	0.51	0.44	0.45	0.11	0.08
Maryland	0.82	0.99	1.16	1.20	0.95	0.80	0.80	0.29	0.41
Lake states									
Michigan	0.76	1.62	2.08	0.90	0.81	1.21	1.43	1.59	3.30
Wisconsin	0.50	1.04	1.49	1.54	1.78	1.88	2.03	1.18	2.14
Minnesota	0.42	0.70	1.45	1.49	1.54	1.35	1.69	0.42	0.81
Corn belt									
Ohio	0.64	1.11	1.89	1.01	0.79	0.89	1.08	0.48	0.78
Indiana	0.62	1.08	2.27	1.18	0.99	0.92	1.34	0.36	0.65
Illinois	0.31	0.55	1.20	1.18	1.19	1.28	1.44	0.64	1.10
Iowa	0.33	0.52	1.14	1.26	1.20	1.19	1.50	0.53	0.99
Missouri	0.25	0.34	0.98	0.98	0.82	0.95	0.82	0.31	0.37
Northern plains									
North Dakota	0.44	1.11	1.70	1.70	1.45	1.18	1.21	0.47	0.67
South Dakota	0.30	0.66	1.41	1.98	1.32	1.22	1.38	0.81	0.87
Nebraska	0.31	0.52	0.85	1.35	1.09	1.22	1.31	0.75	1.35
Kansas	0.41	0.68	1.24	1.23	1.09	1.23	1.25	0.43	0.55

Appalachia									
Virginia	0.36	0.43	0.75	0.65	0.56	0.60	0.54	0.38	0.47
West Virginia	0.41	0.77	1.26	0.50	0.38	0.41	0.41	0.11	0.19
North Carolina	0.28	0.71	1.48	0.95	0.52	0.54	0.53	0.31	0.48
Kentucky	0.51	0.73	1.08	0.84	0.78	0.54	0.55	0.22	0.28
Tennessee	0.56	0.89	1.23	1.03	0.61	0.50	0.59	0.34	0.42
Southeast									
South Carolina	0.51	0.66	1.26	0.94	0.55	0.52	0.46	0.24	0.37
Georgia	0.55	0.79	1.27	0.66	0.75	0.43	0.58	0.40	0.55
Florida	0.38	0.86	0.89	0.82	0.94	0.66	0.84	0.46	0.57
Alabama	0.56	0.82	0.98	0.93	0.52	0.33	0.25	0.11	0.16
Delta									
Mississippi	0.70	1.69	2.10	1.32	0.67	0.40	0.44	0.20	0.29
Arkansas	0.72	0.91	1.12	1.07	0.53	0.64	0.52	0.22	0.40
Louisiana	0.59	1.41	1.40	0.86	0.48	0.39	0.39	0.13	0.28
Southern plains									
Oklahoma	0.54	0.92	1.39	0.98	0.69	0.58	0.54	0.25	0.37
Texas	0.29	0.55	0.92	0.71	0.56	0.55	0.59	0.32	0.52
Mountain									
Montana	0.32	0.75	1.36	1.42	1.14	0.82	1.03	0.50	0.62
Idaho	0.37	0.98	1.64	1.34	1.09	0.96	0.81	0.38	0.51
Wyoming	0.26	0.55	1.12	0.94	0.91	0.72	0.80	0.37	0.47
Colorado	0.34	0.81	1.43	1.53	1.02	1.06	0.96	0.35	0.66
New Mexico	0.21	0.64	1.12	0.70	0.44	0.48	0.53	0.10	0.21
Arizona	0.16	0.71	1.33	1.11	0.94	0.55	1.00	0.42	2.10
Utah	0.38	1.19	1.54	1.31	0.93	0.86	1.00	0.25	0.42
Nevada	0.38	0.84	1.02	1.14	0.88	0.66	0.79	0.18	0.27
Pacific									
Washington	0.50	1.01	1.44	0.80	0.68	0.84	0.91	0.43	0.64
Oregon	0.33	0.73	1.17	1.15	1.27	1.68	1.24	0.54	1.04
California	0.57	0.86	1.10	1.15	1.16	1.04	1.76	0.49	0.63
Hawaii	—	—	—	—	—	0.72	0.58	0.33	0.59
United States	0.47	0.79	1.31	1.18	1.00	0.97	1.08	0.49	0.78

Index